Gravity Rules!

Tracey Lieder
Ronald Koop · Rene'e Mason
John Ervin · AIMS · Johann Weber
Betty Cordel · Project Team · Jim Wilson

AIMS Project Team

This book contains materials developed by the AIMS Education Foundation. **AIMS** (**A**ctivities **I**ntegrating **M**athematics and **S**cience) began in 1981 with a grant from the National Science Foundation. The non-profit AIMS Education Foundation publishes hands-on instructional materials (books and the monthly magazine) that integrate curricular disciplines such as mathematics, science, language arts, and social studies. The Foundation sponsors a national program of professional development through which educators may gain both an understanding of the AIMS philosophy and expertise in teaching by integrated, hands-on methods.

ISBN **1-881431-75-4**

Printed in the United States of America

I Hear and I Forget,

I See and I Remember,

I Do and I Understand.

— Chinese Proverb

Table Of Contents

Gravity Rules!

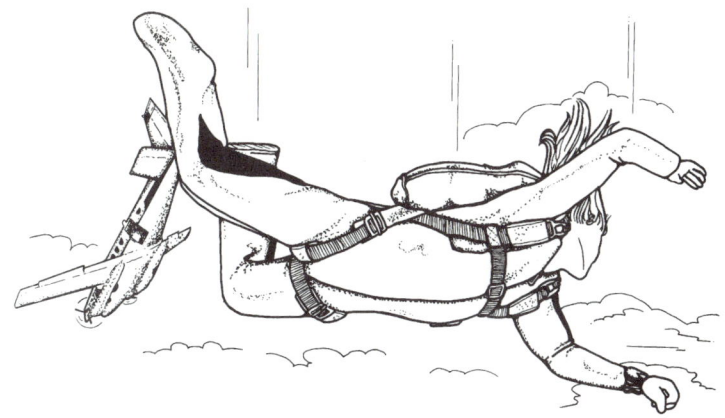

Introduction

Gravity Rules! is a pioneering effort by the AIMS Education Foundation to package an instructional video to accompany our hands-on, integrated mathematics and science activities. *Gravity Rules!* uses the context of modern sport parachuting — called *skydiving* — to observe and study the science topics of *force* and *motion*.

Our primary goal in creating the video portion of the package was to take students to a real-world location — via video — and let them observe and collect data, in real-time, of real-world objects. This data is then used to compute a physical characteristic (e.g., velocity) of the real-world object.

Our goal in developing the correlated hands-on, integrated science and math activities was to duplicate, in the student's classroom, much of what they observed in the video. One method for achieving this direct link between the classroom and the real-world is to have students model in paper the skydivers, their parachutes, and their motions as seen in the video. Often, the same type of data collected from the video is collected from the paper models and used to compute the same physical characteristic. Another method has students collect time and distance measurements to compute how fast they can walk and run. They determine their own terminal velocities in much the same way they collected time and distance data on a real skydiver to compute the skydiver's freefall terminal velocity.

The video and hands-on activities are rich in observation opportunities. This makes classroom discussion an enriching experience for teachers and students.

Each activity is guided by the Project 2061 *Benchmarks for Science Literacy* published by the American Association for the Advancement of Science, the *National Science Education Standards* published by the National Research Council, and the *Curriculum and Evaluation Standards for School Mathematics* published by the National Council of Teachers of Mathematics.

The activities *Skydiver*, *Canopy Pilot*, and *Terminal Velocity* allow students to use a paper model to duplicate many of the actions they observe real skydivers do, thousands of feet in the air, at speeds in excess of one hundred miles per hour. The activities *Fall-timeters*, *Glide Ratio*, and *Terminal Velocity — Take Two* and *BASE Jumpers* are *video investigations*. Real-time video sequences of skydivers in freefall and flying their canopies provide a real-world context for making measurements and then using these measurements to compute ratios and rates.

Most of the *Gravity Rules!* video was shot at the Air Adventures West drop zone located just east of Taft, California.

Skydiver	paper model
How Fast Can You Walk?	personal measurements
How Fast Can You Run?	personal measurements
Climbing To Altitude	video measurements
Fall-Timeters	video measurements
Glide Ratio	video measurements
Canopy Pilot	paper model/measurements
Terminal Velocity	paper model/measurements
Terminal Velocity — Take Two	paper model/measurements
Base Jumper	video measurements
The Race	measurements

Activity
Grade Level Guide

A check mark in a grade level column next to an activity indicates that the activity is generally appropriate for that grade-level.

The Race activity has no connection with the sport of skydiving. It is designed to help students develop, in a logical and sequential manner, the ability to use a distance-time graph. This graph is the basic tool for mathematically representing motion.

The activities How Fast Can You Walk? and How Fast Can You Run? also have no direct connection to the sport of skydiving. These activities ask students to measure and compute a personal physical quantity, their fastest walking and running velocities. These activities provide introductory experiences helpful for interpreting and understanding the remaining activities that are placed within a skydiving context.

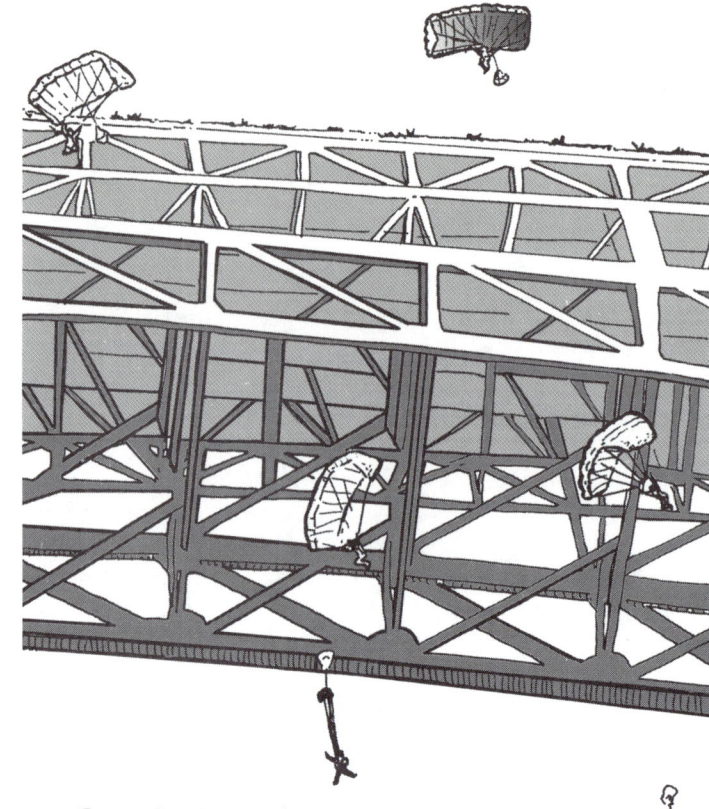

Grade Levels

	5	6	7	8	9	10	11	12
Skydiver!	✔	✔	✔	✔	✔	✔	✔	✔
How Fast Can You Walk?	✔	✔	✔	✔	✔	✔	✔	✔
How Fast Can You Run?	✔	✔	✔	✔	✔	✔	✔	✔
Climbing to Altitude			✔	✔	✔	✔	✔	✔
Fall-timeters			✔	✔	✔	✔	✔	✔
Terminal Velocity			✔	✔	✔	✔	✔	✔
Terminal Velocity — Take Two	✔	✔	✔	✔	✔	✔	✔	✔
Canopy Pilot	✔	✔	✔	✔	✔	✔	✔	✔
Glide Ratio		✔	✔	✔	✔	✔	✔	✔
Rolling Rectangles	✔	✔	✔	✔	✔	✔	✔	✔
BASE Jumping			✔	✔	✔	✔	✔	✔
The Race		✔	✔	✔	✔	✔	✔	✔

Skydiver

Focus
Forces and motion

Key Question
What forces act on a skydiver in freefall and how does the skydiver use these forces to move forwards, backwards, turn left, turn right, and change the rate of fall?

Focus
Students will observe a real skydiver in freefall perform basic flight maneuvers. Students will then cut, fold, and drop a paper skydiver to duplicate the maneuvers of the real skydiver.

Guiding Documents
Project 2061 Benchmarks
- *In the absence of retarding forces such as friction, an object will keep its direction of motion and its speed. Whenever an object is seen to speed up, slow down, or change direction, it can be assumed that an unbalanced force is acting on it [ed. Newton's first law of motion.]*
- *The change in motion of an object is proportional to the applied force and inversely proportional to the mass. [ed. Newton's second law of motion.]*
- *Things near the earth fall to the ground unless something holds them up.*

NRC Standards
- *The position of an object can be described by locating it relative to another object or the background.*
- *Whenever one object exerts force on another, a force equal in magnitude and opposite in direction is exerted on the first object. [ed. Newton's third law of motion.]*
- *Gravitation is a universal force that each mass exerts on any other mass. The strength of the gravitational attractive force between two masses is proportional to the masses and inversely proportional the square of the distance between them.*

NCTM Standard
- *Formulate problems from situations within and outside mathematics*

Math
Geometry and spatial sense
  symmetry
    line of symmetry

Science
Physical science
  Newton's laws of motion
  gravity
    center of gravity
  air resistance

Integrated Processes
Observing
Identifying and controlling variables
Comparing and contrasting
Generalizing relationships

Materials
For the class:
  Gravity Rules! video
For each pair of students:
  6 copies of the paper skydiver in the *Face-to-Earth Position*
  2 copies of the paper skydiver in the *Forward or Track Position*
  scissors
  ruler
  transparent tape

Background Information
Skydiving is a gravity-powered sport. Once the skydiver leaves the airplane, the attractive force of *gravity* pulls the skydiver towards the ground. The weight of the skydiver is a measure of this force (see *Skydiving, A Gravity Powered Sport!* in the *Appendix* for additional background information). As the downward velocity of the skydiver increases, a retarding force caused by the friction of falling through the air pushes upwards against the skydiver. This force is called *air resistance*.

After approximately 12 seconds of freefall, the forces acting on the skydiver are balanced and the skydiver continues to fall at a constant velocity called *terminal velocity* (see *What Is Terminal Velocity* in the *Appendix*).

A paper skydiver duplicates many of the motions of a real skydiver because the *forces* acting on a falling paper skydiver are essentially the same as the forces acting on a real skydiver in freefall. For example, in the section of the activity called *Hard Arch*, the paper skydiver — due to its light weight — reaches terminal velocity very quickly and falls straight down just like a real skydiver.

Skydivers can increase or decrease their terminal velocity by changing the area of their body facing the stream of air flowing past it. This air stream is called the *relative wind*. Arms and legs can be used to deflect the relative wind causing the skydiver to turn left or right, and move forward and backward. Use the *Boy On A Raft* and *How A Skydiver Flies* pages throughout your discussions with students to help them practice thinking about how skydivers apply Newton's third law of motion.

Arching the body (or the paper skydiver) makes the skydiver fall face-to-Earth, stable, and in control. From this position, the skydiver can make controlled turns, do flips, move forward or backward, fall faster

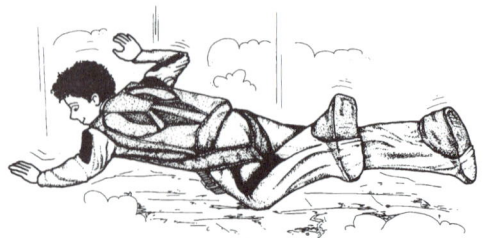

or slower, and maintain a clear view of the ground. In the arched face-to-Earth position, the center of gravity of a skydiver is located a few inches below the navel.

The video sequence (*Part III-2c*) shows Shelly opening her parachute. To many observers, she *appears* to go up! This sequence is an excellent visual example of *relative motion. Extension 6* describes an activity that gives students a simple method for simulating and understanding why Shelly *appears* to go up.

Management

1. Schedule at least two class sessions for this activity. The first session is for viewing and discussing the video. Preview *Parts I* through *VIII* (approximately eight minutes in length) of the *Gravity Rules!* video. These video sequences are designed to create student interest in the sport of skydiving, stimulate questions, and serve as a source of real-world actions for repeated and refined observations.

2. The second session is for cutting, folding, and testing the paper skydivers. Preview *Part IX, Resource Section,* of the video. In *Part IX* students observe one or more skydivers performing a freefall maneuver at normal speed and in slow motion. *Part IX* should be shown to students as they cut and fold a paper skydiver so that when dropped, it duplicates the motion of the real skydiver.

3. Although students may want to color their skydivers, the crayons and inks can affect the way their skydivers fall. Have them delay coloring until the activity is concluded.

4. Test the pause control on the video player you will be using. If possible, use a video player that pauses the picture without blurring the image.

5. Good observation skills are basic to good science. The ability to make scientific observations is a skill acquired (like any other skill) through practice. Do not assume students have good observation skills. It is essential that students *critically* observe the video. This may require repeated viewings.

6. Make overhead transparencies of the pages *Boy on a Raft – Newton's Third Law of Motion* and *How a Skydiver "Flies."*

Procedure

Part 1: Observing the video

1. Prior to showing the video, make certain that students have paper and pencil in order to write down any questions they have, and, if possible, the observation that triggered the question.

2. Show *Parts I* through *VIII* of the video and discuss students' observations and questions.

3. Use the following *Did You See …?* questions to facilitate further discussion.

Did You See …?

- **a skydiver ride something out the door of the airplane?**
  [Cory Maples rides his surfboard out the door (*Part I - 1*).]

- **two skydivers flying upside down?**
  [Eli Thompson and Fritz Pfnur fly in the head-down position. Speed in excess of 200 miles per hour can be achieved by head-down flyers (*Part I-6*).]

- **a condensation trail (contrail) left by a high-flying jet?**
  [Eli and Fritz are seen flying in the head-down position with a contrail above them. (*Part I-6*).]

- **a skysurfer spin upside down?**
  [Skysurfer Tanya Garcia does the helicopter maneuver (*Part I-9*).]

- **a skydiver on her back and then flip over?**
  [Shelly falls on her back and then flips over to a face-to-Earth position (*Part VI-2e*).]

- **an important message to skydivers written on the ground?**
  [PULL is plowed into the ground (*Part III-2a*).]

- **a commercial written on the ground visible to flyers-by?**
  [SKYDIVE is plowed into the ground. (*Part III-2a*).]

- **a skydiver looking at his/her wrist?**
  [The skydiver is checking the wrist-mounted altimeter (*Part III-2c*).]

- **Shelly move her hand and turn?**
  [Shelly uses her left hand to divert the airflow causing her to make a left turn (*Part VI-2-b*).]

- **a skydiver falling up?**
  [Shelly opens her parachute after performing a set of basic maneuvers. Shelly slows down *relative* to the videographer making it *appear* she goes up (*Part X*).]

- **two skydivers spiral their canopies down?**
  [Skydivers use their steering controls to make turns as they descend (*Part VIII-4*).]

- **two people using the same parachute?**
  [Tandem jumpmaster Jerry Cook has a passenger attached to his chest with a special

harness. An extra large canopy is used to make a tandem skydive (*Part I-10*).]

- **a message painted on the bottom of a board?**
  [Steve has painted *Gravity Rules!* on the bottom of his surfboard (*Part VIII-11*).]
- **flapping cheeks on the face of a skydiver?**
  [The tandem passenger's face shows the effects of the air flowing over her face while in freefall (*Part I - 10*).]

Part 2: The paper skydiver
Uncontrolled Tumbling
  1. Show *Part IX-1* of the video.
  2. Pair the students and demonstrate how to make all cuts and folds.
  3. Distribute copies of the paper skydiver in the *Face-to-Earth Position*.
  4. Have the students cut around the skydiver figure just outside the heavy line.
  5. Show students how to hold the paper skydiver, as demonstrated in the video, vertically between thumb and forefinger.

  6. Have students drop their paper skydivers several times and then record their general observation on their student record sheet.

Discussion
Uncontrolled Tumbling
  1. Describe the motion of your falling paper skydiver. [Its fall wasn't predicable.]
  2. How was its motion like Shelly's? [The paper skydiver tumbles.] How was its motion different than Shelly's? [The paper skydiver often falls with a side-to-side, falling leaf motion.]
  3. What forces were acting on the paper skydiver as it fell? [Gravity pulled it towards the ground and its shape caused air to flow unevenly over its surface. This caused it to fall erratically.]

Procedure
Hard Arch: Finding the paper skydiver's center of gravity
  1. Have students locate the paper skydiver's vertical line of symmetry indicated by the broken lines labeled *a*.

  2. With the paper skydiver face down, instruct students to fold up and crease the skydiver along this line of symmetry.

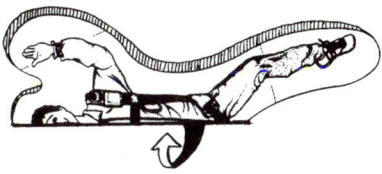

  3. With the skydiver in this folded position, have students cut around their skydiver, just inside the heavy line. As they cut, ask them, "Why this step?" [It insures the same amount of paper, both in area and mass, on both sides of the line of symmetry.]
  4. Tell them to open the folded skydiver, turn it over, and place the point of a pencil inside the figure on the line of symmetry. Have them move the pencil left or right until the skydiver balances in a horizontal position on the pencil point. As they do this, ask them, "Why this step?" [It insures the same amount of paper, both in mass and area, on the left and right side of the figure.

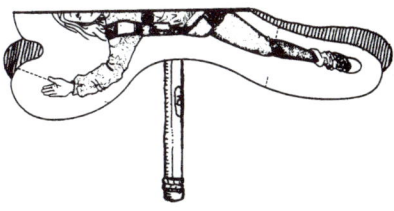

  5. Tell the students to mark the center of gravity point on the line of symmetry.
  6. Have them open the figure and place it down on the desk or table top. Instruct them to fold the paper skydiver up, along a line that passes through the marked center of gravity point and is perpendicular to the line of symmetry. The paper skydiver now has two perpendicular crease lines that intersect at the diver's center of gravity.

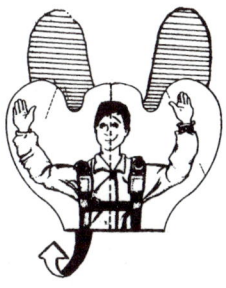

  7. With the paper skydiver face down, unfold the diver so that there is a slight upward slant along both crease lines. The diver's center of gravity is now slightly lower than any other part of the figure.
  8. Show *Part IX-2, Hard Arch* of the video.

9. Demonstrate for students that the proper release method, as shown in the video, is to hold the paper skydiver at shoulder height, face down, and parallel to the floor. With the skydiver balanced lightly on the fingers of both hands, release it by moving the hands to the sides, allowing the skydiver to slide off the fingertips.

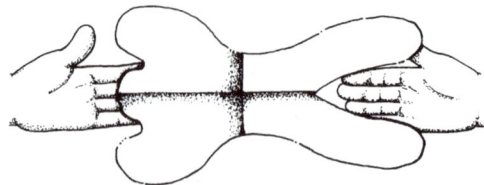

10. Allow students the opportunity to drop their paper skydivers several times and record their general observation on their student page.

Discussion
Hard Arch
1. Describe the motion of your falling paper skydiver. [It falls slowly along a straight-line path to the ground.]
2. How was its motion like Shelly's? [It fell face-to-Earth. Its motion was straight down and controlled.] How was its motion different than Shelly's? [It will sometimes slowly turn to the left or right. It will sometimes rock front-to-back or side-to-side. (This slightly unstable motion is called *potato chipping*.)]
3. How do the area and mass of the top half of the paper skydiver compare to the bottom half? [To balance on the point of the pencil, there must be the same amount of paper on both sides of the line perpendicular to the line of symmetry.]
4. What forces were acting on the paper skydiver as it fell? [Gravity and air resistance. The arch lowered the paper skydiver's center of gravity and the symmetrical arm and leg positions allowed air to flow evenly over its surface. (Use the *How A Skydiver "Flies."*)]
5. Why is falling face-to-Earth in a stable body position so important?

Procedure
Get Off My Back
1. Show *Part IX-3* of the video.
2. Have students drop their skydivers as shown in the video. Be sure they maintain the arch on their skydiver. (This time the center of gravity will be higher than any other part of the figure.)

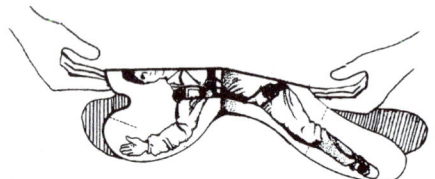

3. Let students drop their paper skydivers several times and record their observations on their record sheet.

Discussion
Get Off My Back
1. Describe the motion of your falling paper skydiver. [It fell a short distance and then flipped over, off its back, to a face-to-Earth position.]
2. How was its motion like Sherry's or Jason's? [Its flip-over motion appeared to be as fast as Sherry's or Jason's.] How was its motion different than Sherry's or Jason's? [The paper skydiver didn't get as stable. It rocked back and forth.]
3. What forces were acting on the paper skydiver as it fell? [There were two forces — gravity and air resistance. Gravity lowered the figure's center of gravity causing it to flip over. (Use the *How A Skydiver "Flies."*)]

Procedure
Left and Right Turns
1. Watch *Part IX-4* of the video.
2. Have students bend down the left or right arm of the paper skydiver along the broken line.
3. Instruct students to use the *Hard Arch* release to drop their paper skydiver. Let them drop their paper skydivers several times and record their observations on their record sheet.

Discussion
Left and Right Turns
1. Describe the motion of your falling paper skydiver. [It fell face-to-Earth and turned in the direction of the bent arm: right arm down, skydiver turns to the right; left arm down, skydiver turns to the left.]
2. How was its motion like Shelly's? [The down position of the paper skydiver's arm diverted air causing it to turn just like Shelly did when she dropped her arm. (Use the *Boy on a Raft – Newton's Third Law of Motion* and *How a Skydiver "Flies."*)] How was its motion different than Shelly's? [It spun faster and couldn't stop the turn like Shelly could.]
3. What forces were acting on the paper skydiver as it fell? [There were two forces — gravity and air resistance. The direction of the air flowing over the figure was diverted to cause the figure to turn.]

Procedure
Move Back — Backslide
1. Show *Part IX-5* of the video.
2. Have students cut out a new paper skydiver, find its center of gravity, and crease it so that it has an arch. Then, direct them to fold up and crease the legs along the broken lines.

3. Allow students to drop their skydivers several times and record their observations on their record sheet.

Discussion
Move Back — Backsliding
1. Describe the motion of your falling paper skydiver. [It moved backwards as it fell.]
2. How was its motion like Shelly's? [It moved backwards.] How was it different? [Sometimes it moved backwards in a left or right turn. (Slight adjustments to either or both legs usually corrects the turn.)]
3. What forces were acting on the paper skydiver as it fell? [The forces of gravity and air resistance. More air was diverted by the front of the paper skydiver causing it to move backwards. (Use the *How A Skydiver "Flies."*)]

Procedure
Move Forward — Tracking
1. Show *Part IX-6* of the video.
2. Distribute copies of the paper skydiver page, *Move Forward or Track Position.*
3. Instruct students to follow the instructions on their page. The easiest way to trim the paper skydiver is to tape enough paper strips to the head so that it dives towards the ground (nose heavy). A good track can then be obtained by cutting one small section of the paper strip at a time until a long, straight track is achieved.
4. Have students release the paper skydiver as shown in the video. (A very gentle push with the head slightly below the horizontal gives the best flight.) Allow plenty of time for students to adjust and test their tracking paper skydivers.
5. Direct them to drop test their skydiver several times and record their observations on their record sheet.

Discussion
Move Forward — Tracking
1. Describe the motion of your falling paper skydiver. [It moved along a straight or slightly curved horizontal path to the ground.]
2. How was its motion like Shelly's? [Its head went down and it flew away from the release point, not straight down.] How was it different? [It stayed in the track position until it hit the ground. The skydivers opened their parachutes after tracking away from each other.]
3. What forces were acting on the paper skydiver as it fell? [There were two forces — gravity and air resistance. (Use the *How A Skydiver "Flies."*)]

Procedure
Two-Way and Three-Way Formations
Funneled Exit
1. Show *Part IX, 7, 8,* and *9* of the video.
2. Have students tape skydivers together. Limit them to either two-way or three-way formations.
3. Be sure students find the center of gravity and crease the arch for each paper skydiver in the formation.
4. Have students predict on their record sheet what they think will happen when their skydiver formation is dropped.
5. Have students drop their paper skydivers several times and record their observations on their record sheet.

Discussion
Funneled Exit
1. Describe the motion of your falling paper skydivers. [Their path wasn't predictable.]
2. How was its motion like the three-way? [They fell out of control.] How was its motion different? [The paper skydivers never recovered into face-to-Earth positions.]
3. What forces were acting on the paper skydivers as they fell? [There were two forces — gravity and air resistance.]

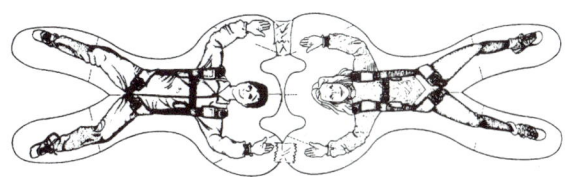

Two-Way Formation

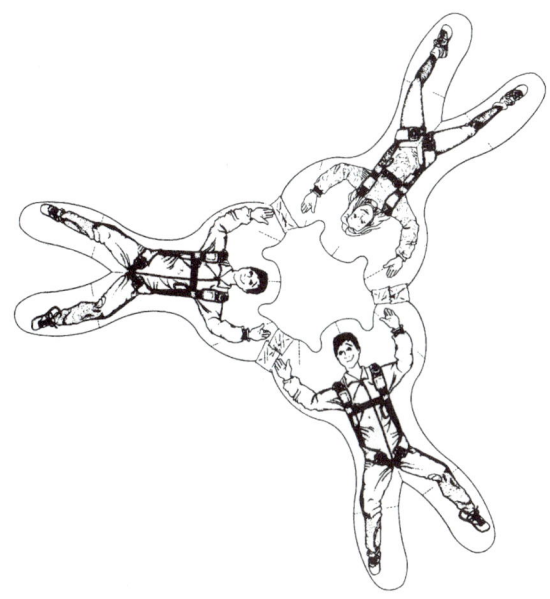

Three-Way Formation

Procedure
Two-Way and Three-Way Formations
Normal Flight
1. Have students predict on their record sheet what they think will happen when their skydiver formations are dropped for normal flight.
2. Have them drop their paper skydivers several times and record their observation on their record sheet.

Discussion
Normal Flight
1. Describe the motion of your falling paper skydivers. [They generally fell face-to-Earth along a straight path to the ground.]
2. How was their motion like the three-way? [They fell face-to-Earth.] How was it different? [The paper skydivers never changed positions.]
3. What forces were acting on the paper skydivers as they fell? [There were two forces — gravity and air resistance.]
4. Which was easier to fly, the two-way or three-way formation? [The three-way flies better because its symmetry makes for a more stable formation.]

Middle and Secondary School
Ask students to describe a skydive using Newton's three laws of motion. (Review the *Background Information* section.) [The force of gravity accelerates (Newton's second law, f=ma) the skydiver until terminal velocity is reached (Newton's first and second law). The skydiver diverts the air flowing over the body (Newton's third law) and uses the reaction force to maneuver.]

Extensions
1. Have students test different weights of paper for the paper skydiver. (Heavier paper takes longer to reach terminal velocity and will have to be dropped from much higher heights.)
2. Encourage them to fold different combinations of arms and legs and observe how the paper skydiver falls. For example, challenge students to get the paper skydiver to move sideways.
3. Direct the students to cut out one of the face-to-Earth paper skydivers *as exactly along the edge* of the figure as possible. Have them fold a hard arch and test drop it. The figure will probably spin rapidly. Why? Can the spin be controlled?
4. Have students build and test four-way, and even larger, formations. Explore the effects of symmetry on large formations.
5. Have a tracking contest. The current record for a straight line flight is just over 19 feet! The paper skydiver was dropped from a height of six feet.
6. Let students simulate the relative motion event of Dave, the freefall cameraman, videoing the opening of Shelly's parachute.

Have students work in pairs. Give one member of each pair a piece of cardboard with a six inch by four inch rectangular hole cut in its center. This student is going to be Dave, the freefall cameraman.

Find an open area where students can walk, side by side, in a straight line for at least 50 feet.

Direct the students to start walking at a constant speed. Have the camera person view the other through the hole in the cardboard. On the signal "ready, set, pull," have the walker playing Shelly's role, *pull* and slow down but the camera person keep walking at the same constant speed, keeping Shelly framed in the rectangular hole.

The camera person will have to continually turn towards the other walker to keep him/her framed in the cardboard. This creates the illusion that the walker is moving backwards when in fact, the walker has only slowed down relative to the camera person.

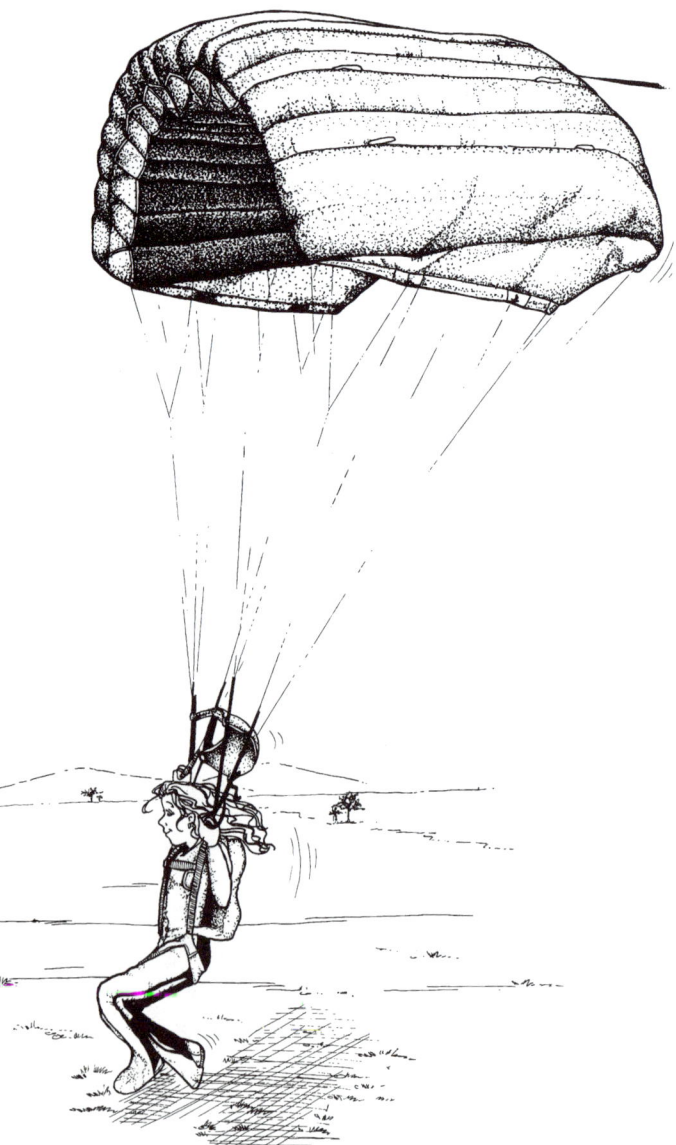

Paper Skydiver
Face-to-Earth Position

Uncontrolled Tumbling
Cut out the figure, cutting outside the bold solid line.

Hard Arch and Get Off My Back
Place the figure face down and fold up along the broken line *a*. With the figure folded in half, cut along the bold solid line. Find the skydiver's center of gravity.

Left and Right Turns
Fold down either arm using the broken lines as a guide.

Move Back
Fold up the legs using the broken lines as a guide.

Two-Way and
Three-Way Formations
Cut and fold two or more figures as described in *Hard Arch*.

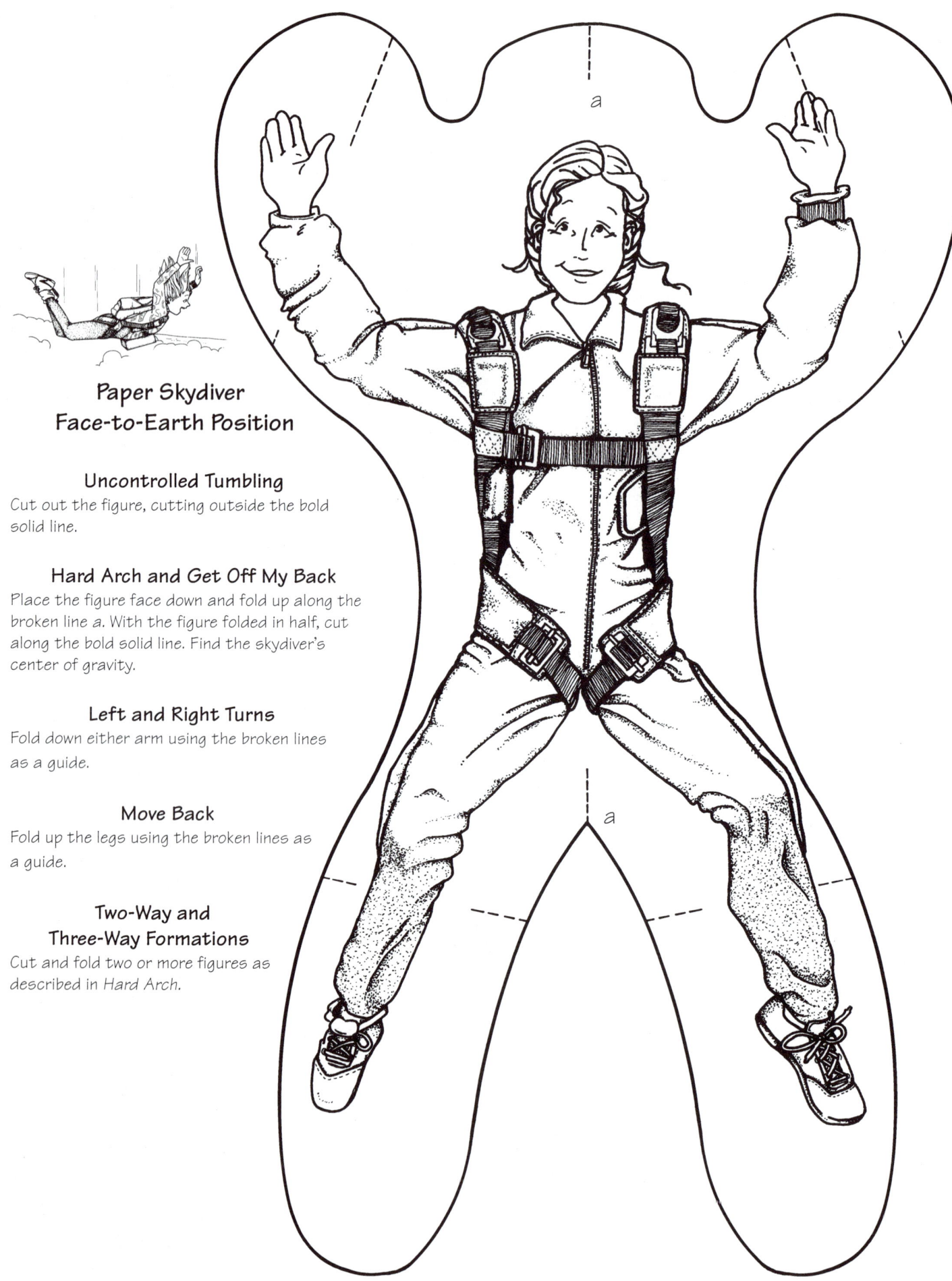

Paper Skydiver
Face-to-Earth Position

Uncontrolled Tumbling
Cut out the figure, cutting outside the bold solid line.

Hard Arch and Get Off My Back
Place the figure face down and fold up along the broken line a. With the figure folded in half, cut along the bold solid line. Find the skydiver's center of gravity.

Left and Right Turns
Fold down either arm using the broken lines as a guide.

Move Back
Fold up the legs using the broken lines as a guide.

Two-Way and
Three-Way Formations
Cut and fold two or more figures as described in *Hard Arch.*

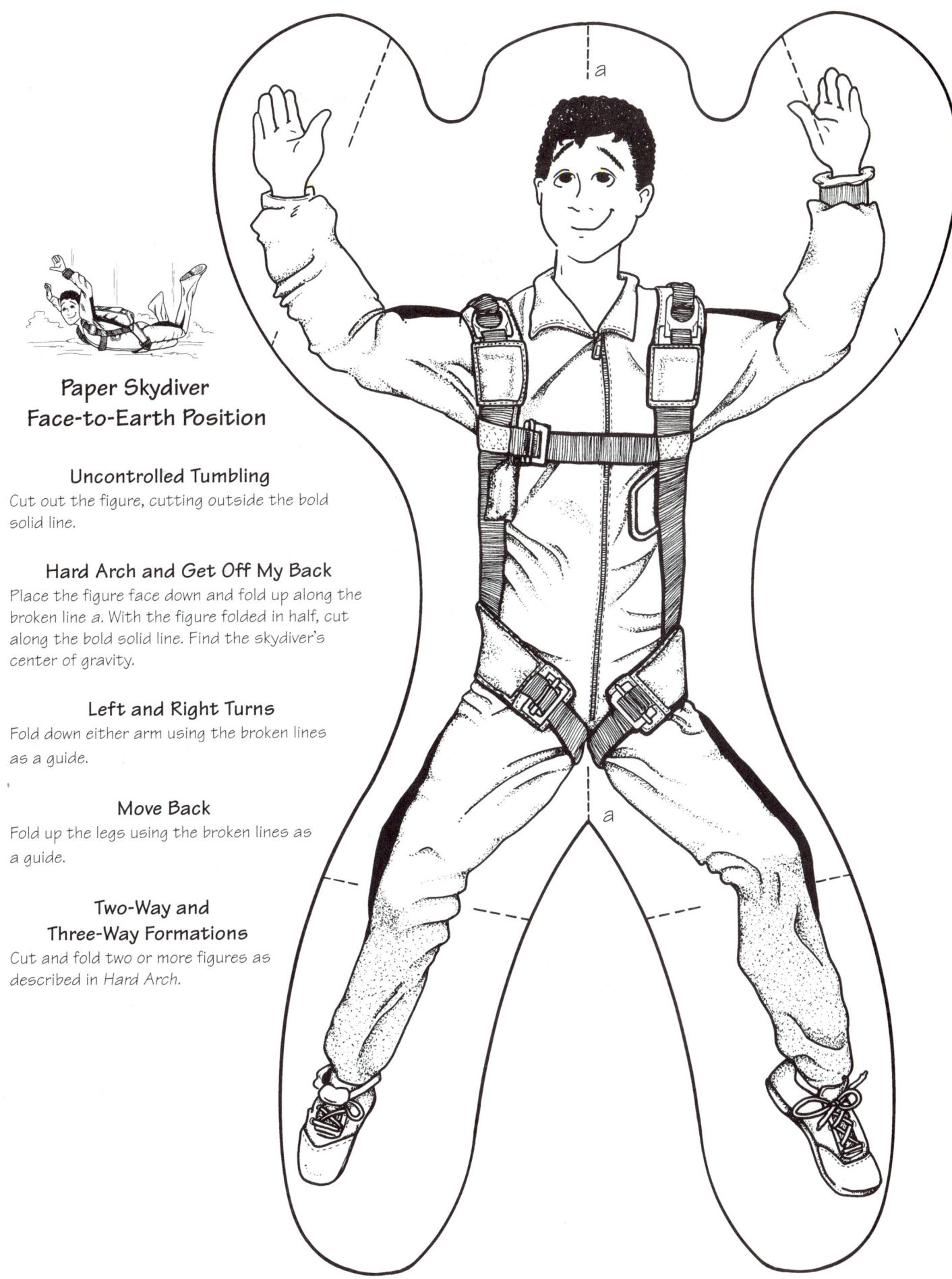

**Paper Skydiver
Face-to-Earth Position**

Uncontrolled Tumbling
Cut out the figure, cutting outside the bold solid line.

Hard Arch and Get Off My Back
Place the figure face down and fold up along the broken line *a*. With the figure folded in half, cut along the bold solid line. Find the skydiver's center of gravity.

Left and Right Turns
Fold down either arm using the broken lines as a guide.

Move Back
Fold up the legs using the broken lines as a guide.

Two-Way and
Three-Way Formations
Cut and fold two or more figures as described in *Hard Arch.*

GRAVITY RULES!
9
© 1998 AIMS Education Foundation

Paper Skydiver
Move Forward or Track Position

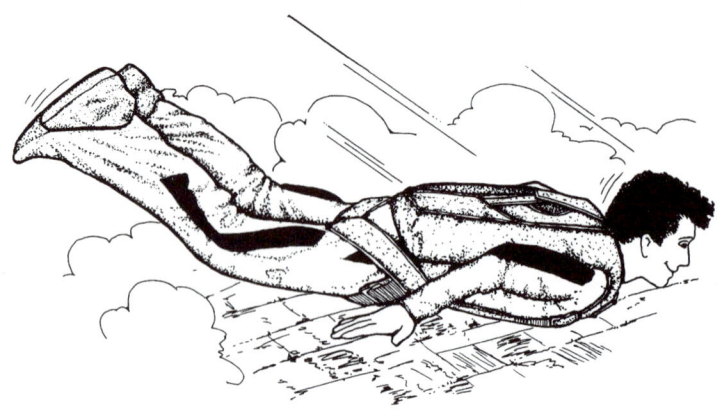

Cut out the skydiver, cutting **outside** the bold solid line. Place the skydiver face down. Fold up along the broken lines. With the skydiver now folded in half, cut along the bold solid line. This insures the same amount of paper on both sides of the broken line.

Cut out the two rectangular strips. Fold each strip in half, three times. On the backside of the skydiver, tape a folded strip to the head position.

Test fly the skydiver by gripping the feet between thumb, first, and second finger. With the skydiver slightly head down, give it a gentle horizontal push.

If the skydiver noses down, cut one section off the paper strip. If the skydiver noses up, add additional strips.

Extra Strips for the Track Position Paper Skydiver

The weight of the paper used to copy the track position skydiver will determine the number of paper strips needed to properly balance the paper skydiver. It is possible that four or more strips will be required.

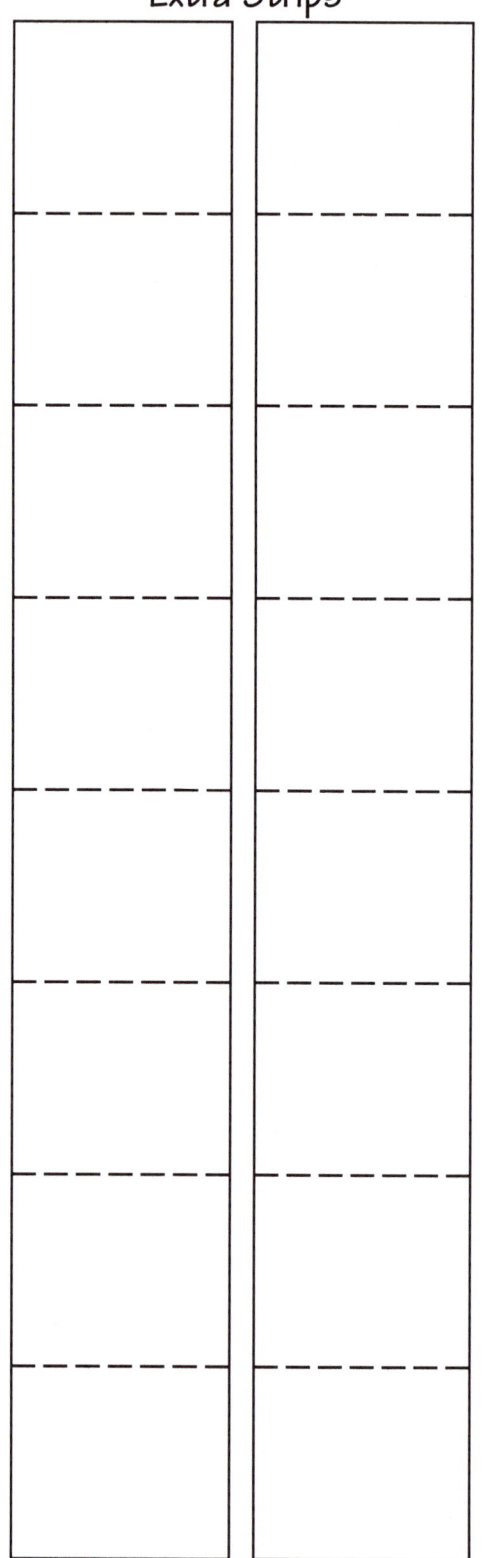

Extra Strips

Paper Skydiver
Move Forward or
Track Position

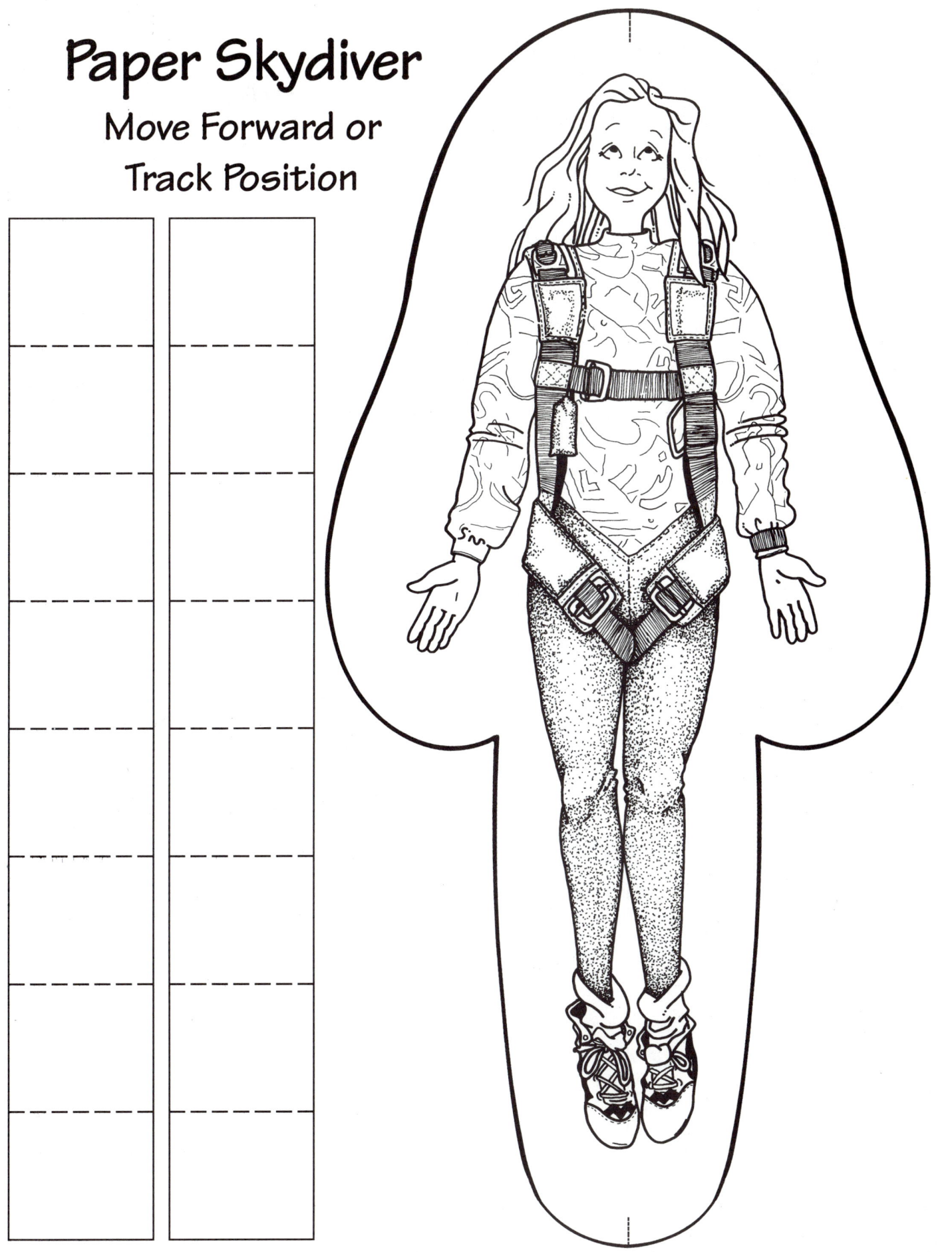

Paper Skydiver

Move Forward or
Track Position

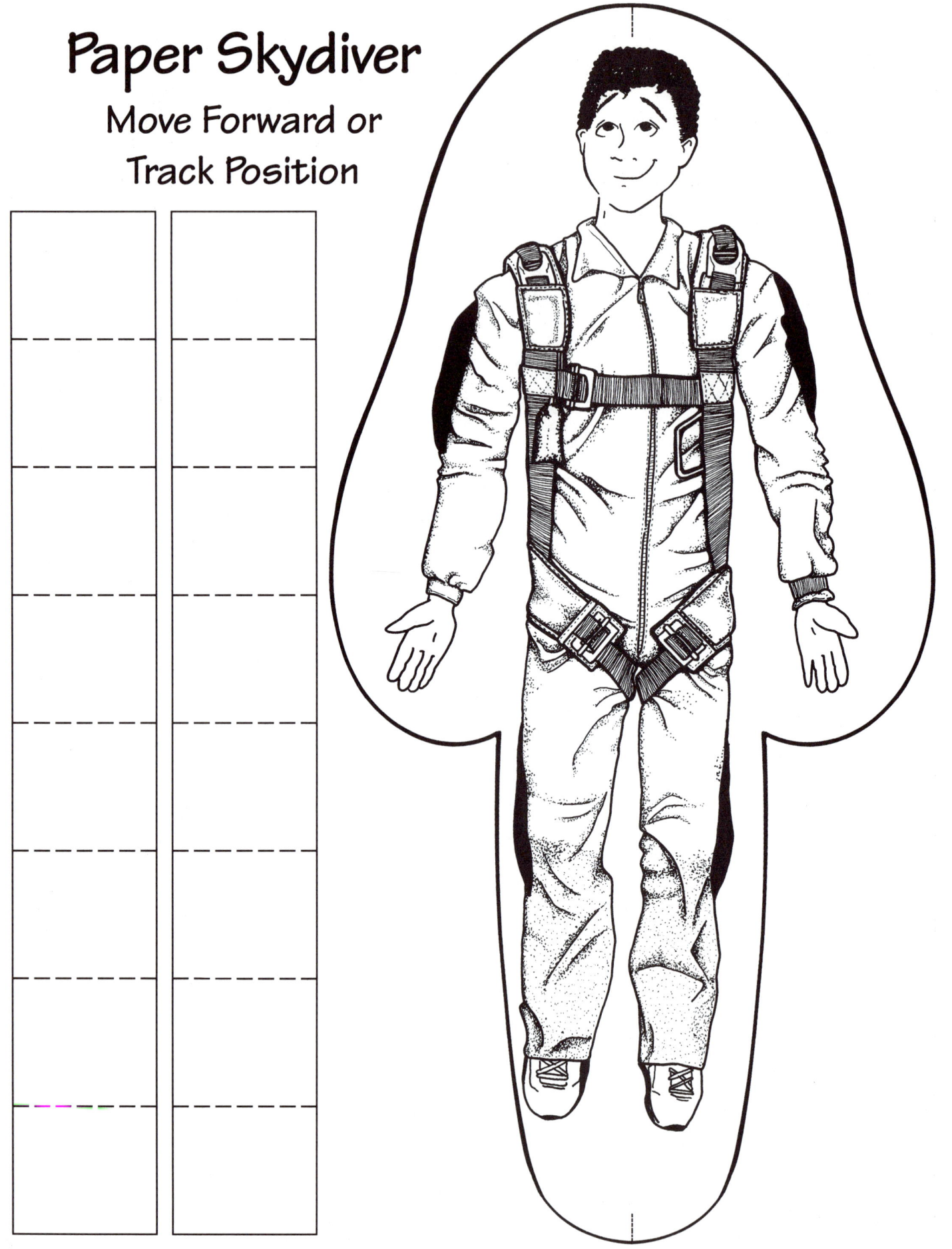

Extra Strips for the Track Position Paper Skydiver

The weight of the paper used to copy the track position skydiver will determine the number of paper strips needed to properly balance the paper skydiver. It is possible that four or more strips will be required.

Skydiver

Make several trials then record your observations.

Uncontrolled Tumbling

Hard Arch

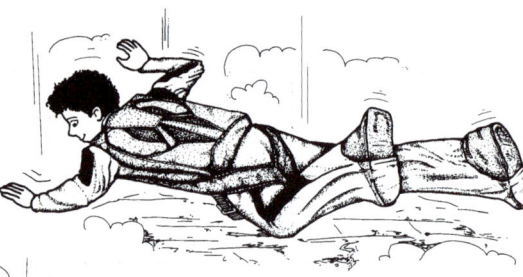

Left and Right Turns

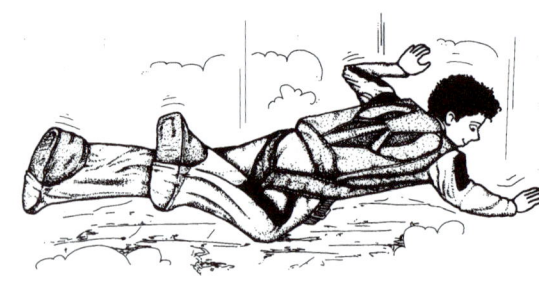

Get Off My Back

Move Back – Backslide

Skydiver

Make several trials then record your observations.

Normal
Flight

Two-Way and Three-Way Formations

Move Forward – Tracking

Normal
Flight

Funneled Exit

Boy On A Raft — Newton's Third Law of Motion

Newton's third law of motion states:

If two objects interact, the force exerted on Object 1 by Object 2 is equal in magnitude and opposite in direction to the force exerted on Object 2 by Object 1.

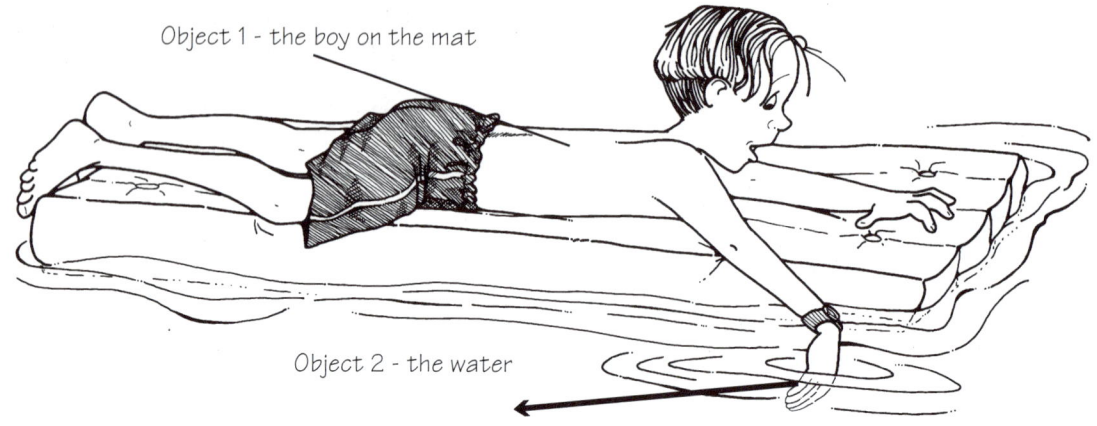

Object 1 - the boy on the mat

Object 2 - the water

If the boy on the floating mat is Object 1, and the water is Object 2, then, by Newton's third law of motion, when the boy exerts a force with his hand on the water, the water (Object 2) exerts an equal but opposite force on the boy's hand.

Newton's law is often stated this way: for every action there is an opposite but equal reaction. Stating the law this way hides the crucial fact that the *action force is on one object* while the *reaction force is on another object*. The action-reaction forces are *not on the same object!*

A boy floating on a mat is able to turn right or left, move forward or backward by exerting a force on the water.

Questions:

1. In the first picture the boy pushes water with his right hand in the direction shown by the arrow. In which direction will the floating mat and the boy move? [The boy and mat will turn to his left.]
2. In the second picture, the boy pushes water with his left hand in the direction shown by the arrow. In which direction will the floating mat and the boy move? [The boy and mat will turn to his right.]
3. What motions would the boy make with his hands to go forward? ... backward?

How A Skydiver "Flies"

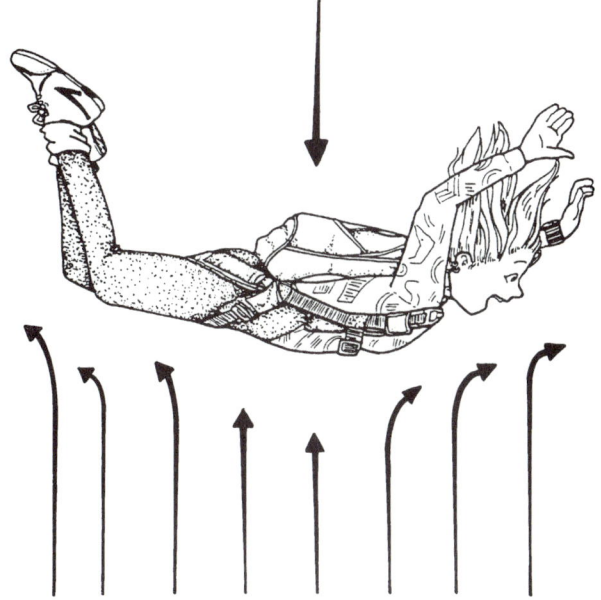

Newton's third law of motion states:

If two objects interact, the force exerted on Object 1 by Object 2 is equal in magnitude and opposite in direction to the force exerted on Object 2 by Object 1.

If the skydiver is Object 1, and the air passing over the skydiver is Object 2, then, by Newton's third law of motion, when the skydiver exerts a force on the air flowing past him/her, the air (Object 2) exerts an equal but opposite force on the skydiver.

A skydiver is able to fall straight down, turn left or right, move forward or backward by exerting a force (deflecting) on the air passing over his/her body. The reaction force on the skydiver then changes the direction of motion or position of the skydiver.

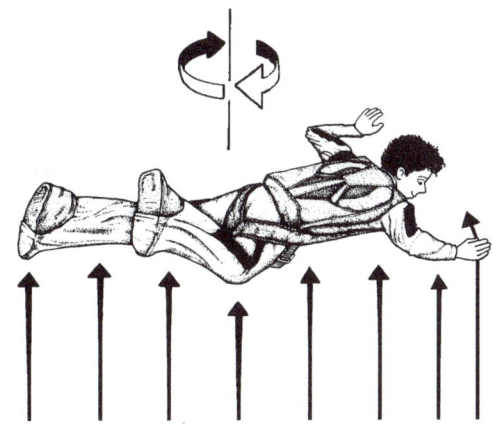

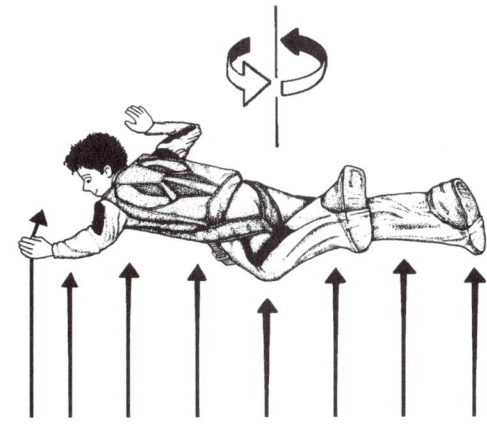

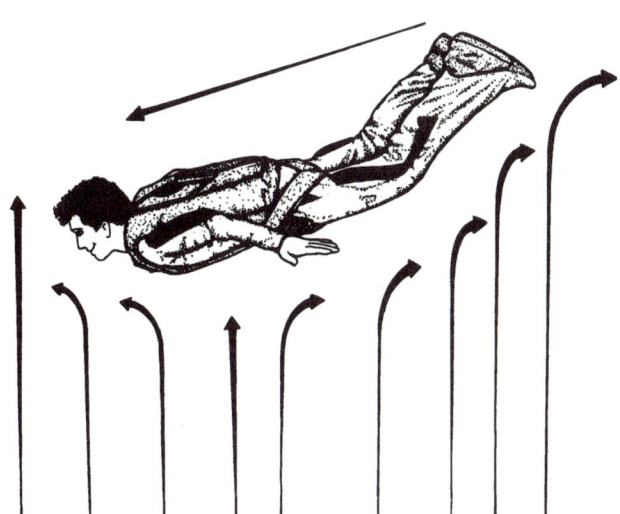

Tiny Broadwick and Bill Booth — Parachuting Pioneers

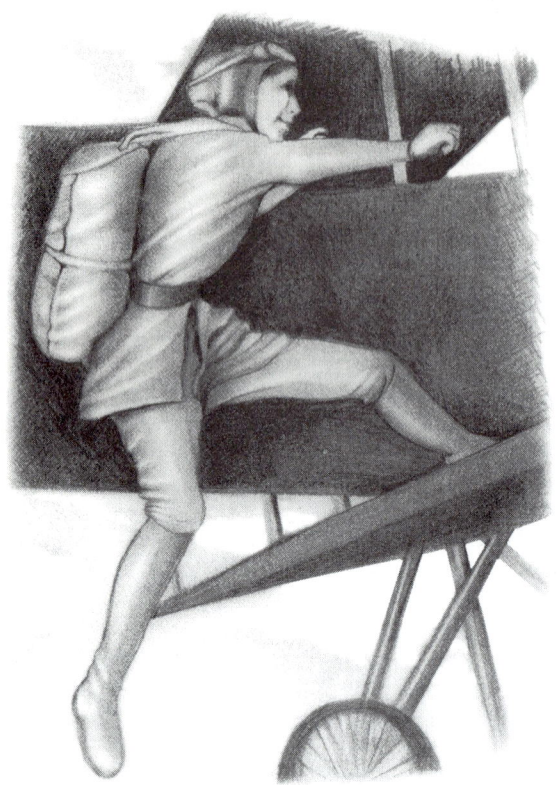

You have seen Shelly Jones jump from an airplane, freefall for almost one minute, and then throw out the pilot chute to open her parachute.

It was another young lady, Georgia "Tiny" Broadwick, who made the first freefall parachute jump.

The year was 1914. Tiny (she was four feet tall and weighed eighty-five pounds) was demonstrating the capabilities of a parachute to observers from the United States government.

Tiny's parachute was opened by a line called a static line. The static line connected her packed parachute to the airplane. As Tiny fell, the line stretched tight and opened her parachute pack. On her fourth jump, the static line snared a part on the airplane. For her fifth jump, Tiny cut the static line from the airplane, trimmed the end to within a foot or two of her packed parachute, and held the trimmed end tightly in her hand. Tiny jumped from the wing of the airplane. When clear of the airplane and while in freefall, Tiny pulled the line to open her parachute pack and thereby secured her position in the history of parachuting.

By the 1970s inventors and innovators were rapidly improving the parachuting equipment used by the growing number of sport parachutists. A revolutionary advance was made in 1976 when Bill Booth introduced the 3-ring main canopy release system. A parachutist with a main canopy malfunction needs a quick and reliable method for releasing the main canopy from the harness so that the reserve canopy can open without entangling with a still-attached main canopy. The 3-ring system (one system for each of the two risers) uses three interlocking rings which work like levers to decrease the suspended load on the release cable. The parachutist, when faced with an emergency requiring a main canopy cutaway, pulls the cutaway release cable to free the small ring to rotate through the middle ring. The middle ring, which is attached to the end of the riser, rotates through the large ring, freeing the riser from the harness. The large ring stays attached to the harness. The 3-ring release replaced a system that required four separate motions to activate. During the time it took to activate the old system, the skydiver lost several hundred feet of precious altitude.

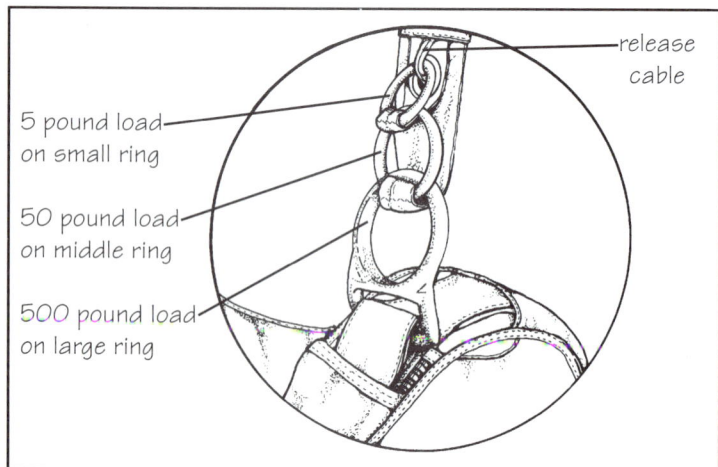

release cable

5 pound load on small ring

50 pound load on middle ring

500 pound load on large ring

3-ring release system

Bill Booth and Tiny Broadwick

Video Companion
for
Skydiver

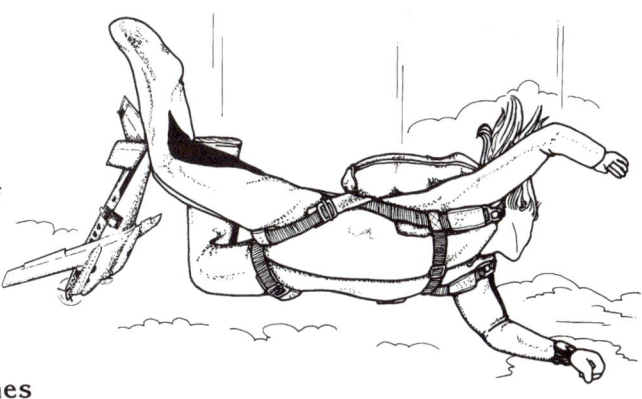

Note: Refer to the *Gravity Rules! Glossary* for definitions of skydiving words and phrases heard in the video.

> **Time = 01 minutes: 10 seconds**

I. **Opening Sequence — A Montage of Skydiving Scenes**
    1. Skysurfer Cory Maples exits the airplane at an altitude of 13,500 feet.
    2. A tandem passenger gets her first look from an open airplane door at 13,500 feet.
    3. Two red-suited jumpmasters exit holding onto the sides of a student skydiver.
    4. Dave Chrouch, a skydiving videographer, is taking the pictures. In this scene, he watches the airplane as he falls away and it flies away.
    5. Tandem jumpmaster Jerry Cook and a tandem passenger exit the airplane.
    6. A condensation trail made by a high-flying jet is in the background *above* Eli Thompson and cameraman Fritz Pfnur as they fly in the head-down position. They high-five each other as they fly.
    7. Eli flies in the stand-up position, flips to the head-down position, and goes back to the stand-up position as Fritz flies to the camera.
    8. Skysurfer Tanya (Cha Cha) Garcia spins against a setting sun background.
    9. Tanya performs the helicopter maneuver.
    10. The tandem pair clown for the camera. Notice the flapping cheeks on the passenger.

> **Time = 01 minute: 41 seconds**

II. **Shelly Describes a Skydiver's Equipment**

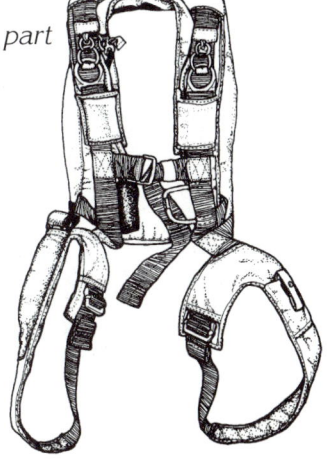

> *"The parachute is the most important part of the skydiver's equipment. This part of the parachute that my legs and arms fit through is called the harness."*

1. **The harness**
    a. The black strap across Shelly's chest is the chest strap.
    b. Shelly touches a leg strap.
    c. Shelly touches a shoulder strap.
    > *"This part of my parachute, on my back, is called the container."*
2. **The container**
    > *"My main parachute is packed in the bottom of the container."*
    a. Where the main parachute is packed
    > *"My reserve parachute is packed in the top."*
    b. Where the reserve parachute is packed
3. **Pilot chute**
    > *"This small parachute is called the pilot chute."*
    a. The pilot chute is tied to the end of the bridle.
    > *"I throw it into the air stream, it inflates and pulls the main pin, which pulls the deployment bag from the container."*
    b. The bridle pulls the main release pin, opening the container. The deployment bag is then pulled out of the container.
    > *"The suspension lines break free of the rubber bands holding them to the deployment bag."*
    c. The suspension lines are neatly attached to the deployment bag with rubber bands. The suspension lines break loose of the rubber bands in sequence. This keeps the lines from getting tangled.
    > *"When you get line stretch the main parachute is pulled from the bag. My main parachute, we call them canopies, opens."*
    d. When the lines are stretched out, the main canopy is pulled from the deployment bag.

4. **Steering lines**
   "I use the steering lines to fly it for a nice soft landing on the ground."
   a. Shelly has her hands in the loops (called toggles) at the lower ends of the steering lines.
5. **Cutaway handle**
   "If something goes wrong with my main parachute I pull this purple cutaway handle which releases it from the harness."
   a. Shelly pulls the cutaway handle which activates the three-ring releases allowing the main canopy to detach from the harness.
6. **Reserve handle**
   "And then I pull this handle to open my reserve parachute."
   a. Shelly pulls the reserve handle. The spring-loaded pilot chute pops out into the air stream.
7. **Altimeter**
   "This instrument that looks like a clock is called an altimeter. It tells me what altitude I'm at."
   a. The red zone of the dial is to warn Shelly that she is near the ground.

> Time = 02 minutes: 50 seconds

III. **Why A Skydiver Learns to Fall Face-to-Earth**
   1. **Vic Logan, a certified Accelerated Freefall (AFF) jumpmaster instructs an AFF student, Kyle Adden, on the proper way to exit an airplane in order to be in a face-to-Earth body position.**
   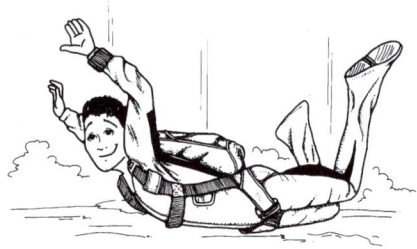
      "The most important freefall skill a skydiver learns is to fall face-to-Earth in a stable position. And there's at least three good reasons why."
   2. **The three good reasons**
      "First, the skydiver can see the Earth. This helps in judging altitude."
      a. The skydiver can see the ground which helps maintain altitude awareness.
      "Second, tumbling through the air can be dangerous. The skydiver can easily become disoriented and loose track of time and altitude. Falling face-to-Earth, and stable, provides a safe starting position for further maneuvering."
      b. Tumbling is disorienting to the skydiver.
      "And third, when it's time to open the parachute, a face-to-Earth position provides a clear path for the parachute to open without wrapping itself around the skydiver."
      c. Face-to-Earth is the best body position for opening the parachute.

> Time = 03 minutes: 33 seconds

IV. **Learning to Arch**
      "Falling face-to-Earth is easy to do but it is more natural for a falling person to flail their arms and pedal their legs. A skydiver arches their [sic] back to get into a face-to-Earth position."
   1. **Jumpmaster Vic teaches Kyle how to arch his body.**

> Time = 03 minutes: 46 seconds

V. **Shelly Uses a Creeper to Demonstrate Basic Flight Maneuvers**
   1. **Left and right turns**
      "Once you're in a face-to-Earth stable body position you can use your arms and legs like the controls of an airplane to move left, or to turn right"
      a. Shelly does a left turn followed by a right turn.
   2. **Forward and backward movement**
      "You can also use your arms and legs to move forward, and backward."
      a. Shelly moves forward and then backward.

3. **Controlling fall rate to fall faster or fall slower**

   "You can also change the area your body presents to the relative wind to slow your fall rate, or speed up your fall rate." (There's a good hard arch shot here.)

   a. Shelly increases the frontal area of her body facing the relative wind to slow her fall rate.

   b. Shelly decreases the frontal area of her body facing the relative wind to speed up her fall rate.

4. **Shelly explains why skydiving is fun**

   "You don't have to just fall like a rock. That's what makes skydiving so much fun. You fly like a pilot controls an airplane — to fly!"

> Time = 04 minutes: 20 seconds

VI. **Shelly Demonstrates Basic Movements in the Air**

1. **Getting to altitude**

   a. The Beechcraft King Air lands to pick up the next load of skydivers.

   b. Shelly and Dave, on their way to the airplane, joke about the upcoming dive.

   c. Shelly and Dave ride in the truck that takes them to meet the airplane at the end of the runway.

   d. The Beechcraft King Air taxies to a stop and picks up the next load of skydivers.

   e. The Beechcraft King Air takes off.

   f. The skydivers clown for the camera.

   g. Michael Jackson, the pilot, checks his instruments.

   h. The airplane lines up for jump run.

   i. The skydivers get ready to jump.

   j. Shelly tumbles out of the airplane.

2. **Narration and further description**

   a. *"Tumbling out of the aircraft, Shelly arches her back to get into a face-to-Earth position.*

   b. *By moving her hands and arms she is able to turn left or right.*

   c. *She can also change her body position in order to fall faster or to fall slower.*

   d. *By flexing her knees Shelly is able to move backward; pulling her arms behind her and straightening her legs enables her to move forwards.*

   e. *After altering her center of gravity, she flips onto her back then rolls back over into a face-to-Earth position.*

   f. *At about four thousand feet, Shelly throws her pilot chute into the air, opening her main chute."*

   g. Shelly opens her parachute.

   h. Dave opens his purple-colored canopy and looks up to check that it is inflated properly.

   i. Shelly as seen by Dave from the air.

   j. Shelly as seen from the ground.

   k. Shelly lines up to land.

   l. Shelly flares her canopy, lands, and gives a "thumbs up" signaling that she had a good dive.

   m. Dave lands after Shelly.

> Time = 06 minutes: 28 seconds

VII. **Shelly Describes her First Skydive**

   "When I made my first skydive, or tried to make my first skydive, I was seventeen. I went up with my father — my father was my jumpmaster — and we got up in the plane and I was ready to go ...

and I got out on the step and my gut is all in a big knot and my heart is pounding through my chest and I looked back at my dad … with my goggles filled with tears and water and I told him 'I can't do it' … he said, 'That's okay' … and he pulled me back inside the plane and said, 'I'm going skydiving anyway.' He jumped out … and I landed with the plane. And it took me three years to try again … and when I tried again, it was the most incredible feeling … when you leave the plane … and you're looking up and you're falling away from the airplane and you know that you've done it … that you did it … and it was great."

Time = 07 minutes: 21 seconds

VIII. Closing Sequence
1. Eli exits the airplane doing a barrel roll maneuver.
2. Fritz flies head-down then goes to the stand-up position.
3. The tandem opens. Who pulled the ripcord — the Jumpmaster or the passenger?
4. Two skydivers spiral down together.
5. Tandems are preparing to land.
6. Jason Jasnos swoops over the camera.
7. A tandem is close to touching down.
8. Two skydivers land together.
9. Sherry Jones has fun landing her parachute.
10. Jason gathers his parachute and heads for the packing area.
11. Skysurfer Steve Clark reminds us that, *"Yes, gravity does rule."*

Time = 09 minutes: 00 seconds

IX. Resource Section
Skydiver Activity
1. **Uncontrolled tumbling**
   a. Shelly tumbles as she exits the plane.
   b. Slow motion replay
   c. Releasing the paper skydiver
   d. A paper skydiver duplicates the motion
   e. Replay of paper skydiver
2. **Hard arch**
   a. Kyle gets into the *hard arch* position.
   b. A slow motion replay
   c. Shelly arches in the air, followed by a slow motion replay.
   d. Releasing the paper skydiver
   e. A paper skydiver duplicates the motion.
3. **Get off my back**
   a. Sherry, Shelly, and Jason perform hard arches to get off their backs.
   b. A slow motion replay
   c. Releasing the paper skydiver
   d. A paper skydiver duplicates the motion.
4. **Left and right turns**
   a. Claudia Vargas and Jason use a creeper to practice a left turn followed by a right turn.
   b. Shelly in the air does a left turn followed by a right turn.
   c. A slow motion replay
   d. A paper skydiver duplicates the motions.

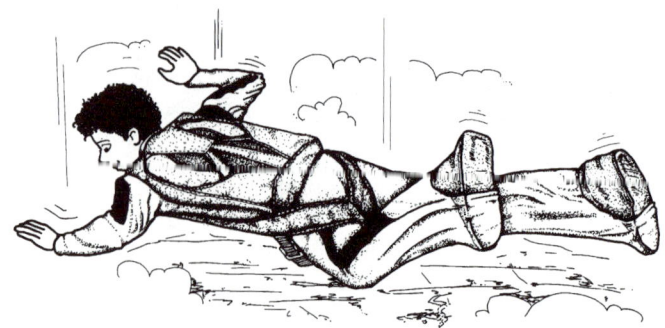

5. **Backslide**
   a. Claudia and Jason use a creeper to practice a backslide.
   b. Shelly in the air moves backwards.
   c. A slow motion replay
   d. A paper skydiver duplicates the backward motion.
6. **Tracking**
   a. Claudia and Jason use a creeper to practice tracking.
   b. Shelly, Sherry, and Jason track in the air.
   c. Shelly moves forward in the air.
   d. A slow motion replay
   e. Releasing the paper skydiver
   f. A paper skydiver duplicates the forward motion.

7. **3-Way formation**
   a. Shelly, Sherry, and Jason dirt dive a three-way door exit.
   b. They dirt dive the freefall maneuvers.
   c. Shelly, Sherry, and Jason are on the step. Shelly counts the exit, *"Ready, Set, GO."*
8. **Funneled exit**
   a. The three-way skydive begins with a funneled exit.
   b. Slow motion replay
   c. A three-way of paper skydivers duplicates the funneled exit.
9. **3-Way point flying**
   a. Shelly, Sherry, and Jason perform point maneuvers in the air. In competition, each formation change earns the team one point.
   b. Slow motion replay
   c. Three-way point flying release position for the paper skydivers
   d. The three paper skydivers fall in a stable formation.

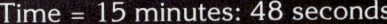

Time = 15 minutes: 48 seconds

X. **Opening the Parachute**
   1. **Shelly throws her pilot chute into the air stream which opens her parachute.**
   2. **A slow motion replay**
      a. The pilot chute inflates.
      b. The bridle pulls open the container.
      c. The deployment bag is pulled from the container.
      d. The suspension lines pull free of the deployment bag.
      e. Shelly grabs the risers as line stretch is reached.
      f. The slider starts down the suspension lines.
      g. The canopy inflates.

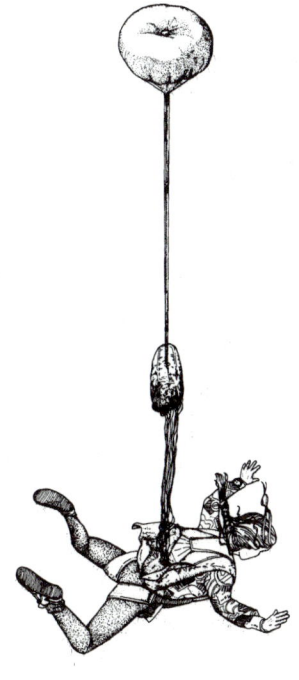

23

How  Fast Can You Walk?

Topic
Speed and velocity

Key Question
How fast can you walk?

Focus
Students will measure the time interval it takes them to walk, at their fastest rate, through a known distance. They will use this data to compute their fastest walking velocity.

Guiding Documents
Project 2061 Benchmark
- *Something that is moving may move steadily or change its direction. The greater the force is, the greater the change in motion will be. The more massive an object is, the less effect a given force will have.*

NRC Standard
- *The motion of an object can be described by its position, direction of motion, and speed. That motion can be measured and represented on a graph.*

NCTM Standard
- *Develop the concepts of rates and other derived and indirect measurements*

Math
Measurement
   length
   time
Rational numbers
   decimals
Estimation
   rounding

Science
Physical science
   average velocity, speed

Integrated Processes
Observing
Collecting and recording data
Interpreting data

Materials
Masking tape
Stopwatch, sports watch with a timer function, or a clock with a second hand

Background Information
To compute the average speed of a walker, divide the total distance traveled by the elapsed time.

The relationship between average speed, distance, and time is expressed in the following equation.

$$\text{average speed} = \frac{\text{total distance traveled}}{\text{interval of time}}$$

The *distance traveled* in the numerator of the formula is the *total distance traveled* during the time interval. Suppose you leave home in your car to travel to a destination exactly 50 miles away. As you're driving towards your destination you can't remember if you locked the door. You turn around, drive home and check the door, and start on your trip again. To compute the average *speed* of your trip, the return trip distance is part of the total distance traveled.

Although the words *speed* and *velocity* are used interchangeably in everyday language, a distinction is made in physics.

Velocity is speed in a known direction and the distance traveled is the *net* distance.

$$\text{average velocity} = \frac{\text{net distance traveled}}{\text{interval of time}}$$

Think back to the car trip example. If it's exactly 50 miles from your home to your destination, the *net* distance traveled is 50 miles. The distance traveled during your return to home is not part of the net distance. In physics, the net distance is called *the displacement*.

For a detailed discussion of *average velocity*, see the activity *The Race*.

The objectives of this activity are to help students develop the concepts of speed, velocity, and *terminal velocity. How Fast Can You Walk?* has students walk as fast as they can, measure the time taken to traverse a known distance, in a known direction, and then compute their personal "terminal velocity." If they're walking as fast as they can, they cannot be speeding up (accelerating) or slowing down (decelerating) so they must be moving at a constant velocity which means their acceleration is zero. They have reached their walking terminal velocity! (See the *What Is Terminal Velocity?* in the *Appendix*.)

Management
1. Locate a level sidewalk, corridor, or playing field at least 150 feet long. A playground or a football

field or track is an ideal location. Do not select a location with a slick floor covering like linoleum.

2. Lay a strip of masking tape 88 feet long along the course. If tape isn't practical, mark the lines of the course with chalk. Place a short piece of masking tape perpendicular to this tape at one end. This is the *Start* line. Lay another perpendicular strip of tape at the other end. This is the *Finish* line.

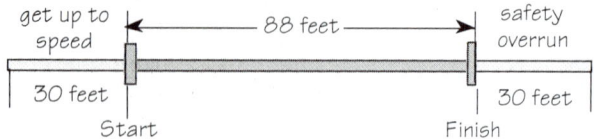

Allow a 30 foot *get up to speed* section before the *Start* line and a 30 foot *safety overrun* section after the *Finish* line.

3. Test the course to be sure there's sufficient unobstructed space to walk and safely slow down.

4. Measure your own terminal walking velocity. For example, if your best time for walking the length of a football field were 43 seconds (timed with a stopwatch), then your average velocity would be determined like this:

$$\text{velocity} = \frac{300 \text{ feet}}{43 \text{ seconds}} = 6.97 \frac{\text{feet}}{\text{second}}$$

To the nearest foot per second, your *walking terminal velocity* is 7 feet per second. Students will feel challenged to beat your walking terminal velocity.

5. Determine the approximate direction the course will be walked. For example, north to south.

6. Round all time measurements to the nearest second. Round all *velocity measurements* to the nearest foot per second.

7. Group students in pairs.

8. If stopwatches are not available, have students use the one-thousand, two-thousand, three-thousand, etc. count as an approximation of one-second intervals.

9. Discuss the common usages of the word *terminal*. Students often have one usage in mind and are sometimes confused by its combination with the word *velocity*. Students are sometimes thinking of an airport or bus *terminal* or an illness that is incurable and ends in death.

Procedure

1. Instruct students to use the *get up to speed* portion of the course to get to their fastest, sustained, walking velocity. Define this velocity as that walking velocity reached where, to go any faster, the walker would have to break into a run.

2. Direct them to take time measurements at the *Start* and *Finish* lines.

3. Have students record the direction of the course on their page.

4. Instruct the students to take turns walking and timing each other through the measured distance.

Discussion

While you and your students are at the course, stand on the *Start* line, point to the *Finish* line, and tell your students, "If you could walk from this *Start* line to the *Finish* line, 88 feet away, in exactly one second, you would be traveling at 60 miles per hour."

Give students the opportunity to respond to your statement and ask additional questions. Most people have never thought about the relationship between time, distance, and speed even though they all have traveled on the highway at speeds in excess of 60 miles per hour.

Procedure

1. Once you and your students have returned to the classroom, have the students compute their walking velocities in feet per second and record the results.

2. Instruct them to record their *fastest* walking velocity as their walking terminal velocity.

3. Ask students to list things they might do to raise their walking terminal velocity.

4. Distribute the *Terminal Velocity Graph* page. Have students record their *walking terminal velocity* from the previous page and use this data to complete the table at the top of their page.

5. Instruct them to make a line graph of the data in the table. The vertical scale of the graph was selected so that the *running terminal velocity* and Shelly's *terminal velocity*, to be measured and computed in the next two activities, can be added to the graph.

6. Distribute the *Terminal Velocity Graph Questions* page. Have students answer questions three and four. Assign questions five through nine only to those students that have studied the slope-intercept form, $y = mx+b$, of an algebraic linear equation.

7. Distribute the *Conversion Graph* page. Work through the example at the top of the page. Point out to students that, in the example, 88 is 44 doubled and 60 is 30 doubled. Instruct students to complete the table, draw the line graph, and answer questions one through four at the bottom of the page.

Discussion

1. What is the difference between speed and velocity? [Velocity is speed in a known direction.] Inform the students that many speed records, for example the land speed automobile record, have to be run in both directions to balance out the speed boost obtained by running with the wind.

2. Define *terminal velocity*. [It means you can't go any faster.]

3. Have students identify as many instances of *terminal velocity* as they can. [If any student responds to this question by giving *running* as an example, tell them that that's the next activity!]

4. Ask students what they think they could do to raise their walking terminal velocity.

5. Responses to the *Terminal Velocity Graph Questions* will vary. For question number 4, given a walking terminal velocity of 7 feet per second, one could walk 420 feet in one minute, 4,200 feet in ten minutes (almost one mile), and 25,200 feet in one hour. Unfortunately, for walks of one hour and one day, one's terminal velocity would rapidly decrease to a value much lower than 7 feet per second.

Responses to questions five through seven will depend on each individual's walking terminal velocity. The general method is as follows.

$$\text{Let the coordinates of } P = (X_1 , Y_1)$$
$$\text{and the coordinates of } Q = (X_2, Y_2)$$
$$\text{The slope } m = \frac{(Y_2 - Y_1)}{(X_2 - X_1)}$$

The response to question eight is that the slope represents the *walking terminal velocity*.

The response to question number nine will take the form $y = mx$ with m equal to the student's *walking terminal velocity*.

How *Fast* Can You *Walk*?

1. Record the distance in feet between the *Start* line and the *Finish* line.
2. For each of three trials, record the time it took you to walk the measured distance.
3. For each of your three trials, compute your velocity in feet per second. Use the relationship, *average velocity equals distance divided by time.*

	time	distance
Trial 1		
Trial 2		
Trial 3		

$$\text{average velocity} = \frac{\text{distance}}{\text{time}}$$

Direction of course: _____ to _____

Trial 1 average velocity = $\dfrac{\underline{\hspace{2cm}} \text{ feet}}{\underline{\hspace{2cm}} \text{ seconds}}$ = $\dfrac{\underline{\hspace{2cm}} \text{ feet}}{1 \text{ second}}$

Trial 2 average velocity = $\dfrac{\underline{\hspace{2cm}} \text{ feet}}{\underline{\hspace{2cm}} \text{ seconds}}$ = $\dfrac{\underline{\hspace{2cm}} \text{ feet}}{1 \text{ second}}$

Trial 3 average velocity = $\dfrac{\underline{\hspace{2cm}} \text{ feet}}{\underline{\hspace{2cm}} \text{ seconds}}$ = $\dfrac{\underline{\hspace{2cm}} \text{ feet}}{1 \text{ second}}$

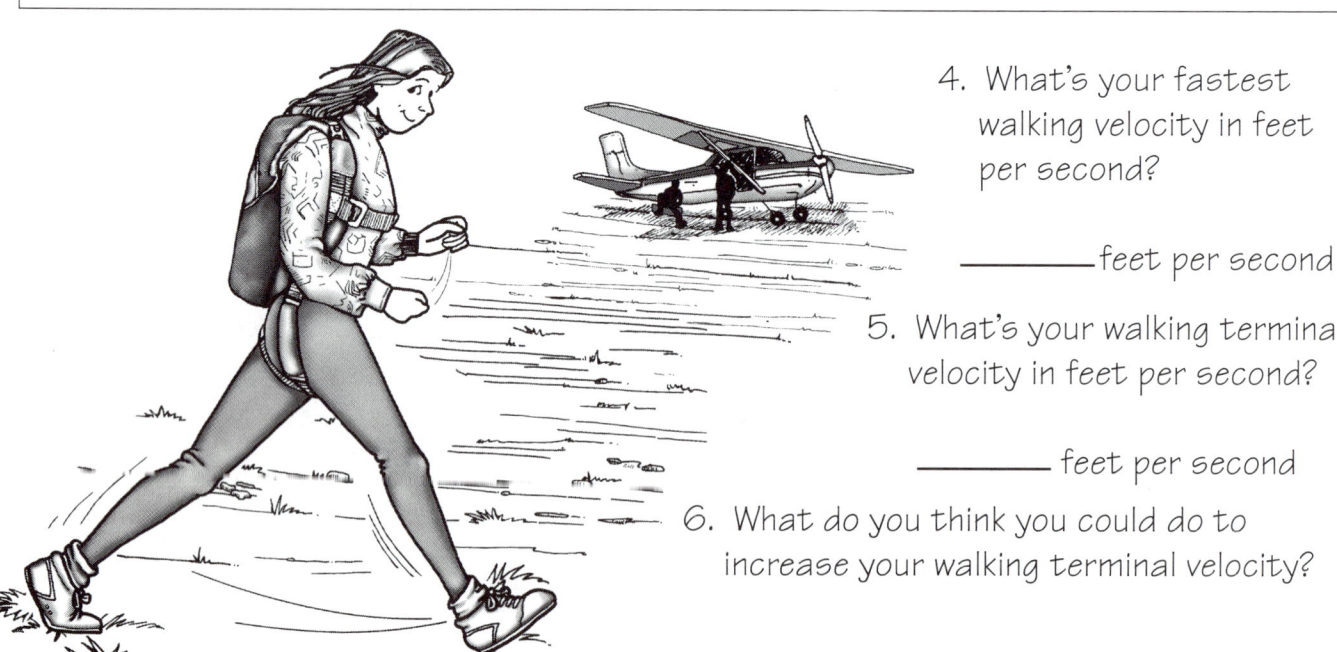

4. What's your fastest walking velocity in feet per second?

_____ feet per second

5. What's your walking terminal velocity in feet per second?

_____ feet per second

6. What do you think you could do to increase your walking terminal velocity?

How *Fast* Can You *Walk*?
Terminal Velocity Graph

Your walking terminal velocity = ——————— $\dfrac{\text{feet}}{\text{seconds}}$

1. Use your *terminal walking velocity*, the distance you can walk in one second, to complete the table.

time (seconds)	0	1	2	3	4	5	6	7	8	9	10
distance (feet)											

2. Graph the data in the table.

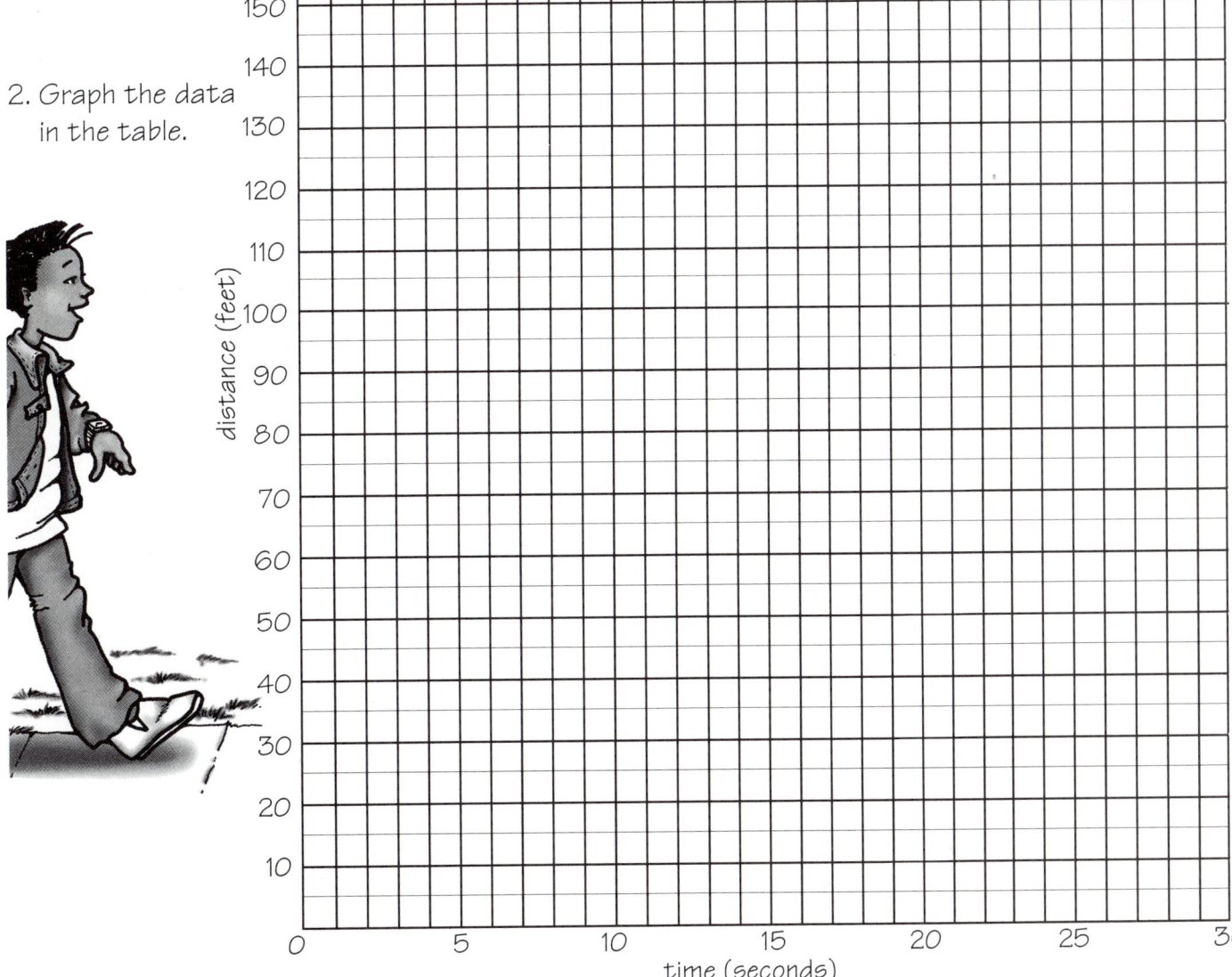

How  Fast Can You Walk?
Terminal Velocity Graph Questions

3. Project your graph to the edge of the grid.

4. At your walking terminal velocity, how far could you walk in one minute?

. . . in ten minutes?

. . . in one hour?

. . . in one day?

5. Pick a point on your line graph with an x-coordinate between 0 and 5 seconds. Label this P. Record the coordinates of this point.

P: (_____ , _____)

6. Pick a second point on your line graph with an x-coordinate between 15 and 25 seconds. Label this point Q. Record the coordinates of this point.

Q: (_____ , _____)

7. Compute the slope of the line segment $\overline{PQ}$.

8. What does the slope represent?

9. What is the equation of the line?

How **Fast** Can You **Walk**?
Conversion Graph

Use the fact that a speed of 44 feet per second is proportional to a speed of 30 miles per hour to complete the following table. Graph the data in the table to make a conversion graph that converts *feet per second* to *miles per hour* or *miles per hour* to *feet per second*.

Example: $\dfrac{44 \text{ feet per second}}{30 \text{ miles per hour}} = \dfrac{88 \text{ feet per second}}{Y \text{ miles per hour}}$, $\dfrac{44}{30} = \dfrac{88}{Y}$, $\dfrac{44}{30} = \dfrac{88}{60}$

X feet per second	0	5.5	11	22	44	88
Y miles per hour					30	

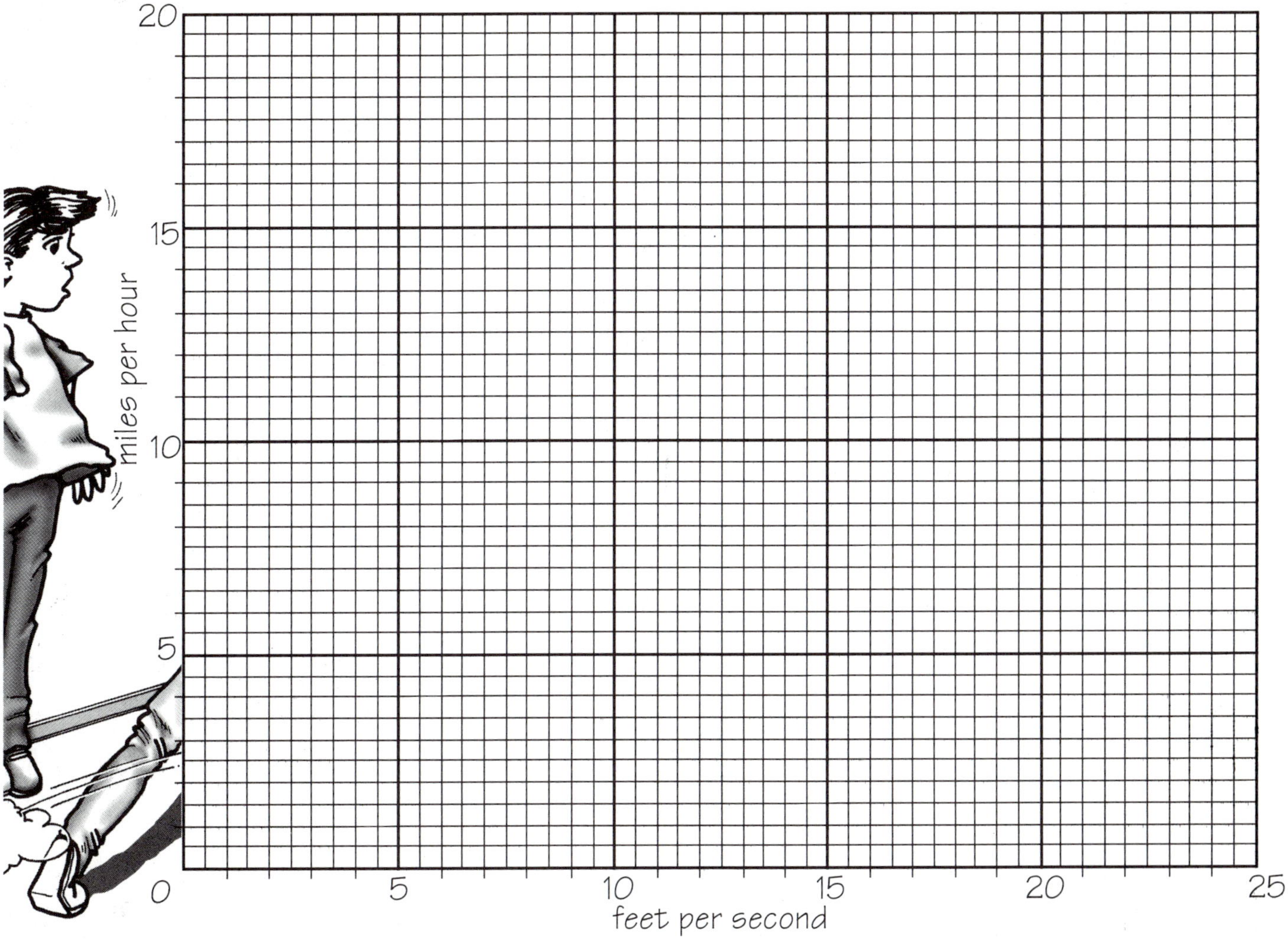

(graph: y-axis: miles per hour, 0 to 20; x-axis: feet per second, 0 to 25)

1. What's your walking terminal velocity in miles per hour?

2. What's your running terminal velocity (*see How Fast Can You Run?*) in miles per hour?

3. What's the highway speed limit in your state in miles per hour?

4. What's the highway speed limit in your state in feet per second?

How **FAST** Can You **RUN**?

Topic
Speed and velocity

Key Question
How fast can you run?

Focus
Students will measure the time interval it takes them to run, at their fastest rate, through a known distance. They will then use the collected data to compute their fastest running speed and velocity.

Guiding Documents
Project 2061 Benchmark
- *Something that is moving may move steadily or change its direction. The greater the force is, the greater the change in motion will be. The more massive an object is, the less effect a given force will have.*

NRC Standard
- *The motion of an object can be described by its position, direction of motion, and speed. That motion can be measured and represented on a graph.*

NCTM Standard
- *Develop the concepts of rates and other derived and indirect measurements*

Math
Measurement
   length
   time
Rational numbers
   decimals
Estimation
   rounding

Science
Physical science
   average velocity, speed

Integrated Processes
Observing
Collecting and recording data
Interpreting data

Materials
Masking tape
Stopwatch, sports watch with a timer function, or a clock with a seconds hand

Background Information
In this activity students will measure the elapsed time it takes to run a measured course and then compute their *running terminal velocity*. When compared to their walking terminal velocity, their running terminal velocity should be much higher. Computing their personal walking and running terminal velocities sets the stage for their understanding Shelly's *falling terminal velocity* as a general answer to the question, *How Fast Can You Fall?*

It may not be possible or convenient to take your class outdoors to measure their terminal running velocity. As an alternative, the terminal velocity of a Hot Wheels® car can be computed or measured in your classroom. See *Extension 2*.

Management
1. Locate a level sidewalk, corridor, or playing field at least 150 feet long. A playground or a football field or track is an ideal location. Do not select a location with a slick floor covering like linoleum.
2. Lay a strip of masking tape 88 feet long along the course. (If tape isn't practical, mark the lines of the course with chalk.) Place a short piece of masking tape perpendicular to this tape at one end. This is the *Start* line. Lay another perpendicular strip of tape at the other end. This is the *Finish* line.

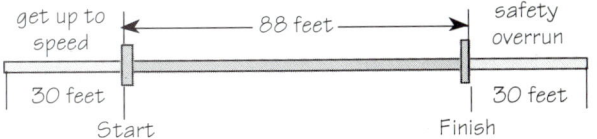

Allow a 30 foot *get up to speed* section before the *Start* line and a 30 foot *safety overrun* section after the *Finish* line.
3. Test the course to be sure there's sufficient unobstructed space to run the course and safely slow down.

4. Measure your own terminal running velocity. For example, if your fastest time for running the length of a football field were 18 seconds (timed with a stopwatch) then your average velocity, to the nearest foot per second, can be determined like this:

$$velocity = \frac{300 \text{ feet}}{18 \text{ seconds}} = 17 \frac{feet}{second}$$

Students will feel challenged to beat your fastest running terminal velocity.

5. Determine the approximate direction the course will be run. For example, north to south.
6. Round all time measurements to the nearest second. Round all *velocity* measurements to the nearest foot per second.
7. Group students in pairs.
8. If stopwatches are not available, have students use the one-thousand, two-thousand, three-thousand etc. count as an approximation of one-second intervals.
9. Inform the class that the reason for using feet per second and miles per hour as speed units in this activity is to be consistent with the units understood and used by the skydivers and pilots seen in the video. Also, state and national speed limits are predominately posted (and understood) in *miles per hour*.

Procedure

1. Instruct students to use the *get up to speed* portion of the course to get to their fastest, sustainable, running velocity. Define this velocity as that running velocity reached where they can't run any faster.
2. Direct students to take time measurements at the *Start* and *Finish* lines.
3. Have students record the direction of the course on their page.
4. Instruct the students to take turns running and timing each other through the measured course.
5. Have the students compute their running velocities in feet per second and record the results.
6. Instruct them to record their *fastest* running velocity as their running terminal velocity.
7. Ask students to list things they might do to raise their running terminal velocity.
8. Have students add the line graph of their *running terminal velocity* to the *Terminal Velocity Graph* of *How Fast Can You Walk?*
9. Instruct students to use the *Conversion Graph* to convert their running terminal velocity from *feet per second* to *miles per hour* and record the result.

Discussion

1. Have the students compare their walking terminal velocities to their running terminal velocities.
2. Ask students what they think they could do to raise their running terminal velocity. (Will those $100 sport shoes really help?)

3. Discuss whether or not *speed limit* signs should be described as *velocity limit* signs.
4. Ask students what a car's speedometer measures. Have them identify and design the components of a velocity meter. [Such a device would essentially be a compass connected to a speedometer.] What might such a device be used for? [Perhaps as the heart of an automated guidance system.]
5. How can you justify the use of measuring *elapsed time* to determine winners of track and swimming events? [The races are run over a predetermined course of known length. Distance is therefore a constant for every competitor.]
6. Are runners, swimmers, and other athletes always going as fast as they can? Explain.
7. Most schools have school and/or inter-school track meets. Give students with recorded "times" for any running event the opportunity to compute their average speeds, in *meters per second,* and share their results with the class.

Extensions

1. Secondary students enrolled (or planning to enroll) in a pre-calculus or calculus class should explore the effects of shortening the distance interval being measured. (Shortening the time interval shortens the distance interval. At some point in the real world, it becomes impractical to measure the time interval because it's so short. Theoretically, the limit of the distance/time ratio, as the time interval approaches zero, is defined as the *instantaneous* velocity.)
2. For students that have a strong algebra background or are taking a physics class, measuring the terminal velocity of a Hot Wheels® car can either substitute for or extend the measurement of a person's running terminal velocity. See *Computing and Measuring the Terminal Velocity of A Hot Wheels® Car* in the *Appendix*.

How FAST Can You RUN?

	time	distance
Trial 1		
Trial 2		
Trial 3		

1. Record the distance in feet between the *Start* line and the *Finish* line.

2. For each of three trials, record the time it took you to run the measured distance.

3. For each of your three trials, compute your average velocity in feet per second.

$$\text{average velocity} = \frac{\text{distance}}{\text{time}}$$

Direction of course: _____ to _____

Trial 1   average velocity = $\dfrac{\underline{\hspace{2cm}} \text{ feet}}{\text{seconds}}$ = $\dfrac{\underline{\hspace{2cm}} \text{ feet}}{1 \quad \text{second}}$

Trial 2   average velocity = $\dfrac{\underline{\hspace{2cm}} \text{ feet}}{\text{seconds}}$ = $\dfrac{\underline{\hspace{2cm}} \text{ feet}}{1 \quad \text{second}}$

Trial 3   average velocity = $\dfrac{\underline{\hspace{2cm}} \text{ feet}}{\text{seconds}}$ = $\dfrac{\underline{\hspace{2cm}} \text{ feet}}{1 \quad \text{second}}$

4. What's your best running velocity in feet per second? _____ feet per second

5. What's your running terminal velocity in feet per second? _____ feet per second

6. What do you think you could do to raise your running *terminal velocity*?

7. Compare your walking terminal velocity to your running *terminal velocity*.

8. Add a line graph of your running *terminal velocity* to the *Terminal Velocity Graph*.

Climbing To Altitude

Topic
Force and motion

Key Question
How long does it take an airplane carrying skydivers to takeoff, climb to jump run altitude, and then descend to a landing?

Focus
Students will learn how to read an *Instantaneous Vertical Speed Indicator* (IVSI), an *Altimeter*, and an *Airspeed Indicator*. An airplane with a load of skydivers takes off, climbs to altitude, discharges the load of jumpers, and then descends. At one-minute intervals students will observe and record altimeter, IVSI, and airspeed readings. These readings form an *altitude-time* data table. From the table students construct an *altitude-time* graph of the climb to altitude, jump run, and descent of the airplane.

Guiding Documents
Project 2061 Benchmark
- *Read analog and digital meters on instruments used to make direct measurements of length, volume, weight, elapsed time, rates, and temperature, and choose appropriate units for reporting various magnitudes.*

NRC Standard
- *The motion of an object can be described by its position, direction of motion, and speed. That motion can be measured and represented on a graph.*

NCTM Standards
- *Construct, read, and interpret tables, charts, and graphs*
- *Develop the concepts of rates and other derived and indirect measurements*
- *Understand and apply reasoning processes, with special attention to spatial reasoning and reasoning with proportions and graphs*
- *Represent situations and number patterns with tables, graphs, verbal rules, and equations and explore the interrelationships of these representations*
- *Understand the concepts of variable, expression, and equation*

Math
Ratio and proportion

Graphs
Estimation
  rounding
Function

Science
Physical science
  average velocity

Integrated Processes
Observing
Collecting and recording data
Interpreting data
Applying

Materials
Gravity Rules! video
  Climbing to Altitude sequence
Student pages
Scissors
Transparent tape or glue sticks

Background Information
The *Climbing to Altitude* video sequence begins with an explanation of the flight group instruments followed by the airplane's take off and slow climb to altitude. It then transitions to a one-minute *jump run*. At the end of the jump run, the skydivers jump out of the airplane. After the jumpers are clear, the airplane rapidly descends to a landing. The pilot's basic flight instruments are visible throughout the whole sequence.

Soon after take off, Mike Jackson, the pilot, sets the engine throttles and flight controls so that the airplane climbs at a constant rate to jump altitude. One of the instruments Mike uses to check his *rate of climb* is called the Instantaneous Vertical Speed Indicator (IVSI).

There is another vertical speed indicator on Mike's instrument panel (not seen in the video) that has a six- to nine-second lag time between indicating the *trend* — going up or going down — to settling down and indicating the *rate* of vertical speed. It's used as a backup to the IVSI.

Directly above the IVSI is the altimeter. An aircraft altimeter is more of a precision instrument than a sky-diving altimeter. The aircraft altimeter can be adjusted to barometric (atmospheric) pressure. Mike typically sets the airplane's altimeter to local barometric pressure as reported by the air traffic controller with whom Mike communicates as he flies. Setting the altimeter to field barometric pressure, while the airplane is on the ground, sets the altimeter to read *altitude above mean sea level.*

Mike usually takes off to the south, turns left, and then circles the drop zone as the airplane climbs to altitude.

He levels the airplane at 13,500 feet and sets up for the jump run. Jump runs normally last two minutes. When Mike gets close to the drop zone, he reduces the speed of the airplane and lowers the flaps. Flaps are the movable, rear sections of a wing located near the fuse-lage (body) of the airplane. Flaps provide more lift at lower airspeeds. This is necessary for the safety of the jumpers. The lowering of the flaps is the signal to a skydiver stationed near the door to open the door, look out, and visually locate the drop zone. From his knowl-edge of the wind velocities, both at altitude and near the ground, Mike determines the *spot*. The spot is the point over the ground where Mike turns on the green light visible to the skydivers near the open door. The green light is their signal to jump. A good spot allows every jumper the opportunity to land on or near the drop zone.

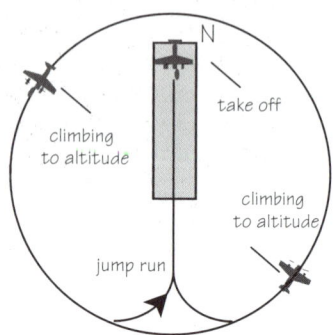

After the jumpers are away, Mike raises the flaps and reduces the power on the engines with the throttles. Without the power of the engines, the Beechcraft King Air, falls rapidly. The altimeter can be seen to, as pilots say, *unwind*. When the airspeed builds up to around 200 knots (see the *Reading an Airspeed Indicator* page), Mike pulls back on the controls to decrease the descent rate of the airplane. He lands, south to north, and waits at the end of the runway for the next load of skydivers to arrive.

Management

1. Students should complete the *Gravity Rules!* activity before attempting *Climbing to Altitude.*
2. Take the time to view the related video sequence, *Climbing to Altitude*, to set the stage for the activity.
3. Consider taking data from the video as a challenge. Scientists and engineers are often faced with less than perfect experimental or project conditions. The space program provides numerous examples of equipment that broke down and instruments that malfunctioned. Still, the scientists and engineers that work in the space program take great pride in their ability to, in their own jargon, *work around the problem*. The instruments are not always clearly seen in the video, but the tape can be stopped, rewound, played in slow motion, and stop-framed to *work around the problem*. It's hard to imagine real scientists and engineers making only *one pass* through the data record.
4. You have the option to do the activity *without* collecting data from the video. With this option, students compute *average* ascent and descent rates. See *Procedure: Doing the Activity Without Collecting Data from the Video.*
5. If you choose to have students collect data from the video, group them in teams of three.
6. If the video is difficult for students in the back of your class to view, have them, in groups of nine, gather near the video player and monitor to gather their data. It takes approximately three minutes to gather the data. Those not recording data could complete the *Rate of Climb Table* page.

Procedure
Reading An Instantaneous Vertical Speed Indicator
1. Make a transparency of *The Instantaneous Vertical Speed Indicator* page.
2. Distribute the *The Instantaneous Vertical Speed Indicator* page.
3. Point out the different scale divisions and explain how to read the Instantaneous Vertical Speed Indicator. The IVSI is indicating a 1000 feet per minute rate of climb.

4. Instruct students to answer the questions on the page.

Answers to the *Instantaneous Vertical Speed Indicator* student page
1. Climbing at 600 feet per minute
2. Descending at 2000 feet per minute
3. The white lines indicate the limits of the IVSI. The maximum indicated rate of climb and descent is 3500 feet per minute. If these limits are reached, a pilot would say the IVSI is *pegged*.
4. The most obvious action is to look out the window. If most of what you see is sky, then you're climbing at a rate of at least 3500 feet per minute. If most of what you see is ground, then you're descending at a rate at least 3500 feet per minute. Other actions could include listening to the sound of the engines, or checking the altimeter to see if it's unwinding (going down) or winding (going up).

Procedure
Reading an Aircraft Altimeter
1. Make a transparency of the *Aircraft Altimeter* page.
2. Distribute the *Aircraft Altimeter* page.
3. Point out the different scale divisions and explain how to read the altimeter. The altimeter at the top of the page indicates an altitude of almost 520 feet above mean sea level. This is what the altimeter indicates, in the video, just before taking off.
4. Instruct students to answer the questions on the page.

[*Optional: Collecting airspeed data is not required to complete the activity. It is included because the airspeed, as seen in the video, does change dramatically.*]

Answers to the *Reading an Aircraft Altimeter* student page
1. 5520 feet
2. 13,500 feet
3. 39,000 feet

Procedure
Reading an Airspeed Indicator
1. Make a transparency of the *Airspeed Indicator* page.

2. Distribute the *Airspeed Indicator* page.
3. Point out the different scale divisions and explain how to read the airspeed indicator.
4. Instruct students to answer the questions on the page.

Answers to the *Reading the Airspeed Indicator* student page
1. 180 knots; 207 miles per hour
2. 110 knots; 126.5 miles per hour
3. 60 knots; 69 miles per hour

Procedure
Doing the Activity Without Collecting Data from the Video
1. Distribute the *Rate of Climb Table* page.
2. Instruct students to use the climb rate of 760 feet per minute to complete the table.
3. Direct the students to complete the page.
4. Distribute the *Climb to Altitude, Jump Run, and Descent Graph* pages.
5. Instruct the students to cut and glue or tape along the indicated lines to make the graph. Direct them to tape on the blank sides of the pages so that the tape doesn't interfere with the graphing.
6. Tell the students to use the data table to make a straight line graph.
7. Have the students indicate on their graphs the point at which Mike levels off at 13,500 feet.
8. Instruct students to draw the horizontal *jump run* line of the graph. At an altitude of 13,500 feet and a time of 18 minutes, Shelly and Dave jump from the airplane.

9. Have the students graph the average descent rate by drawing the straight line from 13,500 feet at 18 minutes to 550 feet at 22.5 minutes.
10. Instruct students to save their graphs for the next activity, *Fall-timeters*.

Doing the Activity Using the Vdeo
1. Distribute the *Climbing to Altitude Data* page.
2. Tell the students to choose one from their group to read the altimeter, another to read the IVSI, and the third to read the airspeed indicator.

3. Inform the students that the video has been edited so that they can obtain their readings approximately five seconds before and five seconds after the whole minute mark. Tell them to take their readings as near to the minute as possible. Direct them to take the readings every 30 seconds from the eighteenth minute through the landing.

4. Have students view the video and collect the data.

   The following data were collected from the video by using a four-head player equipped with slow motion and pause buttons. Use this data as a guide. (Note: At 11 minutes and 41 seconds, the screen blurs due to the camera pointing to the sun.)

Time (minutes : seconds)	Altitude (feet)	Vertical Speed (feet per second)	Airspeed Indicator (knots)
0:00':00":00			
00:00	550	1000	90
01:00	1360	800	90
02:00	2200	1000	90
03:00	3150	1600	90
04:00	3900	1000	90
05:00	4800	1500	90
06:00	5750	1500	90
07:00	6500	1000	90
08:00	7250	1000	90
09:00	8050	1000	90
10:00	8800	1000	90
11:00	9600	1000	90
12:00	10300	1000	90
13:00	10900	1000	90
14:00	11700	1000	90
15:00	12300	1000	90
16:00	12850	600	90
17:00	13600	1000	90
18:00	13400	-3000	120
18:30	9850	-3000	180
19:00	8150	-3000	185
19:30	6900	-3000	170
20:00	5250	-3000	170
20:30	4000	-2500	150
21:00	2900	-2500	140
21:30	2000	-2100	120
22:00	980	-2000	110
22:30	550	0	0

   The automatic focusing mechanism of the camera focuses on the glass lens shield instead of the instrument panel. Specks of dust are clearly visible. The camera operator eventually determines that the sun is blinding the camera and tries to shield the lens. Obtaining data for minutes 12 and 13 is a challenge. Try squinting at the video screen to bring the instrument panel into better focus.

5. Distribute the *Climb to Altitude, Jump Run,* and *Descent Graph* pages.

6. Instruct the students to cut and glue or tape along the indicated lines to make the graph. Direct them to tape on the blank sides of the pages so that the tape doesn't interfere with the graphing.

7. Tell the students to graph the time-altitude data in their table.

8. Instruct them to save their graphs for the next activity, *Fall-timeters.*

Discussion

1. Does the pilot's altimeter correspond to the skydiver's altimeter? [No. Skydivers set their altimeters to indicate *feet above ground level.* Pilots typically set their altimeters to their altitude above mean sea level. This is called *field elevation.*]

2. Could this cause a problem? Explain. [Not really. Since pilots generally fly cross country, they are trained to set their altimeters to local barometric pressure which sets their altimeter to field elevation. On their aeronautical charts, the elevation figures for fixed objects such as mountain peaks, airports, and TV antennas are given in feet above mean sea level.

3. Where do you think the use of *knots* originated? [*Knots,* nautical miles per hour, is the standard distance unit used by sailors. One nautical mile (6076 feet) is equal to one minute of latitude.]

4. What reasons can you give for Mike descending so fast? [Time is money. Getting to the ground as fast as possible means Mike can pick up another load of skydivers. To save even more time, Mike, unless he needs fuel, waits at the end of the runway for a truck to bring the next load of skydivers. During a long summer day, Mike will fly 20 or more loads of skydivers.]

5. *For those that collected data from the video:* How did the IVSI readings correlate to the altimeter readings? What range of readings were seen on the airspeed indicator?

6. For *those that collected data from the video:* What other instruments can you read and interpret on the instrument panel. (Some students may recognize the *Turn Coordinator* to the lower left of the IVSI. The miniature airplane banks in the direction the airplane is rolled. If the ball is kept centered in a turn, the turn is *coordinated.* A coordinated turn rate is three degrees per second. At this rate it takes two minutes to complete a 360 degree turn.

This turn coordinator indicates the airplane is not turning.

This turn coordinator indicates that the airplane is making a coordinated, two minute turn to the left.

Some students may also recognize the *Attitude Indicator* seen to the left of the altimeter. This instrument provides an artificial horizon and is especially useful when the natural horizon can't be seen due to clouds or darkness.

The attitude indicator below shows the airplane flying straight and level.

The following indicator shows the airplane banking to the left. Compare the attitude indicator to the turn coordinator and you'll notice that the airplane symbol moves in the turn coordinator but it's the artificial horizon that moves in the attitude indicator.

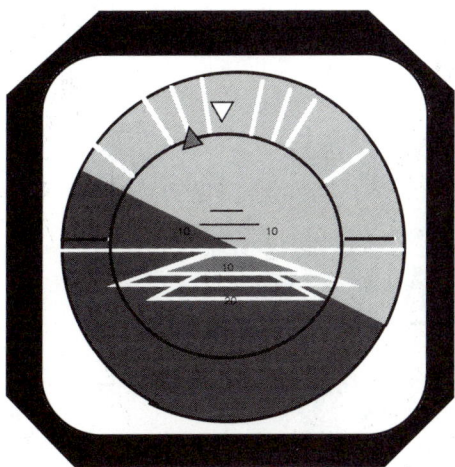

7. Describe the actual path, over the ground, the airplane flew, as it climbed to altitude. [an upward spiral]
8. What's the general shape of the graph during the climb to altitude? [a straight line]
9. What's the shape of the graph during jump run? [a straight line] Describe the path Mike was actually flying during jump run? [a straight line]
10. What did the attitude indicator show at the start of the descent? [The attitude indicator shows a

very steep — all ground, no sky — left-hand turn towards the ground.]
11. Describe the movement of the altimeter needle after the last jumper has left the airplane.
12. Describe the descent path. [a steep spiral path to the point where Mike lines the airplane up with the runway for landing]
13. The airplane took off north to south. The sun was in the west. From studying the video, what might this information tell you about the motion of the airplane? [The changing angle of the sun causes light to move across the instrument panel. This gives an indication that the airplane is turning. The direction of the turn can be inferred from the direction the light travels across the instrument panel.]

Middle School and High School
1. Discuss the *Climb to Altitude Graph* as a function. Ask students to identify the *dependent* and *independent* variables. [The altitude is the dependent variable (y) and time is the independent variable (x)]
2. From the table and graph, what linear equation approximates the *Climb to Altitude* portion of the graph? [y=760t, where y is the altitude and t is the time]
3. What's the *domain* of the equation? [$0 \leq t \leq 17$]
4. From the table and graph, what is the equation of the *Jump Run* portion of the graph? [y=13,500]
5. What's the *domain* of the equation? [$17 \leq t \leq 18$]
6. If students completed the *Rate of Climb Table*: Compare the *average* rate of climb and descent to the actual data.

Extensions
1. If students did not complete the *Rate of Climb* table, have them do so and then compare the *average* rate of climb and descent to the actual data.
2. Scientists and engineers are almost always limited by the amount of money, time, and technological tools they have available for an experiment or project. Have students discuss the limitations of the video and what could be done to get better data.
3. If any parents of students happen to be pilots, have them explain to the class what they see in the video and answer any questions students might have.
4. If you have a computer and a flight simulator program, set up a *climb to altitude* simulation. Let students observe how the aircraft instruments respond to control inputs. Two of the most popular computer flight simulators are *Flight Simulator* by Microsoft®and *Flight Unlimited II*™ by Looking Glass Technologies.

Climbing To Altitude

Name _____

The Instantaneous Vertical Speed Indicator (IVSI)

A very important dial on the instrument panel of any airplane is called the *Instantaneous Vertical Speed Indicator* (IVSI). This instrument tells the pilot the rate the airplane is going up or going down. Every whole number is 1000 feet per minute. From 0 feet to 1, the dial is calibrated in units of 100 feet per minute (.5 is 500 feet per minute). Beyond 1 (1000 feet per minute) the dial is calibrated in 500 feet per minute intervals. If the airplane is in level flight, the needle will point to the 0 mark.

Note: The high performance jets flown by the men and women in the Air Force, Navy, and Marine Corps are capable of much higher rates of climb than 2000 feet per minute.

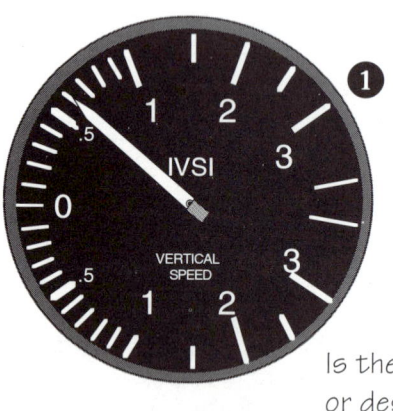

1 What is the indicated vertical motion of the airplane?

_____ feet
―――――
1   minute

Is the airplane climbing or descending? _____

2 What is the indicated vertical motion of the airplane?

_____ feet
―――――
1   minute

Is the airplane climbing or descending? _____

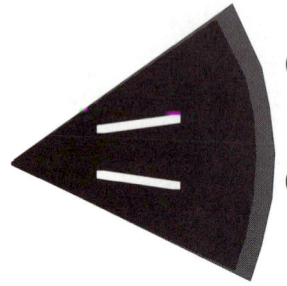

3 What are the white line markers near the right side of the IVSI dial?

4 Besides looking at the IVSI, what other actions could you take to determine whether you are going up or going down?

Climbing To Altitude

Mike Jackson is the pilot of the Beechcraft King Air. Mike is flying Shelly and Dave to an altitude of 13,500 feet for Shelly's altimeter jump. Mike says that on a hot day, with a full load, the King Air can climb to altitude at the **average rate of 760 feet per minute.**

Rate of Climb = $\dfrac{760}{1}$ $\dfrac{feet}{minute}$

❶ Assume the King Air climbs at this constant rate. Complete the *time-altitude table.*

❷ To the nearest minute, at what time did the King Air reach 13,500 feet?

_____ minutes

At 13,500 feet Mike levels off and starts the *jump run.* The jump run lasts one minute.

❸ At the end of the jump run, it takes Mike 4.5 minutes to descend the 13,000 feet to the ground. What's the average descent rate in feet per minute?

_____ feet per minute

Time (minutes)	Altitude (feet)	Time (minutes)	Altitude (feet)
0	550	10	
1		11	
2		12	
3		13	
4		14	
5		15	
6		16	
7		17	
8		18	
9		19	

Climbing To Altitude

Aircraft Altimeter

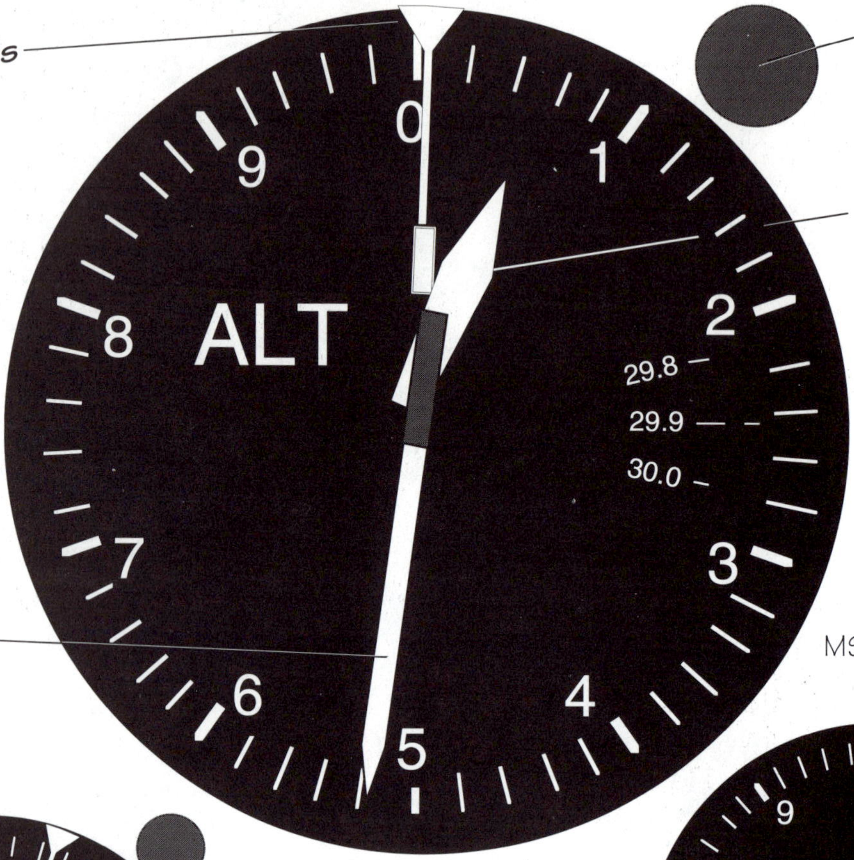

Ten Thousands pointer

Barometric Pressure Adjustment Knob

Thousands pointer

ALT

29.8
29.9
30.0

Barometric Pressure Window

Hundreds pointer

MSL = Mean Sea Level

1

ALT

29.8
29.9
30.0

altitude: _____ feet MSL

2

ALT

29.8
29.9
30.0

altitude: _____ feet MSL

3

ALT

29.8
29.9
30.0

altitude: _____ feet MSL

Mike's airplane could never reach this altitude but a transcontinental airliner could.

Climbing To Altitude

Name _____

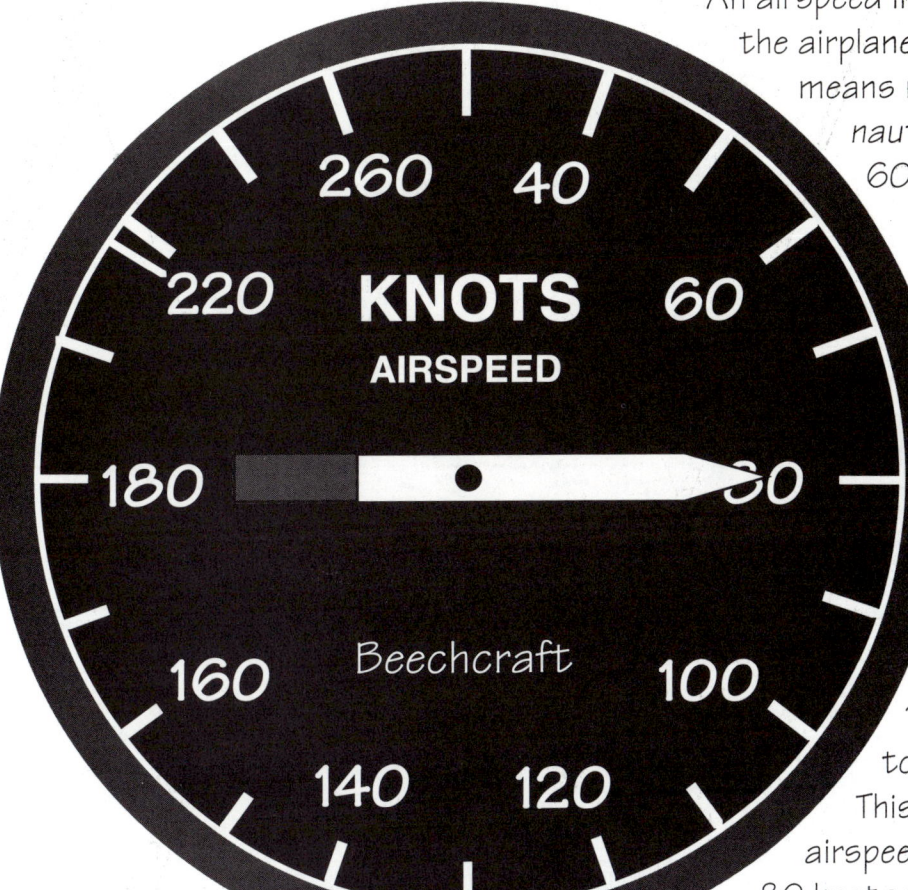

260 40

KNOTS
AIRSPEED

220   60

180   80

160   100

Beechcraft

140   120

An airspeed indicator reports the speed of the airplane in *knots*. The term *knot* means nautical miles per hour. One nautical mile equals 6076 feet.

$$\frac{1 \text{ knot}}{1 \text{ mile}} = \frac{6076 \text{ feet}}{5280 \text{ feet}}$$

1 knot is approximately equal to 1.15 miles per hour.

This instrument is indicating an airspeed of 80 knots.

80 knots x 1.15 miles per hour per knot

80 knots = 92 miles per hour

Record the airspeed indicated by each instrument.

❶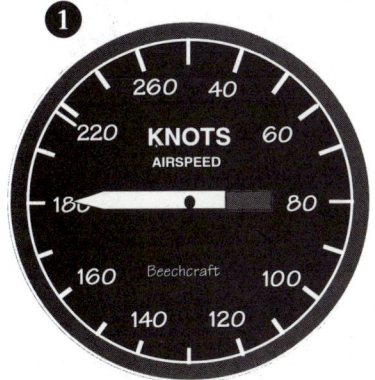

❷

❸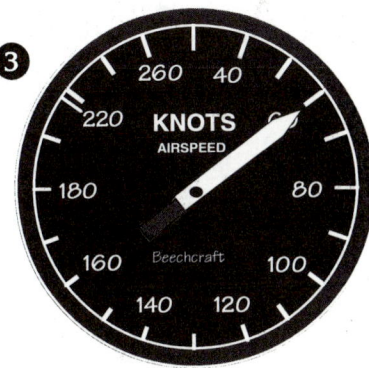

Airspeed = _____ knots

Airspeed = _____ mph

Airspeed = _____ knots

Airspeed = _____ mph

Airspeed = _____ knots

Airspeed = _____ mph

Climbing To Altitude

Data Table

Name _____

Time (minutes : seconds)	Altitude (feet)	Vertical Speed (feet per second)	Airspeed Indicator (knots)
0:00'00": 00	ALT	IVSI VERTICAL SPEED	KNOTS AIRSPEED Beechcraft
00:00			
01:00			
02:00			
03:00			
04:00			
05:00			
06:00			
07:00			
08:00			
09:00			
10:00			
11:00			
12:00			
13:00			
14:00			
15:00			
16:00			
17:00			
18:00			
18:30			
19:00			
19:30			
20:00			
20:30			
21:00			
21:30			
22:00			
22:30			

glue or tape along this tab

Climb to Altitude

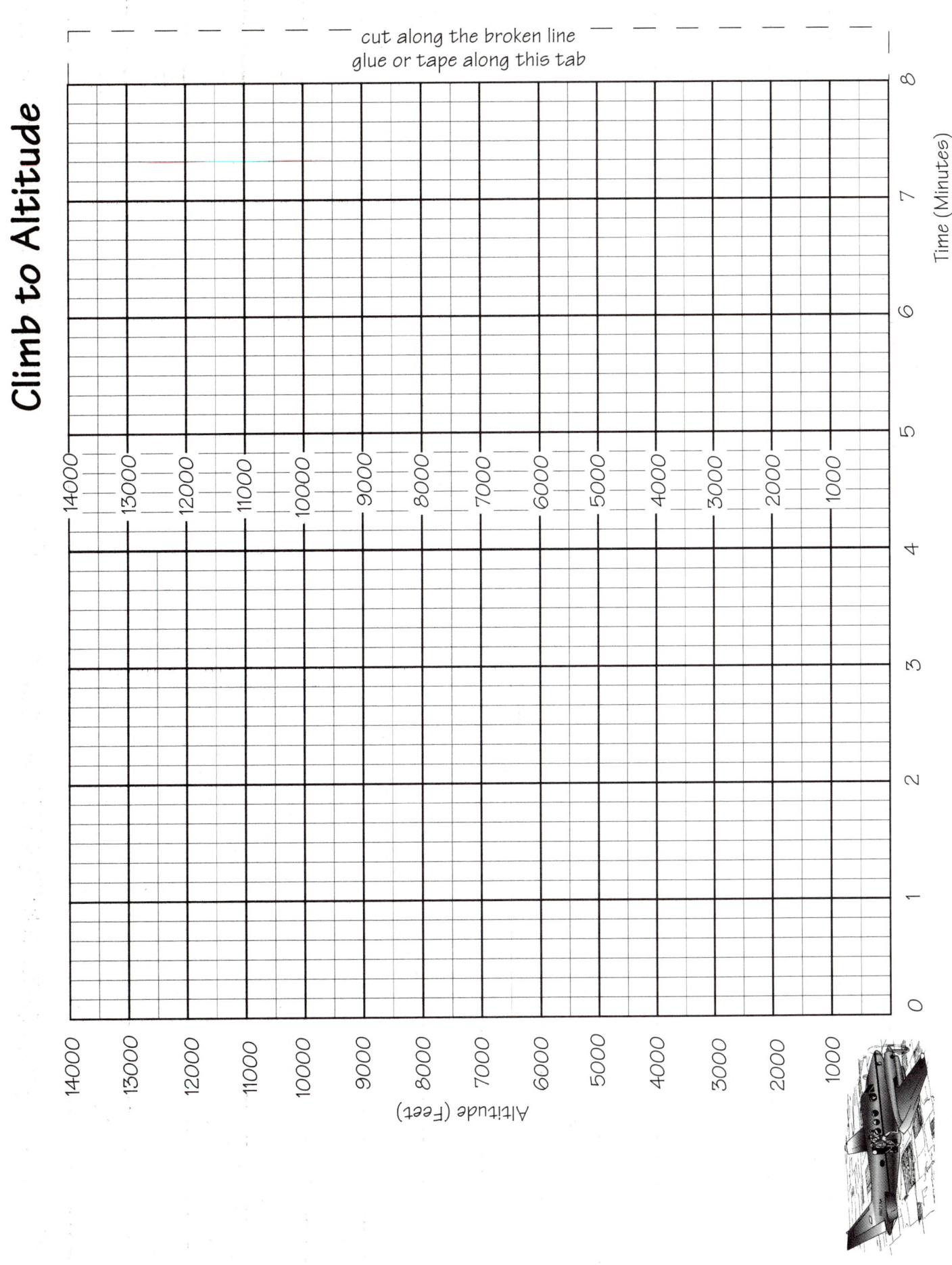

Time (Minutes)

Altitude (Feet)

14000
13000
12000
11000
10000
9000
8000
7000
6000
5000
4000
3000
2000
1000

Jump Run

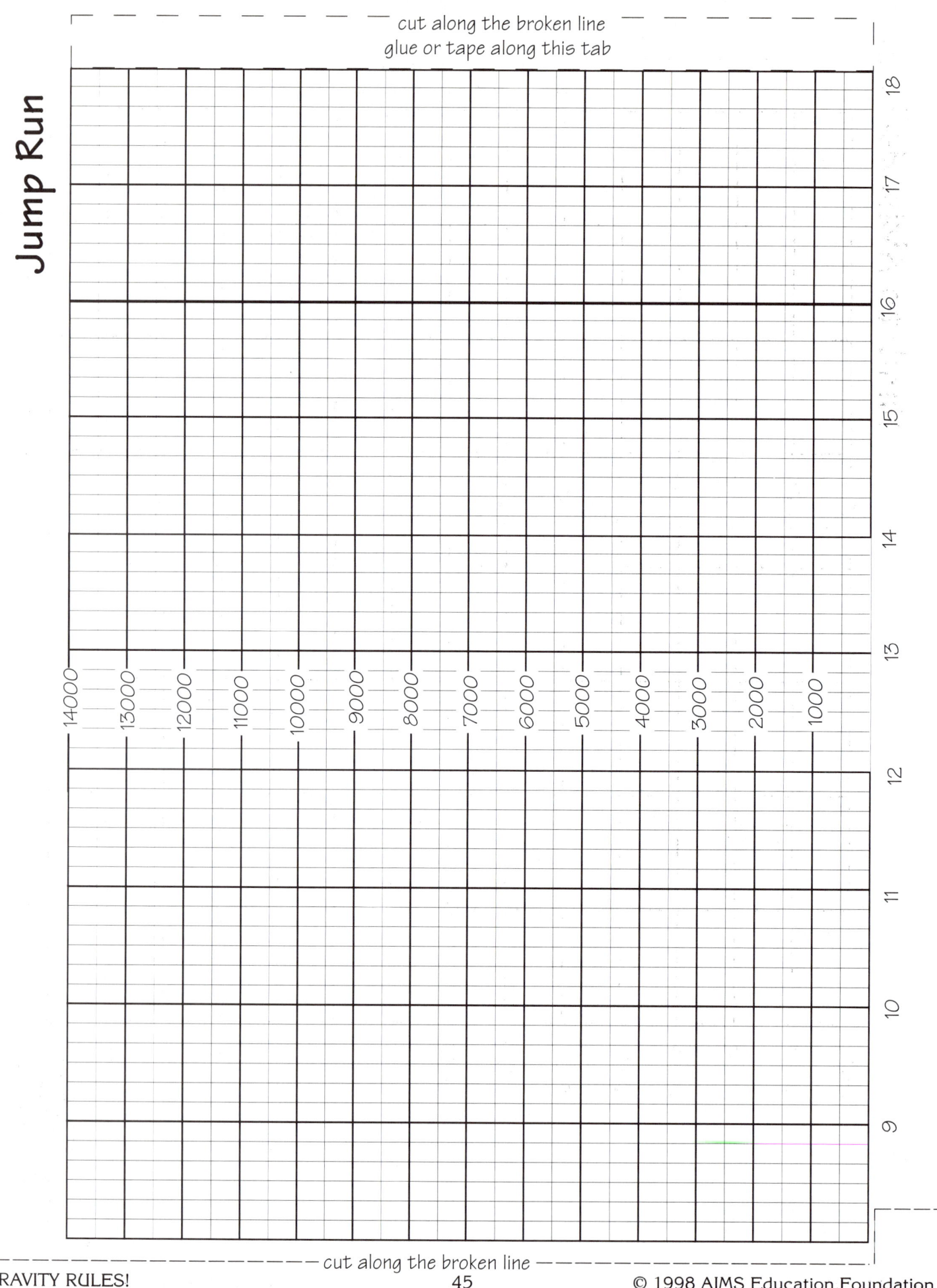

14000
13000
12000
11000
10000
9000
8000
7000
6000
5000
4000
3000
2000
1000

18 17 16 15 14 13 12 11 10 9

GRAVITY RULES!

45

climbing To Altitude

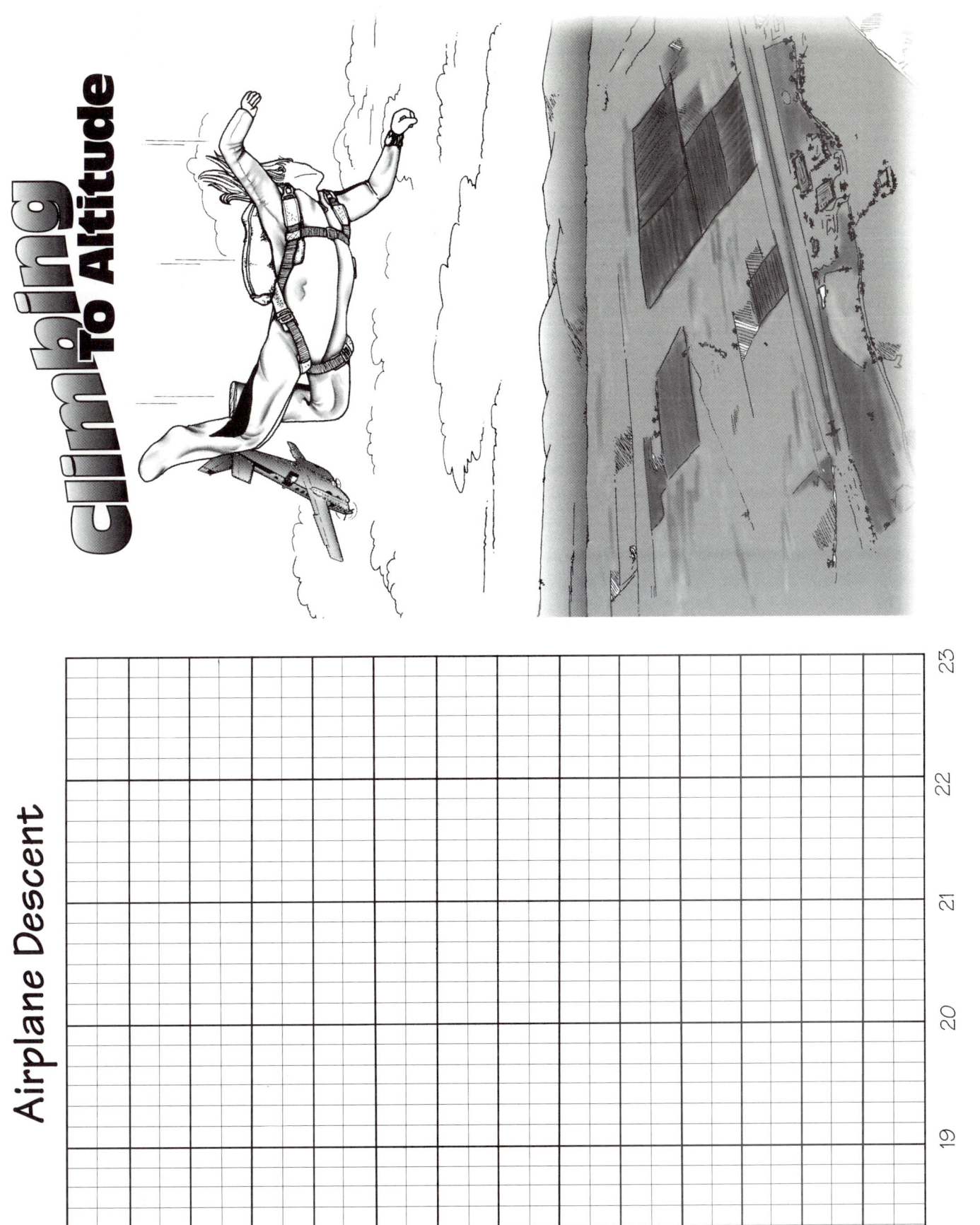

Airplane Descent

cut along the broken line

19   20   21   22   23

Video Companion
for
Climbing To Altitude

Note: Refer to the *Gravity Rules! Glossary* for definitions of skydiving words and phrases heard in the video.

Time = 29 minutes: 17 seconds

I. In the Cockpit of the Beechcraft King Air
Narration:

> *"This is the cockpit and instrument panel in the Beechcraft King Air. These instruments indicate the status of the engines and the electrical and hydraulic systems."*

1. **A yellow orange rectangle surrounds this group of instruments.**
> *"These are the communications radios."*

2. **A yellow orange rectangle surrounds the radios.**
> *"This group of flight instruments is used to fly the airplane."*

3. **A yellow orange rectangle surrounds this group of instruments.**
> *"The airspeed indicator reports the speed, in knots per hour, of the airplane."*

4. **An arrow points to the air speed indicator.**
> *"Here the airspeed increases from approximately 110 knots to 190 knots."*

5. **The needle on the airspeed indicator is seen moving.**
> *"The attitude indicator reports whether the airplane is climbing, descending, turning, or flying straight and level. The blue portion of the instrument represents the sky and the brown portion represents the Earth. The attitude indicator is sometimes called the 'artificial horizon'."*

6. **An arrow points to the attitude indicator.**
> *"The attitude indicator shows a diving left turn."*

7. **The face of the attitude indicator indicates a diving left turn.**
> *"The turn indicator reports the rate at which the airplane is turning. When the wings of the small airplane symbol align with the white marks next to the 'L' and 'R' markings, the airplane is turning at the standard rate of three degrees per second. At this rate, the airplane completes a 360 degree turn in two minutes."*

8. **An arrow points to the turn indicator.**
> *"Here the airplane is in a coordinated left turn"*

9. **The face of the turn indicator indicates a coordinated left turn.**
> *"The altimeter reports the vertical height of the airplane above mean sea level. The long needle shows hundreds of feet, the shorter needle shows thousands of feet, and the shortest needle indicates intervals of ten thousand feet."*

10. **An arrow points to the altimeter.**
> *"This altimeter indicates the airplane is loosing altitude, fast."*

11. **The large needle of the altimeter (hundreds) is seen rapidly moving counterclockwise indicating that the altitude is decreasing.**
> *"The vertical speed indicator reports the rate, in feet per minute, the airplane is climbing or descending."*

12. **An arrow points to the vertical speed indicator.**
> *"This IVSI shows the airplane descending at a rate in excess of 3000 feet per minute"*

13. **The needle of the vertical speed indicator is seen "pegged" on the descent side of the instrument.**

Time =31 minutes: 11 seconds

II. Take Off!

1. The King Air is ready to take off.
2. The high pitched sound of the turbine engines as take off roll begins.
3. Looking straight down the runway as the King Air nears 100 knots.
4. The clock starts at the moment the King Air lifts off. Note the altimeter and rate of climb needles.

A data collection window of five seconds before and after the minute is provided for the first 11 minutes of the climb. Collect data on the minute.

At 11 minutes and 41 seconds into the flight, the screen blurs. Specks of dust are clearly visible on the camera lens. The camera operator eventually determines that the sun is blinding the camera and tries to shield the lens. Obtaining data for minutes 12 and 13 is a challenge. Try squinting at the video screen to bring the instrument panel into better focus.

Minutes 14 – 16, five seconds before and after each minute, collect data.

> Time = 35 minutes: 18 seconds

III. Jump Run

Mike calls *"two minutes"* to start the jump run.

1. An AFF student and two jumpmasters exit first.
2. Tandem master Jerry and passenger exit next.
3. Tandem master Danny and passenger exit last.

> Time = 36 minutes: 18 seconds

IV. Descent

Mike puts the King Air into a dive.

1. Watch the altimeter unwind.
2. It's all brown Earth out the front windshield.
3. Continue to collect data. Watch the airspeed indicator.
4. Notice the attitude indicator shows the airplane is descending in a left-hand spiral.

> Time = 38 minutes: 32 seconds

V. Landing

1. Mike sets ups for landing.
2. Crossing the canal — Notice how narrow the air field appears.
3. Mike lands the Beechcraft King Air at 22 minutes and 31 seconds.
4. Jim asks Mike about the altimeter being set to field elevation.

FALL-TIMETERS

Topic
Terminal velocity

Key Questions
What is the terminal velocity of a skydiver in freefall?
What is the terminal velocity of a skydiver under canopy?

Focus
A skydiving altimeter was mounted in a special box along with a video camera and was worn by a skydiver during a typical skydive. Students will collect and record *time* and *altitude* data directly from the video. They will then graph and analyze the data. The data will be used to compute *average velocities*, including *terminal velocities*.

Guiding Documents
Project 2061 Benchmarks
- *In the absence of retarding forces such as friction, an object will keep its direction of motion and its speed. Whenever an object is seen to speed up, slow down, or change direction, it can be assumed that an unbalanced force is acting on it. [ed. Newton's first law of motion.]*
- *Read analog and digital meters on instruments used to make direct measurements of length, volume, weight, elapsed time, rates, and temperature, and choose appropriate units for reporting various magnitudes.*

NRC Standards
- *The motion of an object can be described by its position, direction of motion, and speed. That motion can be measured and represented on a graph.*
- *If more than one force acts on an object along a straight line, then the forces will reinforce or cancel one another, depending on their direction and magnitude. Unbalanced forces will cause changes in the speed or direction of an object's motion. [ed. Newton's first law of motion.]*

NCTM Standards
- *Systematically collect, organize, and describe data*
- *Construct, read, and interpret tables, charts, and graphs*
- *Develop the concepts of rates and other derived and indirect measurements*

- *Understand and apply reasoning processes, with special attention to spatial reasoning and reasoning with proportions and graphs*

Math
Ratio and proportion
Rational numbers
  percent
  decimals
Measurement
  length
  time
Graphs
Estimation
  rounding

Science
Physical science
  Newton's first law of motion
  Newton's second law of motion
    average velocity
    terminal velocity

Integrated Processes
Observing
Collecting and recording data
Interpreting data

Materials
AIMS *Gravity Rules!* video
  Fall-timeters sequence
Stopwatches or clocks with a second hand, optional

Background Information
    The *Fall-timeters* video is a real-time record of a skydiving altimeter worn by Shelly during a skydive. Dave Chrouch, the freefall videographer seen in the video, designed and built an aluminum box in which he mounted a skydiving altimeter and a small video camera. A strap was attached to the box so Shelly could wear it on her stomach during a skydive. Dave also took video of Shelly.
    The altimeter in the special box is subjected to several shocks and jolts as it is taken from the calm, relatively still air of the airplane's passenger cabin into the 100 plus mile per hour airstream. It accelerates to approximately 140 miles per hour, maintains that velocity for nearly 50 seconds and then

decelerates — from approximately 180 feet per second to 10 feet per second — in less than two seconds.

The altimeter is a mechanical device with accuracy limitations consistent with any device costing less than 200 dollars. There are anomalies in the altimeter's record. Hypotheses should be formed to explain these anomalies.

Management

1. Students should complete the AIMS activity *Skydiver* including viewing its accompanying video before attempting *Fall-timeters*. Students will then have the background knowledge and understanding of the elements of a skydive that underlie *Gravity Rules!* Students should also complete the activities *How Fast Can You Walk?*, and *How Fast Can You Run?* These activities establish a basis for understanding the concept of *average velocity*. These prior experiences allow students to concentrate on analyzing and interpreting the data contained in the *Fall-timeters* video.

2. The video contains three different *Fall-timeters* (exit to ground) video sequences: (a) reduced views of the altimeter, chronograph, and Shelly are displayed against a background of Shelly in the air, (b) reduced views of the altimeter and Shelly are displayed on a background of Shelly in the air, (c) the face of the altimeter fills the screen. Three versions give you maximum flexibility in collecting altitude and time data. For versions b and c, students will need to operate stopwatches to determine the time intervals.

3. There is wide variation in the ability of video players — especially older models — to display clear *stop action* scenes when the *Pause* button is pressed. If the machine you are using isn't clear, check other machines until you find one that is satisfactory.

4. Group students in pairs. Tell students to take turns observing the time and recording the altitude. The timers should say "mark" to their partners when they want them to observe and record a reading.

Procedure

Reading A Skydiving Altimeter

1. Make a transparency of the skydiving altimeter (see *Skydiving Altimeter* page).
2. Point out the different scale divisions.
3. Explain to students the importance of setting the altimeter correctly. (Errors could mislead a skydiver to open the parachute too late.)

4. Distribute the *Reading a Skydiving Altimeter* page.
5. Have students "read" each of the nine altimeters that appear on their page.

Discussion

1. Have students compare their altimeter readings to these:
   1. 0 ft
   2. 2000 ft
   3. 7000 ft
   4. 11,000 ft
   5. 3500 ft
   6. 7250 ft
   7. 12,500 ft
   8. 17,750 ft
   9. 15,500 ft

2. During freefall, how accurately do you think skydivers read their altimeters? [Often, a skydiver quickly glances at the altimeter to determine his/her altitude, to the nearest thousand feet.]

3. Under canopy, how accurately do you think skydivers read the altimeter? [As the skydiver sets up for landing, the hundred feet divisions on the altimeter face become important. Experienced skydivers learn to judge altitudes accurately without having to check the altimeter during landing. Student skydivers are told to learn *what three thousand feet* looks like so they don't become totally dependent upon their altimeters. That's a *survival* estimation skill.]

4. Describe the sections in the video — there's more than one — where you saw a skydiver look at the altimeter.

Procedure

Without Collecting Data

1. View the altimeter video in its entirety. Answer questions about how the skydive was done, etc. Point out the exit, the free fall, opening shock, and the landing portions of the video so that students will be able to identify these portions of the skydive for themselves when they view the video again. Fast-forward or rewind whenever necessary.

Collecting Data

2. Distribute *Data Table 1* and *The Altitude-Time Graph* pages.

3. View the video a second time but this time alert the students to observe and record in *Data Table 1* the altitude (to the nearest 100 feet) at which Shelly exits the airplane and the time (to the nearest second) she lands her canopy.

4. Instruct students to plot their data on the *Altitude-Time Graph* and draw a straight line between the two points.

5. Tell the students to find the *average velocity* during her skydive.

Discussion

1. What is accurate about your graphs? [The exit point and landing point.]

2. What might be misleading about your graphs? [The graph shows Shelly falling *at the same rate*

throughout the skydive, but we know *from watching the needle on the altimeter move* that Shelly fell much slower under canopy than when in freefall.]

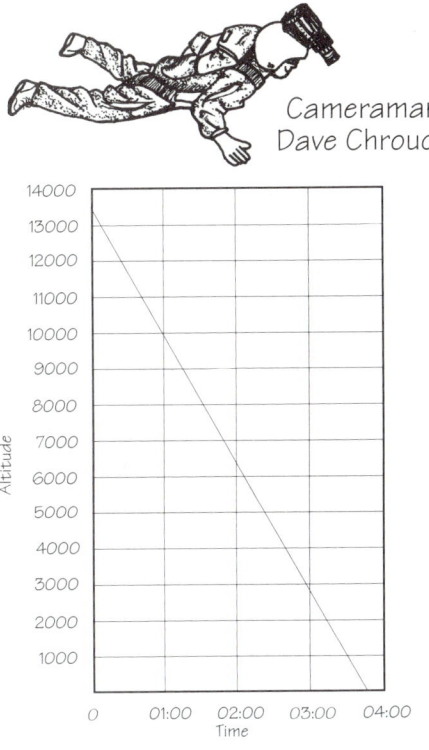

Cameraman
Dave Chrouch

the altitude Shelly exits the airplane and the altitude and time she opens her parachute and lands. The purpose of this second graph is to refine the data. This graph will show that the skydive is divided into two major portions: a) a high-velocity part — 9250 feet fallen in 50 seconds, and b) the long, relatively low velocity canopy flight to the ground. Note: The comparatively short time interval of the opening sequence is recorded in a later graph.]

3. Show students how to compute the *average velocity* for the skydive from the graph. What does the average velocity represent? [The average velocity represents the *constant* velocity an object would have to have in order to traverse the given distance in the given time.]

4. Was the downwards directed velocity constant throughout the skydive? [Shelly started with zero velocity (towards the ground), fell faster until reaching terminal velocity, and slowed down once under canopy. Upon landing, her velocity was again zero.]

Answers to *Data Table* questions on student page
7c. The conversion factor is 88 feet per second which equals 60 miles per hour.
8. The line would be *below* the line on the graph.
9. The line would be *above* the line on the graph.

Procedure
Data Table 2
1. Distribute the *Data Table 2* page.
2. Tell students they are going to view the video again. Instruct them to observe and record in *Data Table 2*

3. Instruct students to plot their data on the *Altitude-Time Graph* and draw a straight line, in a different color from that used for the first line, between the two points.
4. Have students answer the remaining questions.

Answers to *Data Table 2* questions on student page
7. The more data points taken and plotted, the more accurate the graph.
8. Take and plot even more data points, say at five-second intervals.
9. The freefall average velocity is by the far the highest.

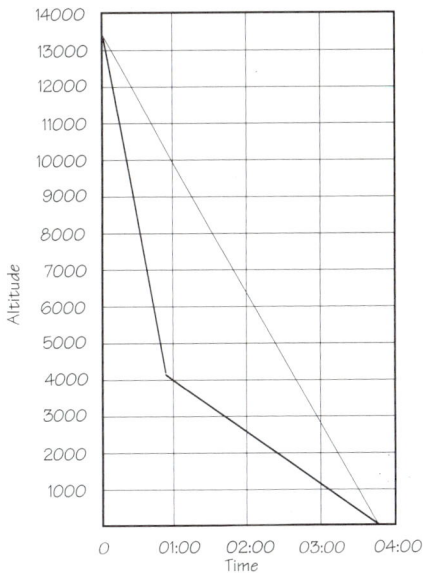

Procedure
Data Table 3
1. Instruct students to view the video again and record in *Data Table 3* the altitude at ten-second intervals.
2. Have students plot their data on the *Altitude-Time Graph* and draw a straight line, in a color different from that used for the first two lines, between the two points.

A four-head video player with stop-frame capability was used to collect the following data. Use this data as a guide.

Data Table 3			
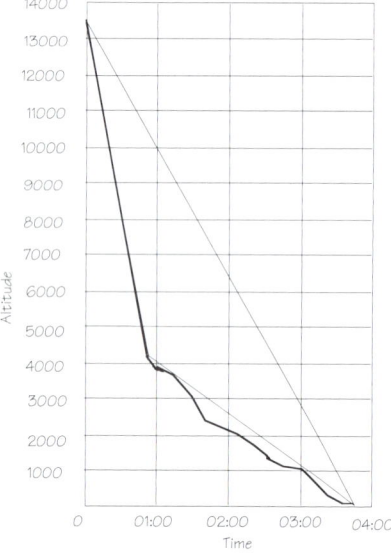Time	Altitude	Time	Altitude
00': 00'': 00	13 500 feet	02': 00'': 00	2 200 feet
00': 10'': 00	11 900 feet	02': 10'': 00	2 100 feet
00': 20'': 00	10 000 feet	02': 20'': 00	1 750 feet
00': 30'': 00	8 500 feet	02': 30'': 00	1 500 feet
00': 40'': 00	6 100 feet	02': 40'': 00	1 300 feet
00': 50'': 00	4 200 feet	02': 50'': 00	1 100 feet
01': 00'': 00	3 900 feet	03': 00'': 00	1 000 feet
01': 10'': 00	3 600 feet	03': 10'': 00	700 feet
01': 20'': 00	3 400 feet	03': 20'': 00	500 feet
01': 30'': 00	2 900 feet	03': 30'': 00	200 feet
01': 40'': 00	2 500 feet	03': 40'': 00	100 feet
01': 50'': 00	2 400 feet	03': 46'': 00	0 feet

Answers to *Data Table 3* questions on student page

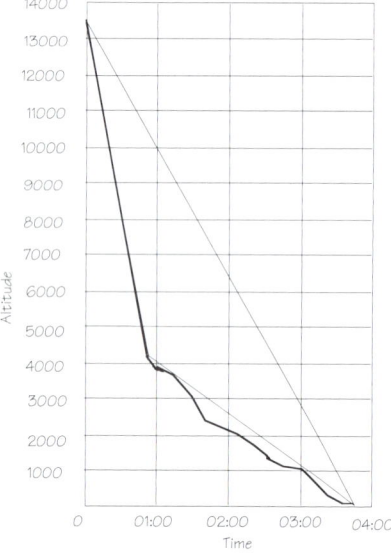

3. The graph shows a variation from the average velocities computed from the first two data tables. Once Shelly reaches *terminal velocity*, at 12,000 feet, her velocity remains almost constant. Notice in the video that she doesn't change body position very much during the freefall portion of the skydive. Under canopy, the graph is not as constant. A ram-air canopy "dives" towards the ground in a turn, losing altitude more rapidly.

4. Take more data points. For example, try to graph the "opening" sequence as accurately as possible. This will require repeated reviewing of the video and deft use of the PAUSE button.

5. Even though Shelly fell for 50 seconds, she didn't continue to fall faster. She reached a terminal velocity of approximately 185 feet per second.

For Secondary Students:
Fall-timeters uses the *average velocity* concept to create successively more accurate graphs of the altitude-time data. Relate this process to the definition of *instantaneous velocity*, v.

$$v = \lim_{\Delta t \to 0} \frac{\Delta x}{\Delta t} = \frac{dx}{dt}$$

Extensions

1. Further analysis of the video using a four-head player and the stop motion key yields this additional data.

The First Nine Seconds	
Time	Altitude
00': 00'': 00	13 500 feet
00': 01'': 00	13 400 feet
00': 02'': 00	13 200 feet
00': 03'': 00	13 100 feet
00': 04'': 00	13 000 feet
00': 05'': 00	12 900 feet
00': 06'': 00	12 600 feet
00': 07'': 00	12 400 feet
00': 08'': 00	12 200 feet
00': 09'': 00	12 000 feet

The four-head, stop motion technique was used in an attempt to get data about Shelly's parachute opening. Reliable time data can be obtained from the video but the mechanical skydiving altimeter can't react to the tremendous change in velocity (deceleration) experienced during the opening of the parachute.

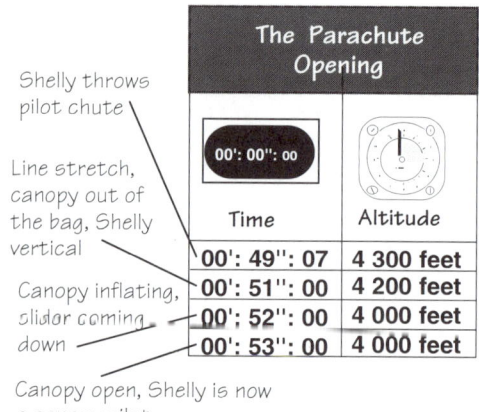

Shelly throws pilot chute

Line stretch, canopy out of the bag, Shelly vertical

Canopy inflating, slider coming down

Canopy open, Shelly is now a canopy pilot

The Parachute Opening	
Time	Altitude
00': 49'': 07	4 300 feet
00': 51'': 00	4 200 feet
00': 52'': 00	4 000 feet
00': 53'': 00	4 000 feet

Ask students what they think could be done to get better data? [The bottom line is time and money. Better devices for measuring time and altitude are available but they cost considerably more than the 20 dollar stopwatch and 200 dollar altimeter used in the video. More time could be spent designing and manufacturing instrument and camera mounts and housings but that would cost money too.]

2. Add the graph of the data in *Table 3* to the *Climbing to Altitude* graph. Distribute the *Freefall and Canopy Flight* graph page and have students regraph the data from *Table 3*. The new graph can then be taped to the *Climbing to Altitude* graph. This provides a complete description of both the airplane and skydiver on the same graph. Have students compare the descent graph of the airplane with Shelly's freefall and canopy flight graph.

3. *Average acceleration* is defined as the ratio of the change in velocity to the elapsed time.

$$\overline{a} = \frac{\Delta v}{\Delta t} = \frac{v_f - v_i}{t_f - t_i}$$

Knowing Shelly's terminal velocity at pull time (v_i), her terminal velocity under canopy (v_f), and the elapsed time ($t_f - t_i$) is enough to compute the average *deceleration* Shelly experienced during the opening of her parachute. If 32 feet per second per second is taken as *one g*, how many *g*s did Shelly experience during opening?

4. The video is interesting in that it is the record of an actual experiment. The focus of this activity has been to look at successively shorter distance and time intervals in order to obtain closer approximations to the *velocity* of the skydiver. Explore other interpretations that perhaps focus on some other dynamic. For example, can an *energy* interpretation be made?

Technology

Secondary Mathematics and Physics

1. The graphing calculator is a powerful tool for quickly looking at data. The last page, *Fall-timeters — A Texas Instruments Graphing Calculator Analysis*, explains how to use a graphing calculator to find the quartric equation, $y = .00001838009x^4 - 0.0119264961x^3 + 2.816305493x^2 - 300.6093116x + 4376.13864$.

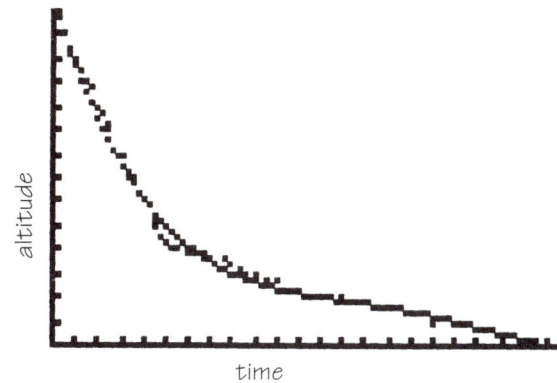

This fourth-degree algebraic equation, when graphed on top of the graph of the data, fits closely except for the acceleration to terminal velocity and the deceleration during the opening of the parachute.

Skydiving Altimeter

Overhead Transparency Page

Adjusting Knob

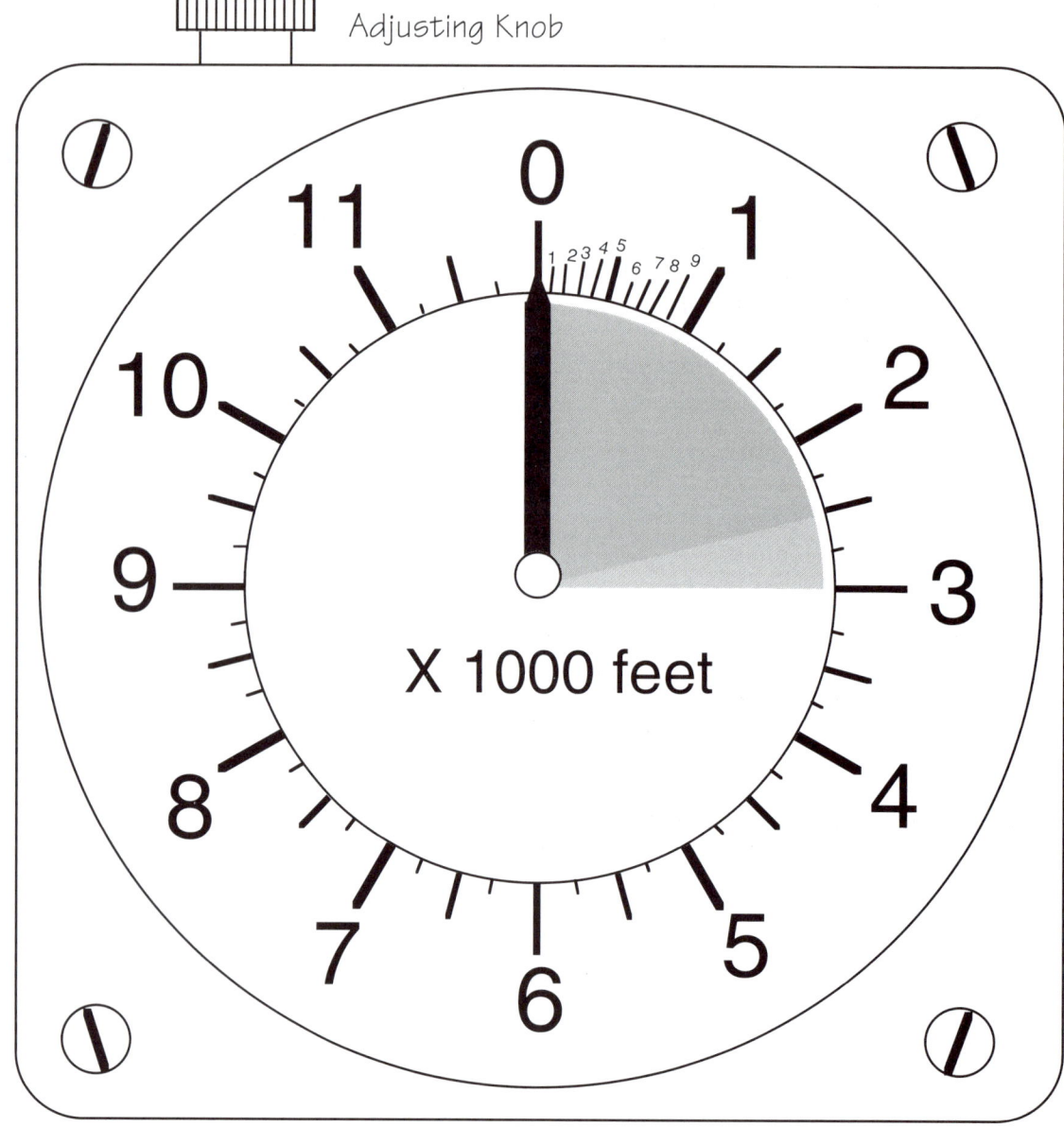

X 1000 feet

Before boarding the airplane, a skydiver turns the adjusting knob left or right to set the needle on the zero mark. From then on, the altimeter will indicate their altitude in feet Above Ground Level (AGL). Sometimes a skydiver lands at a point different from the takeoff point. The altitude at the landing site may be above or below the takeoff altitude. In such a case, the skydiver must know the altitude above Mean Sea Level (MSL) at the landing site and set the altimeter accordingly.

FALL-TIMETERS Reading A Skydiving Altimeter

Altimeters 1-6 are below 12,000 feet. What altitude does each altimeter indicate? Read each needle to the nearest mark.

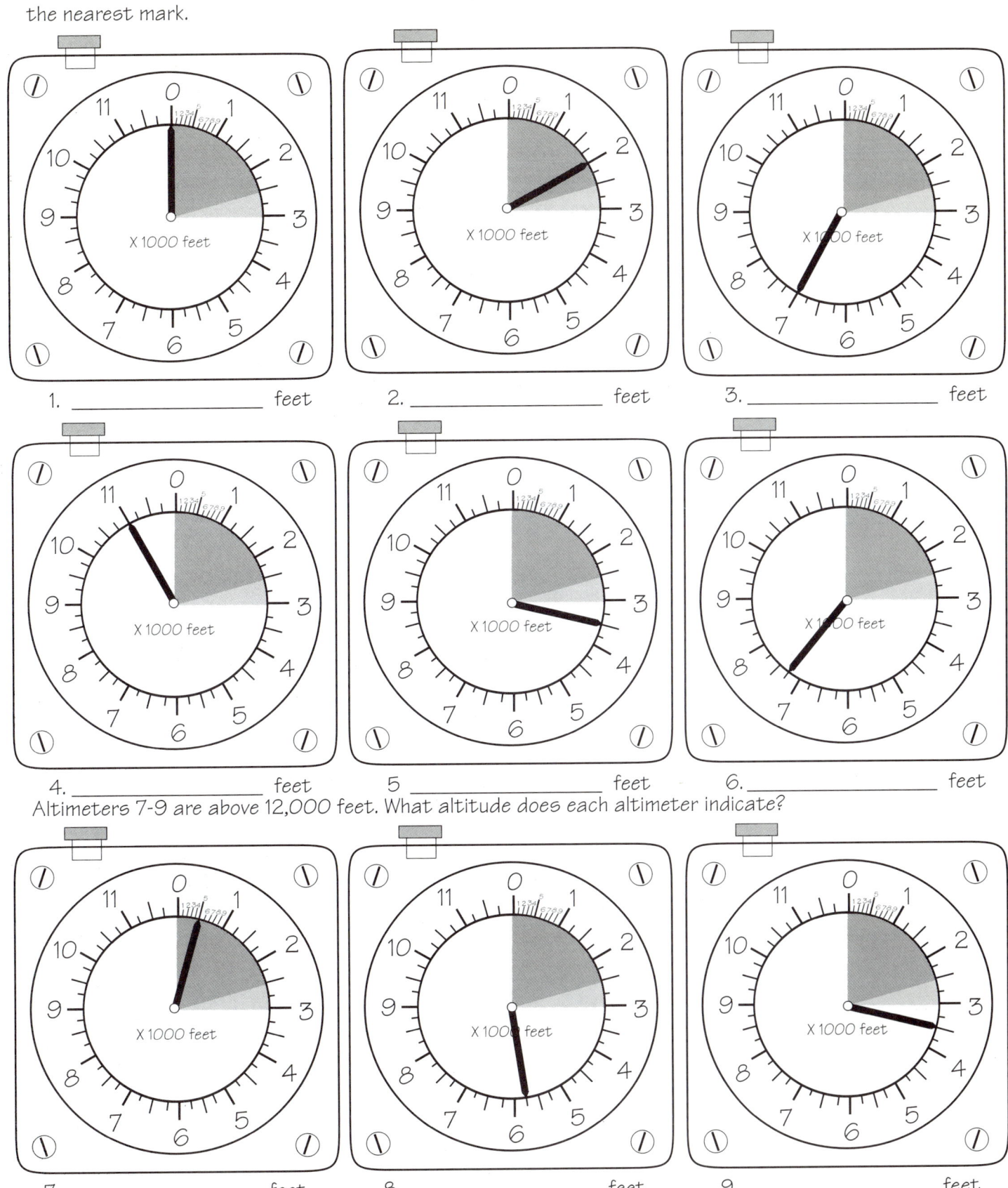

Altimeters 7-9 are above 12,000 feet. What altitude does each altimeter indicate?

1. _____ feet

2. _____ feet

3. _____ feet

4. _____ feet

5. _____ feet

6. _____ feet

7. _____ feet

8. _____ feet

9. _____ feet

FALL-TIMETERS

Procedure: Data Table 1

Data Table 1	a Time minutes : seconds	b Altitude (feet)
Shelly exits airplane	00 : 00	_____ ft
Shelly lands	_____ : _____	_____ 0 ft

1. Start your stopwatch or note the timer in the video when Shelly exits the airplane.
2. Record in column *b* the altitude, to the nearest 100 feet, at which Shelly exits the airplane.
3. Record in column *a* the time, to the nearest second, that Shelly lands her parachute.
4. Plot this data on the Altitude-Time graph. Draw a straight line between the two points.
5. What's accurate about the graph?

6. What is misleading about the graph? Give an example.

7. Compute the average velocity of Shelly's skydive from the formula: **average velocity = $\dfrac{\text{distance}}{\text{time}}$**

   distance = exit altitude - landing altitude = _____ feet − _____ feet = _____ feet

   time = 60 X _____ minutes + _____ seconds = _____ seconds

   a. Divide the distance by the time.
   average velocity = _____ $\dfrac{\text{feet}}{\text{seconds}}$

   b. Round result to the nearest foot.
   average velocity = _____ $\dfrac{\text{feet}}{\text{second}}$

   c. Use the conversion graph from *How Fast Can You Run?* to convert feet per second to miles per hour.
   average velocity = _____ $\dfrac{\text{feet}}{\text{second}}$

   average velocity = _____ $\dfrac{\text{miles}}{\text{hour}}$

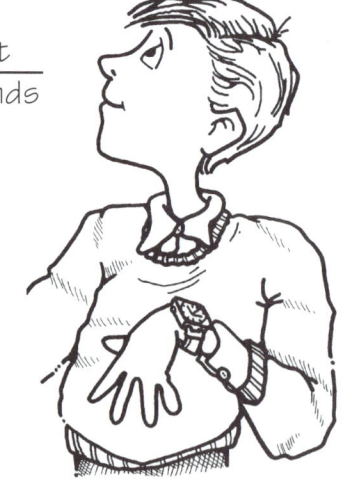

8. If Shelly fell faster, would the line representing the graph of her *average velocity* be above or below the line on your graph?

9. If Shelly fell slower, would the line representing the graph of her *average velocity* be above or below the line on your graph?

FALL-TIMETERS

Procedure:

1. Start your stopwatch or note the timer in the video when Shelly exits the airplane.
2. Record in column b the altitude at which Shelly exits the airplane.
3. Record in column a the time at which Shelly opens her parachute.

Data Table 2	a Time minutes : seconds	b Altitude (feet)
Shelly exits airplane	00 : 00	_____ ft
Shelly opens her parachute	_____ : _____	_____ ft
Shelly lands	_____ : _____	0 ft

4. Record in column b the altitude at which Shelly opens her parachute.
5. Record in column a the time Shelly lands.
6. Plot this data on the Altitude-Time graph. Draw a straight line between the two points.
7. Why is this graph more accurate than the first graph?

8. What could you do to make an even more accurate graph?

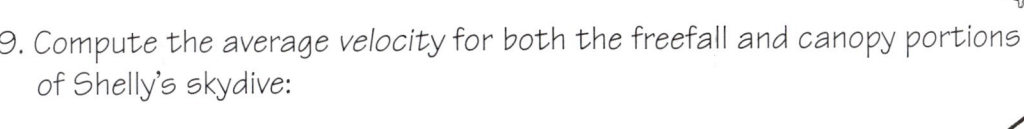

9. Compute the average velocity for both the freefall and canopy portions of Shelly's skydive:

$$\text{average velocity} = \frac{\text{distance}}{\text{time}}$$

Freefall portion of skydive: average velocity = _____ $\frac{\text{feet}}{\text{seconds}}$

Average velocity = _____ $\frac{\text{feet}}{\text{second}}$ Average velocity = _____ $\frac{\text{miles}}{\text{hour}}$

Canopy flight portion of skydive: average velocity = _____ $\frac{\text{feet}}{\text{seconds}}$

Average velocity = _____ $\frac{\text{feet}}{\text{second}}$ Average velocity = _____ $\frac{\text{miles}}{\text{hour}}$

10. Compare these velocities with the average velocity computed from Data Table 1.

GRAVITY RULES!   57   © 1998 AIMS Education Foundation

Name ____________________

FALL-TIMETERS

Altitude - Time Graph

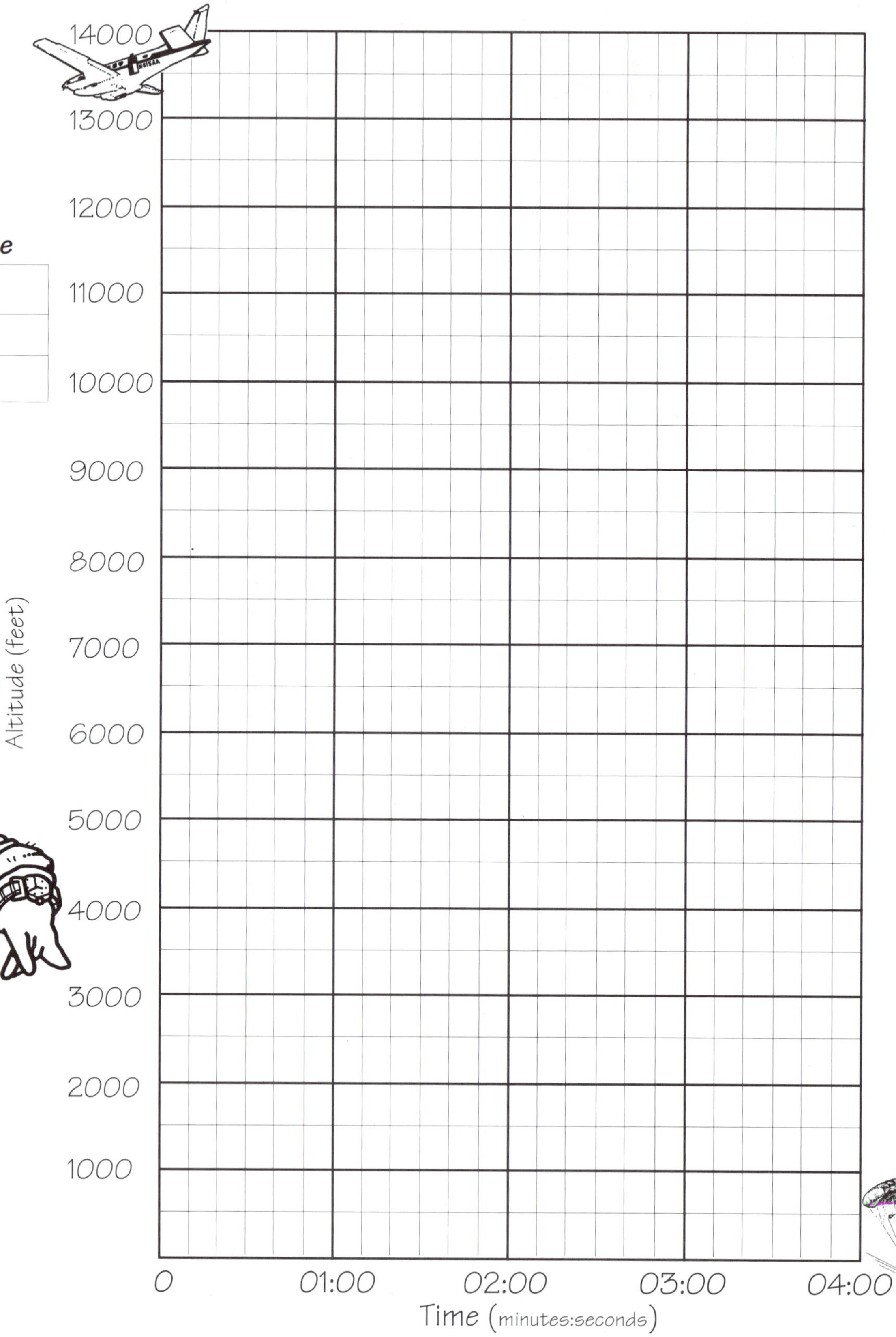

14000
13000
12000
11000
10000
9000
8000
7000
6000
5000
4000
3000
2000
1000
Altitude (feet)
0
01:00
02:00
03:00
04:00
Time (minutes:seconds)

Color Code

Data Table 1	
Data Table 2	
Data Table 3	

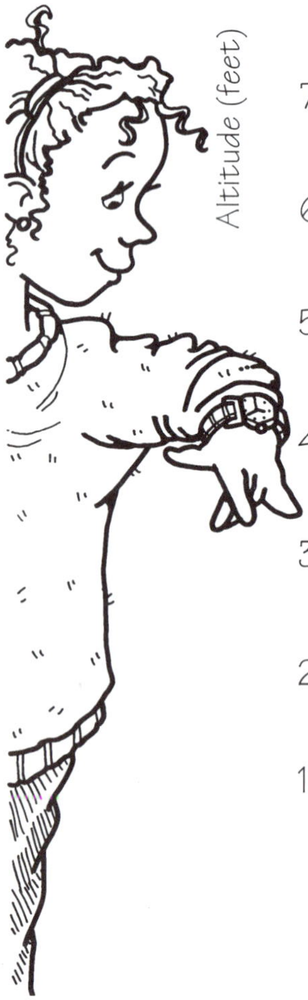

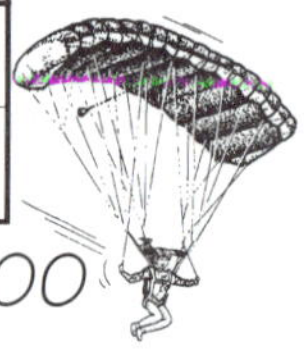

FALL-TIMETERS

1. Record in *Data Table 3* the altitudes at 10 second intervals.
2. Plot the data on the *Altitude-Time* graph. Use a different color to make a line graph of the data.
3. Compare this graph to the other two graphs.

    a. freefall portion

    b. canopy flight portion

4. How would you make an even more accurate graph?

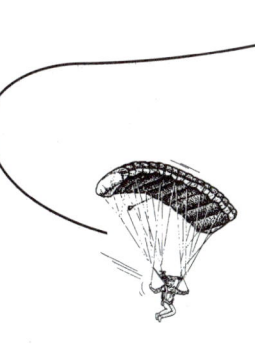

5. Describe in your own words the freefall portion of the graph.

Data Table 3	
Time	Altitude
00': 00": 00	
00': 10": 00	
00': 20": 00	
00': 30": 00	
00': 40": 00	
00': 50": 00	
01': 00": 00	
01': 10": 00	
01': 20": 00	
01': 30": 00	
01': 40": 00	
01': 50": 00	
02': 00": 00	
02': 10": 00	
02': 20": 00	
02': 30": 00	
02': 40": 00	
02': 50": 00	
03': 00": 00	
03': 10": 00	
03': 20": 00	
03': 30": 00	
03': 40": 00	
03': __": 00	

Freefall and Canopy Flight Graph*

Name _____

Data Table 1 color code
Data Table 2 color code
Data Table 3 color code

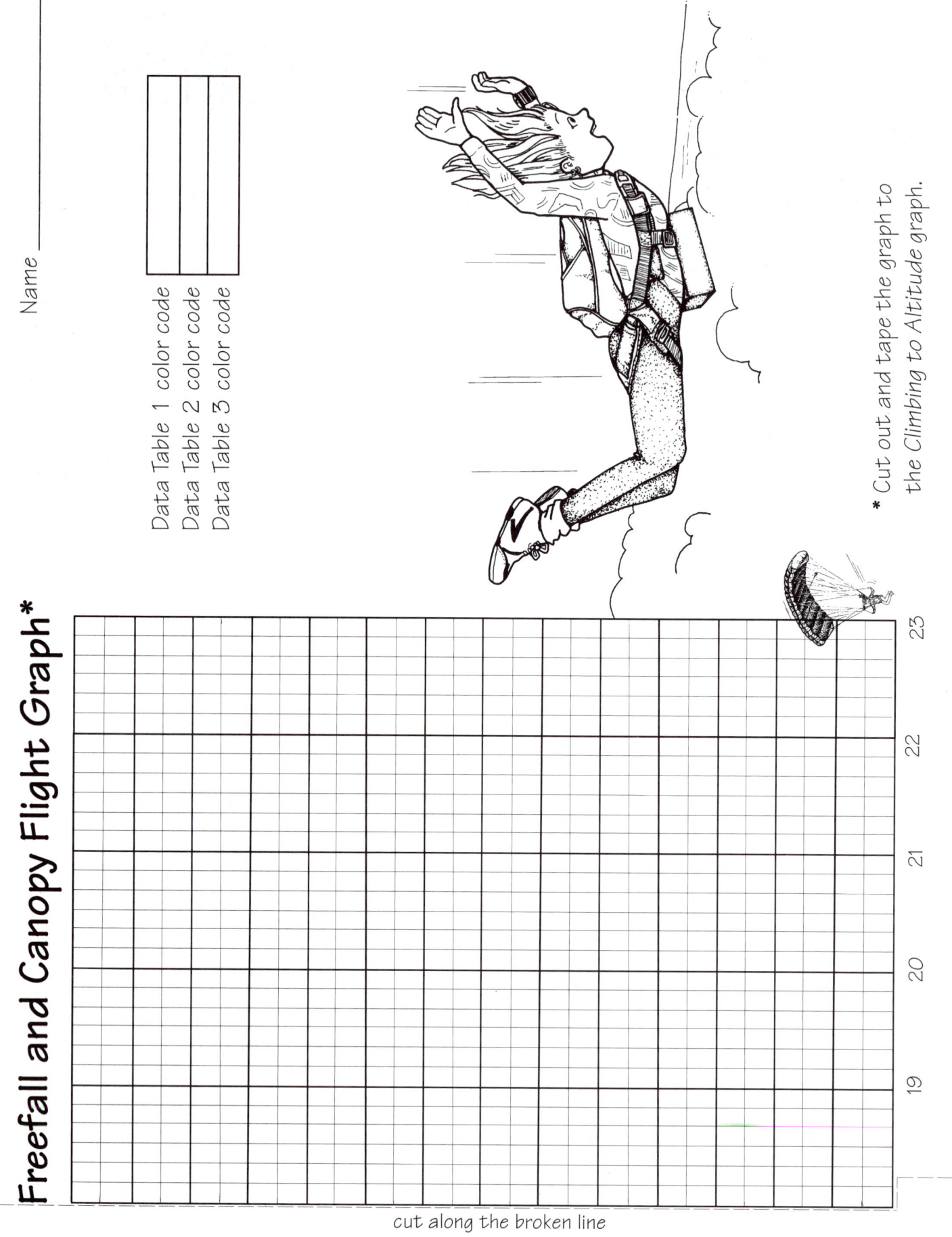

* Cut out and tape the graph to the Climbing to Altitude graph.

cut along the broken line

19   20   21   22   23

Fall-timeters

Texas Instruments - 82
Graphing Calculator Analysis

Time-Altitude Data from Video	
List L₃ [seconds]	List L₄ [feet]
0	13500
2	13200
3	13000
6	12500
8	12250
9	12000
10	12000
12	11500
15	11000
16	10750
20	10000
21	9750
24	9250
25	9000
30	8000
34	7250
35	7000
39	6250
40	6000
45	5250
46	5000
49	4500
50	4250
51	4250
52	4000
55	4000
56	4000
60	3850
63	3750
65	3750
66	3750
70	3600
76	3500
80	3400
83	3250
85	3000
90	2900
95	2750
100	2600
110	2300
120	2100
130	2000
140	1750
150	1500
160	1250
170	1000
180	900
190	750
200	500
210	300
220	100
225	0

1. Collect time-altitude data from the video. Store the time data in one list and the altitude data in another list (see example data).

```
WINDOW FORMAT
  Xmin=0
  Xmax=225
  Xsci=10
  Ymin=0
  Ymax=14000
  Ysci=1000
```

```
Plot 1
On  Off
Typr: [graph icons]
Xlist:L1 L2 L3 L4 L5 L6
Ylist:L1 L2 L3 L4 L5 L6
Mark: = + ▪
```

2. Set the WINDOW variables as shown. The x-axis is the time axis and the y-axis is the altitude axis.

3. Set the Plot menu variables as shown.

4. Press the GRAPH key to display the altitude-time graph.

The circles indicate where better data are needed.

```
CubicReg L3 L4
Cubic Reg
  y=ax³+bx²+cx+d
  a=⁻.0040669928
  b=1.757066708
  c=⁻254.2575582
  d=13970.21749
```

5. Press the STAT key and select CALC from the menu. Select CubicReg from the menu. Enter the name of the lists, x-axis data first, and then press the ENTER key. After a few seconds, the coefficients of the cubic regression will be displayed.

```
VARS
1:Window...
2:Zoom...
3:GDB...
4:Picture...
5:Statistics...
6:Table...
```

```
X/Y Σ EQ BOX PTS
1:a
2:b
3:c
4:d
5:e
6:r
7:RegEQ
```

6. To store the regression equation in the Y= list, press the Y= key and select the location you would like the regression equation stored by putting the cursor after the equals sign. Press the VARS key and select Statistics from the menu. Cursor right to highlight EQ and then select menu item 7, RegEQ. Press the ENTER key and the regression equation will be stored in the Y= list.

7. Press the GRAPH key and the altitude-time data will be plotted plus the regression equation.

```
QuartReg L3,L4
QuarticReg
  y=ax⁴+bx³+...+e
  a=1.8138009ₑ⁻5
  b=⁻.0119264961
  c=2.816305493
  d=⁻300.6093116
  e=14376.13864
```

8. Repeat steps 6 through 8 to do a QuartReg on the data.

```
Y₁=⁻.00406699284
217X^3+1.7570667
07796X^2+⁻254.25
755824297X+13970
.217490842
Y₂=
Y₃=
Y₄=
```

9. Which gives the better fit?

Video Companion
for
Fall-Timeters

Note: Refer to the *Gravity Rules! Glossary* for definitions of skydiving words and phrases.

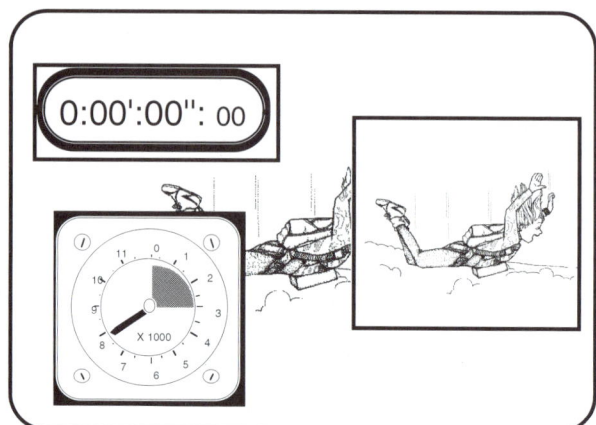

Time = 16 minutes: 29 seconds

I. Altimeter, Skydiver & Chronograph

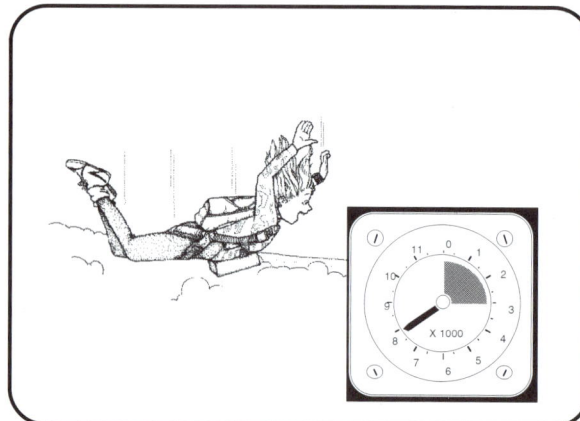

Time = 20 minutes: 53 seconds

II. Altimeter & Skydiver

Time = 25 minutes: 16 seconds

III. Altimeter Only

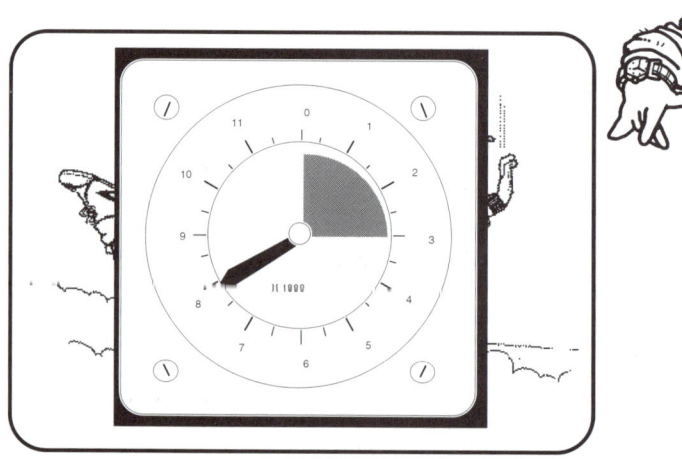

TERMINAL VELOCITY

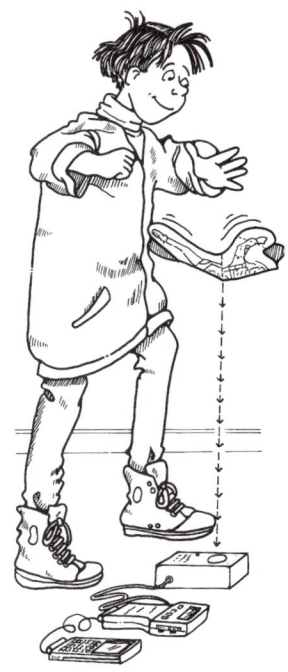

Topic
Terminal velocity

Key Question
How can a graphing calculator and computer technology be used to measure the terminal velocity of a paper skydiver?

Focus
Students will use a graphing calculator, data collector, and motion detector to measure the terminal velocity of a paper skydiver.

Guiding Documents
Project 2961 Benchmarks
- *Read analog and digital meters on instruments used to make direct measurements of length, volume, weight, elapsed time, rates, and temperature, and choose appropriate units for reporting various magnitudes.*
- *In the absence of retarding forces such as friction, an object will keep its direction of motion and its speed. Whenever an object is seen to speed up, slow down, or change direction, it can be assumed that an unbalanced force is acting on it.*

NRC Standards
- *Science and technology are reciprocal. Science helps drive technology, as it addresses questions*

that demand more sophisticated instruments and provides principles for better instrumentation and technique. Technology is essential to science, because it provides instruments and techniques that enable observations of objects and phenomena that are otherwise unobservable due to factors such as quantity, distance, location, size, and speed. Technology also provides tools for investigation, inquiry, and analysis.
- *If more than one force acts on an object along a straight line, then the forces will reinforce or cancel one another, depending on their direction and magnitude. Unbalanced forces will cause changes in the speed or direction of an object's motion.*

NCTM Standards
- *Estimate, make, and use measurements to describe and compare phenomena*
- *Select and use an appropriate method for computing from among mental arithmetic, paper-and-pencil, calculator and computer methods*
- *Develop the concepts of rates and other derived and indirect measurements*

Math
Measurement
  length
  time
Algebra
  equation of a straight line,
    slope-intercept form,
    $y = mx + b$

Science
Physical science
  average velocity

Integrated Processes
Observing
Collecting and recording data
Analyzing data

Materials
For each group of four students:
  Texas Instruments *CBL*™ (Calculator Based Laboratory)
  Texas Instruments graphing calculator compatible with the *CBL*™

Texas Instruments *Graph Link*™ cable and software
(optional)
motion detector
paper skydiver
Gravity Rules! video
Terminal Velocity sequence

Background Information

Terminal velocity, since it is a *constant* velocity, is an excellent real-world example of a linear algebraic equation. The slope-intercept form for a linear equation is $y = mx + b$. The coefficient of x, is m. It is the *slope* of the line. The line intercepts the y axis at b.

The weight of the paper skydiver is small so the paper skydiver reaches terminal velocity very quickly. See *What Is Terminal Velocity?* in the *Appendix* for a discussion of the physics of terminal velocity.

The graphing calculator and data collecting unit (CBL™) used in this activity are products of the Texas Instruments Corporation. A complete description of Texas Instruments' product line can be obtained by writing to the following address, calling their toll-free number, or going to their Internet site.

Texas Instruments
P. O. Box 6118
Temple, Texas 76503-6118
1-800 TI-CARES
www.ti.com

The Ultrasonic Motion Detector (part code MD-CBL™) is available from:

Vernier Software
8565 S. W. Beaverton-Hillsdale Hwy.
Portland, Oregon 97225
503-297-5317
www.vernier.com

The Casio corporation has a system similar to the Texas Instruments system called the *Casio Data Analysis System*. For further information contact:

CASIO
570 Mt. Pleasant Avenue
Dover, NJ 07801
1-800-582-2763
www.casio-usa.com

Management

1. View the *Terminal Velocity* video segment.
2. The BALLDROP and SELECT Texas Instruments programs are printed in the *Experiment Workbook* packaged with the Calculator Based Laboratory (CBL™) unit. The programs are also on a computer disk supplied with the workbook.
3. Load the BALLDROP and SELECT programs into each calculator. If necessary, key each program into one calculator and then use the link cable

supplied with each calculator to load the programs into all the calculators.
4. Connect the motion detector cable to the SONIC port of the CBL™ unit. Use the link cable to connect each CBL™ unit to a calculator.
5. The calculator can be mounted on the CBL™ by stretching two rubber bands around the CBL™ unit as shown in the diagram.

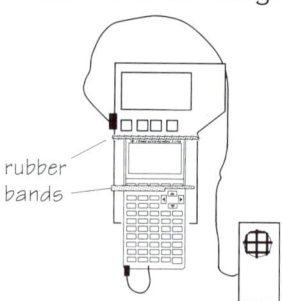

rubber bands

6. The Texas Instruments *Graph Link*™ cable and software enables users to print hard copies of graphs displayed by the calculator. The link can be hooked up to one computer and students can then connect their calculators to the link.
7. Test all hardware and software before attempting this activity.
8. Note that the display of the graphing calculator will dim whenever the calculator is analyzing data.
9. The HEIGHT data (in feet) is stored in the calculator in list L_1 and the TIME data is stored in list L_2.

Procedure

1. Assign three or four students to each group. Students can take turns operating the calculator and the CBL™ data collector, dropping the paper skydiver, and recording the data.

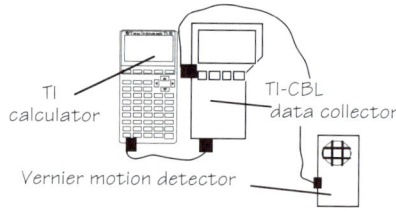

TI calculator   TI-CBL data collector

Vernier motion detector

2. Direct one of the students to place the motion detector on the floor. The gold-colored window of the detector should be face up.
3. Instruct the students controlling the calculators and CBL™ units to turn them on and EXECute the BALLDROP program on the calculator. Tell them to check that the motion detectors are emitting continuous, audible clicks and the red light-emitting diode on its face is glowing.
4. Tell the students to hold the paper skydivers at a height of four to six feet, in a face-to-Earth position, directly over the motion detector's window.

5. On the count of three, have the students release the paper skydivers and press the TRIGGER key on the CBL™ units at the same time. Inform the students that the CBL™ units are now collecting HEIGHT and TIME data. After approximately 1.5 seconds the CBL™ units will send the data to the calculators. The display screen on the calculators will show ANALYZING.... The HEIGHT vs. TIME graphs will then be displayed on the calculators. Below is an actual graph copied from the display screen of a calculator using the *Graph Link*™ hardware and software.

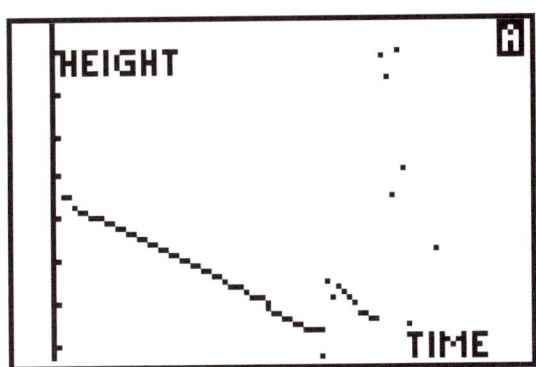

6. Tell students to press the program key on the calculators and EXECute the SELECT program. Explain that the SELECT program allows the user to "select" a continuous section of the graph for further analysis. This permits the removal of spurious data points from the graph. For example, in the above graph there are a few data points on both the left and right sides that are not linear. The points on the right side show the paper skydiver bouncing off the detector and then the detector reading arm movements or some other object directly over the detector.

7. When the SELECT program runs, it asks for the lower bound of the new graph. Instruct students to use the *cursor left* key to move the cursor to the lowest x-value they want to select for the new graph. Tell them to notice both the x and the y coordinates of the cursor's position are displayed at the bottom of the screen.

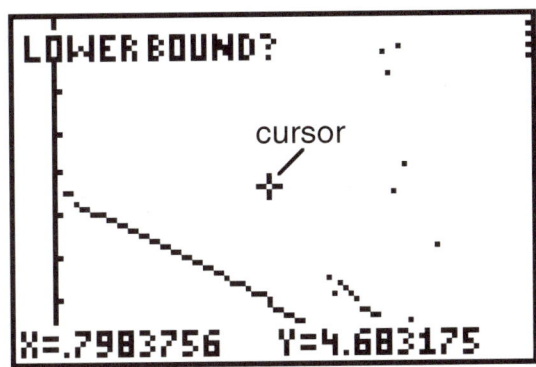

8. Tell the students to Press ENTER and observe that a vertical line appears in their displays indicating the lower bound of the graph and prompts them to select an upper bound for the new graph. Have them now use the cursor key to move the cursor to the greatest x-value.

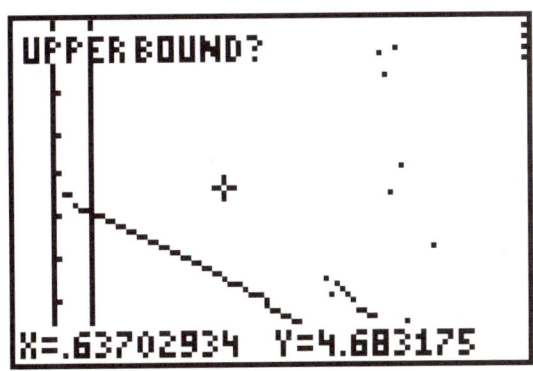

Caution students that if a mistake is made, they should press the ON key to break the SELECT program and start from the beginning. It may be necessary for them to use the ZOOM menu, item 9, ZOOMSTAT, to get the original graph.

9. Tell students that they should see a vertical line, indicating the upper bound, in their calculator display windows. They should also observe the message, ANALYZING..., that appears in the display as the SELECT program puts the height values between the upper and lower bound into list L3 and the time data between the same two bounds into list L4 in the calculator. They should soon see the redrawn graph.

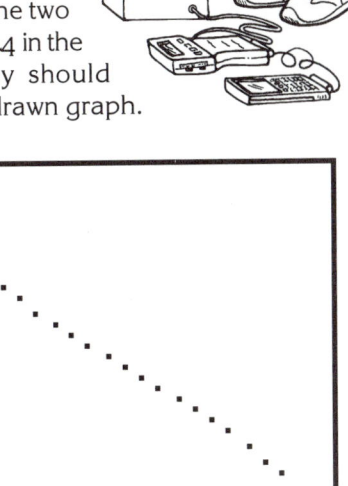

11. Ask the students to determine if the new graph appears to be linear. (If the graph does not appear to be linear, instruct the students to repeat the procedure). Tell them to press the TRACE key and observe the star-shaped cursor that appears at the upper end point of the graph. Instruct them to record the coordinates of the point.

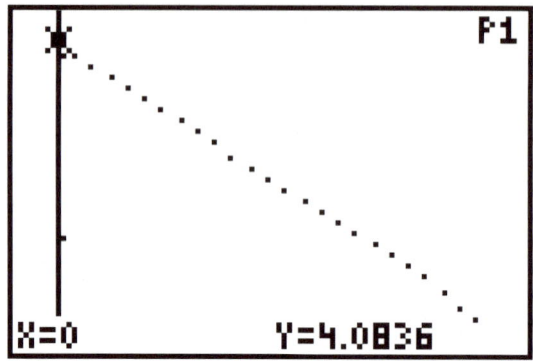

$X_1 = \underline{0}$, $Y_1 = \underline{4.0836}$

12. Have them repeatedly press the *cursor right* key to move the cursor along the graph and select a second point near the right side of the graph. Instruct them to record the coordinates of the point.

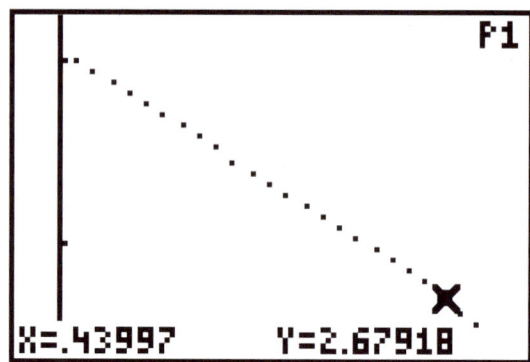

$X_2 = \underline{.43997}$, $Y_2 = \underline{2.67918}$

13. From the coordinates of the two points on the line, tell students to compute *m,* the slope of the line y=mx + b.

$$m = \frac{(Y_2 - Y_1)}{(X_2 - X_1)} = \frac{(2.67918 - 4.0836)}{(.43997 - 0)}$$

$$m = -3.19$$

14. Explain that the slope m, represents the terminal velocity of the paper skydiver. Since the *height* is measured in feet and *time* is measured in seconds, the terminal velocity has the units *feet per second*. The negative sign indicates that the object is falling (a rising object would be increasing height as a function of time).

m = terminal velocity = -3.19 feet per second

Discussion

1. Interpret the data shown on the first graph. How do you interpret the first part of the graph? [The paper skydiver was accelerating to terminal velocity.] From the graph, what was the release height of the paper skydiver? Interpret the middle portion of the graph. [The paper skydiver is falling with a constant velocity called terminal velocity.] How do you interpret the last part of the graph? [The paper skydiver bounced off the detector.]

2. How would you estimate the accuracy of the result for the terminal velocity? [Drop the paper skydiver from a height of six feet and compare a one-thousand, two- thousand, etc. seconds count to your result. The paper skydiver should hit the floor somewhere between 1.5 and 2 seconds.]

Extensions

1. Use the same set up and programs to graph the *height* versus *time* relationship of a softball-sized Wiffle® ball dropped onto the motion detector. To protect the detector, stack books around the detector to deflect the ball. See the *Measuring the Terminal Velocity of a Wiffle® Ball Teacher's Page* in the *Appendix* for sample data and an analysis that includes a quadratic curve fit to the data. A student page, *Measuring the Terminal Velocity of a Wiffle® Ball,* is also included in the *Appendix.*

2. Use a graphing calculator, data collector, and light probe to measure the terminal velocity of a toy car as it reaches the bottom of a ramp. See *Computing and Measuring the Terminal Velocity of A Hot Wheels® Car* in the *Appendix.*

3. Repeat the activity to determine, from the calculator's graph, just how quickly the paper skydiver reaches terminal velocity.

TERMINAL VELOCITY

What is the terminal velocity of a paper skydiver?

Procedure:

1. Load the BALLDROP and SELECT programs into the calculator.
2. Connect the sound detector cable to the SONIC port of the CBL. Connect the calculator to the CBL.
3. Turn on the CBL. EXECute the BALLDROP program. The sonic detector should be emitting continuous audible clicks.
4. Hold the paper skydiver directly over the sonic detector window at a height of 5 to 6 feet.
5. Release the paper skydiver and press TRIGGER on the CBL at the same time. The CBL is now collecting HEIGHT and TIME data. After approximately 1.5 seconds the CBL will send the data to the calculator. The display screen on the calculator will show ANALYZING... The HEIGHT vs. TIME graph will then be displayed on the calculator.
6. Copy the graph into display window 1 or use the Graph Link to get a hard copy and tape it into the window.

display window 1   display window 2

7. Use the SELECT program to capture the linear portion of the graph.
8. Copy the SELECTed graph into display window 2.
9. Press the TRACE key and use the cursor left and cursor right keys to select a point near each end of the graph.
10. Record the coordinates of each point.

$X_1 =$ _____ $x_2 =$ _____,

$y_1 =$ _____ $y_2 =$ _____

11. Use these coordinates to compute the slope m, of the graph.

$$m = \frac{y_2 - y_1}{x_2 - x_1} , \quad m = \text{_____}$$

12. The slope of the line represents the terminal velocity of the paper skydiver.

$m =$ _____ feet per second

Video Companion
for
Terminal Velocity

Note: Refer to the *Gravity Rules! Glossary* for definitions of skydiving words and phrases heard in the video.

Time = 40 minutes: 07 seconds

I. Opening Sequence
Narration:
> *"This human skydiver reaches a terminal velocity of 123 miles per hour."*

1. **A skydiver exits the Beechcraft King Air.**
2. **Notice the King Air diving towards the horizon.**
> *"What's the terminal velocity of a paper skydiver? That's the key question asked in the activity 'Terminal Velocity.' We're going to show you how to use the technology described in the activity to answer that question."*

3. **The real skydiver and the paper skydiver fall side by side.**
> *"These are the materials you'll need. First, you'll need a Texas Instruments data collecting unit called a CBL. CBL is an acronym that stands for Calculator Based Laboratory."*

4. **The CBL unit**
> *"With the CBL you will need a compatible Texas Instruments graphing calculator."*

5. **A Texas Instruments graphing calculator**
> *"Then you'll need a motion detector. The detector connects to the sonic port of the CBL unit."*

6. **A sonic motion detector from the Vernier company**
> *"A Texas Instruments Graph Link cable and software are optional, but highly recommended."*

7. **The cable and software disk**
> *"The final materials needed are a paper skydiver from the 'Skydiver' activity, and the student page from the 'Terminal Velocity' activity. Here's an overview of how the system works."*

Time = 41 minutes: 20 seconds

II. Overview
> *"The calculator has a program stored in its memory. This program is sent to the data collecting unit. The data collecting unit controls the motion detector. The motion detector sends out ultra-sonic sound waves which bounce off the object being measured and are reflected back to the detector. The data collecting unit then sends this data back to the graphing calculator for graphing and analysis."*

Time = 41 minutes: 48 seconds

III. Activity Procedure
> *"We will now go through the activity, step by step, as you would want your students to go through it. There are two ways to load the required programs into the calculator. First, the experiment book that comes with the CBL unit lists all of the book's programs in Appendix A. Someone has to key these programs into the calculator."*

8. **Keying programs into the calculator.**
> *"Fortunately there's a second option. To load programs from the computer into the calculator, you need to follow these steps: First, connect the link cable to the calculator."*

9. **Connecting the link cable.**
> *"Then select the programs BALLDROP and SELECT from the file menu."*

10. **The computer screen displays the program menu.**

  "Third, set the calculator to receive the programs like this … press the 2nd key and the LINK key, and highlight RECEIVE from the menu."

11. **Setting the calculator to receive the BALLDROP and SELECT programs from the computer.**

  "Fourth, select SEND from the computer menu and wait for the programs to load."

12. **The computer sends the programs to the calculator.**

  "That's all there is to it. You can see why the TI-GRAPH LINK cable and software are a nice management option. To load the programs into other calculators, use the link cable supplied with each calculator."

13. **Using the link cable to connect two calculators together so that they can share programs.**

  "Now, connect the calculator to the CBL unit using the supplied cable. Connect the sound detector cable to the SONIC port of the CBL unit. The calculator can be mounted on the CBL by stretching two rubber bands around the CBL unit, like this."

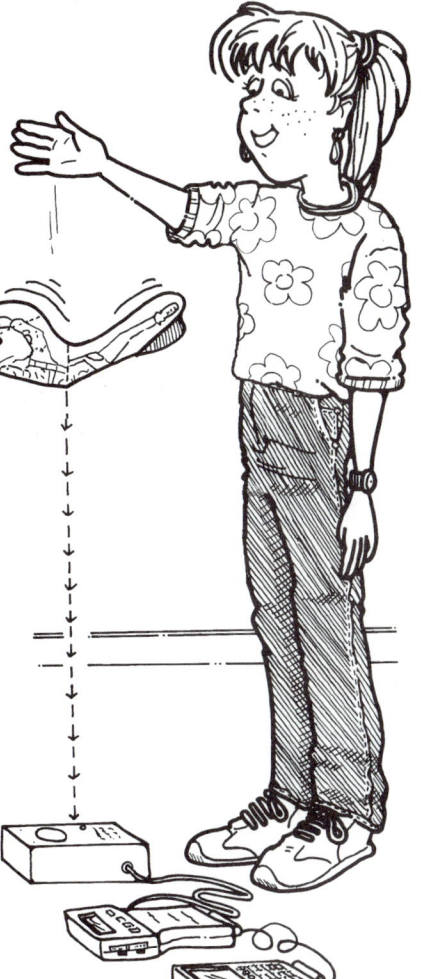

14. **Mounting the calculator to the CBL with rubber bands.**

  "Turn on the CBL unit. Execute the BALLDROP program on the calculator. The motion detector should be emitting continuous, audible clicks and the red light on its face should be glowing."

15. **The red light on the face of the motion detector glows.**

  "Watch carefully while a paper skydiver is dropped at a height of about four to six feet, in a face-to-Earth position, directly over the motion detector window."

16. **Getting ready to measure the terminal velocity.**

  "On a count of three, the paper skydiver is released and the TRIGGER on the CBL is pressed."

17. **The paper skydiver falls onto the motion detector.**

  "The CBL is now collecting HEIGHT and TIME data. After approximately 1.5 seconds, the CBL will send the data to the calculator. The HEIGHT vs. TIME graph is then displayed on the calculator."

18. **The graph as it appears in the calculator's display**

  "The HEIGHT data (in feet) is stored in list L_1 and the TIME data is stored in list L_2 in the calculator."

19. **The contents of the lists L_1 and L_2 are displayed.**

  "From the calculator's program menu, execute the SELECT program. The SELECT program allows the user to 'select' a continuous section of the graph for further analysis."

20. **Choosing the SELECT program from the calculator's program menu.**

  "Use the 'cursor left' key to move the cursor to the lowest x-value that you want to select for the new graph."

21. **The cursor keys on the calculator.**

  "Press the ENTER key and a vertical line appears indicating the lower bound of the graph. The screen also prompts you to select an upper bound. Use the 'cursor' key to move the cursor to the greatest x-value and press the ENTER key again."

22. **Selecting the lower bound.**

  "A vertical line appears in the display at the upper bound. The message, ANALYZING, appears in the display. The graph is then redrawn using the selected points."

23. **The new graph as seen in the calculator's display.**

  "The graph appears to be linear. Use TRACE to locate coordinates of two points on the graph. From these coordinates, compute the slope of the line. The coordinates for the point marked by the cross-shaped cursor are displayed at the bottom of the calculator's display screen. From these two points, we can compute the slope, m. The slope, m, represents the terminal velocity of the paper skydiver."

24. **A "chalkboard" animation of the definition of slope**

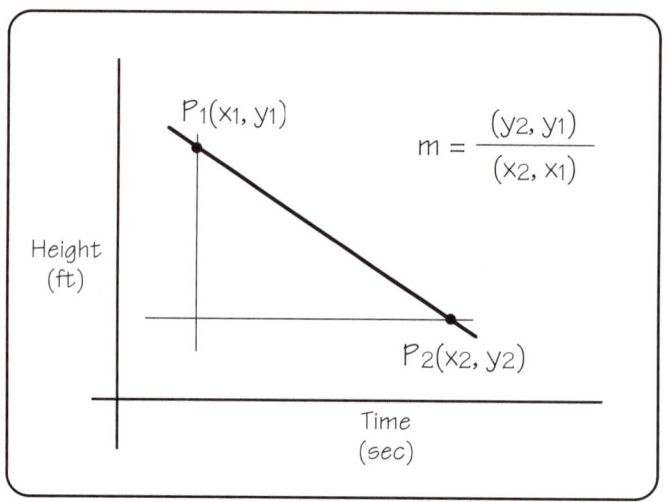

$$m = \frac{(y_2, y_1)}{(x_2, x_1)}$$

P₁(x₁, y₁) ... P₂(x₂, y₂)

Height (ft)

Time (sec)

"Since the height is measured in feet and time is measured in seconds, the terminal velocity has the units feet per second.'

Time = 45 minutes: 26 seconds

IV. Close

"The setup and procedure for this activity is relatively simple. However, to insure success, you'll need to repeat the procedure several times. Measuring the terminal velocity of a paper skydiver is an excellent activity for algebra students. And it connects to the larger context of skydiving in the real world."

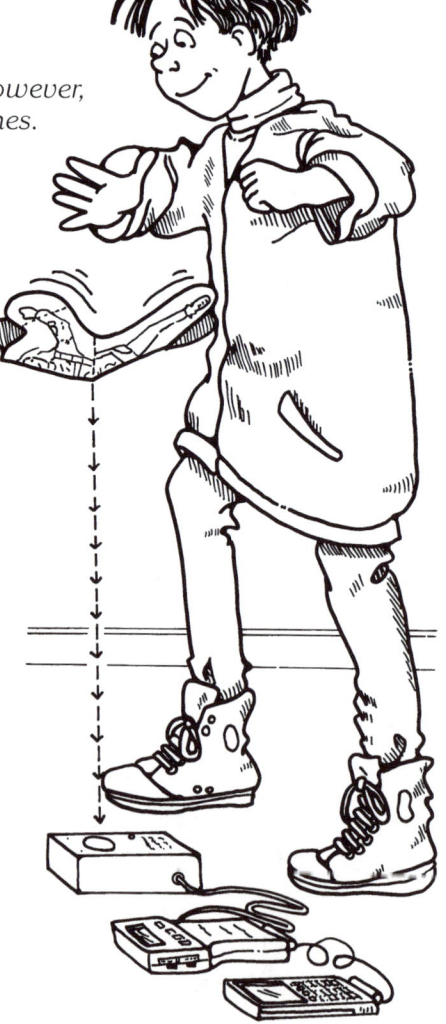

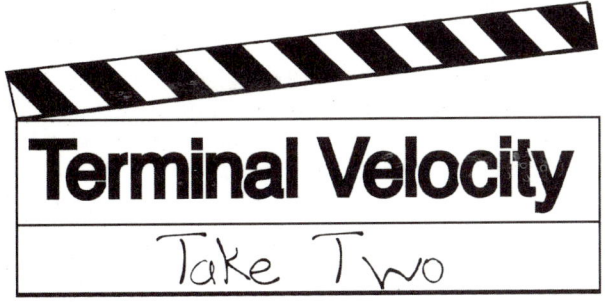

Terminal Velocity

Take Two

Topic
Terminal velocity

Key Question
How can video be used to measure the terminal velocity of a falling paper skydiver?

Focus
Students will view a video of a paper skydiver falling against a blue paper background consisting of horizontal lines spaced at one-foot intervals. Students will measure the time the paper skydiver takes to fall through a vertical height of ten feet. They will then use this data to compute the terminal velocity of the paper skydiver.

Guiding Documents
Project 2961 Benchmarks
- *Read analog and digital meters on instruments used to make direct measurements of length, volume, weight, elapsed time, rates, and temperature, and choose appropriate units for reporting various magnitudes.*
- *In the absence of retarding forces such as friction, an object will keep its direction of motion and its speed. Whenever an object is seen to speed up, slow down, or change direction, it can be assumed that an unbalanced force is acting on it.*

NRC Standard
- *If more than one force acts on an object along a straight line, then the forces will reinforce or cancel one another, depending on their direction and magnitude. Unbalanced forces will cause changes in the speed or direction of an object's motion.*

NCTM Standards
- *Estimate, make, and use measurements to describe and compare phenomena*
- *Select and use an appropriate method for computing from among mental arithmetic, paper-and-pencil, calculator and computer methods*
- *Develop the concepts of rates and other derived and indirect measurements*

Math
Measurement
   time
Statistics and probability
   mean

Science
Physical science
   average velocity
   terminal velocity

Integrated Processes
Observing
Collecting and recording data
Analyzing data

Materials
Gravity Rules! video
 Terminal Velocity - Take Two sequence
Stopwatch or sports watch with timer

Background Information
The paper skydiver reaches terminal velocity very quickly. In the video sequence the paper skydiver is dropped approximately one foot above the first horizontal line of the background scale. This line represents the zero end of the scale. The paper skydiver has *already* reached terminal velocity by the time it crosses this line.

Most students can visually estimate a length of one foot but few students know how to estimate time intervals of one second. Quietly counting one thousand one, one thousand two, one thousand three, is a useful method for estimating seconds.

Viewing the paper skydiver falling against the background convinces most observers that the paper skydiver's fall rate is constant. It doesn't appear to be speeding up or slowing down.

Management
1. View the *Terminal Velocity* video sequence to familiarize yourself with the activity.
2. The video sequence for measuring the time it takes the paper skydiver to fall ten feet is repeated three consecutive times to save rewinding.

Procedure
1. Explain to students that to make the backdrop, three long strips of blue paper were taped together. Masking tape was then applied horizontally, at one-foot intervals, to the paper. This background was then taped to the balcony railing in a gymnasium.
2. Distribute the student page. Show students the introductory video sequence and instruct them to label the vertical scale on the diagram of their page as described in the video.

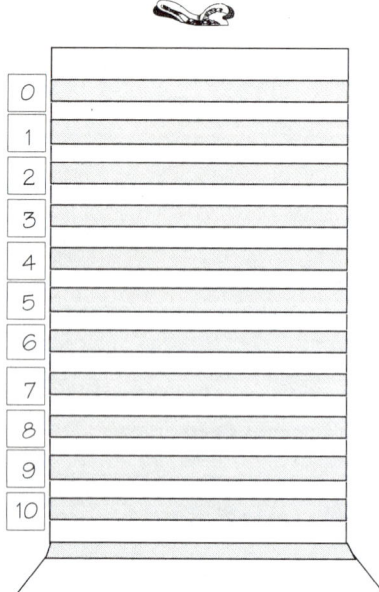

7. Cue the *Measuring the Time* video sequence. Tell the students that they are going to view the same falling skydiver sequence three consecutive times. Each time, they are to measure and record the elapsed time it takes the skydiver to fall through ten vertical feet.
8. Instruct the students to compute the *mean* of the three measured time intervals.
9. Using 10 feet as the *distance* and the computed mean as the average *time,* tell students to compute and record the average terminal velocity of the paper skydiver's fall.
10. Have them compare the *estimated* terminal velocity to the *measured* terminal velocity.

Discussion
1. What did you determine for the estimated average velocity? Discuss the range of results. (The *estimated* average velocity, to the nearest foot per second, should be three feet per second.)
2. Have students compare the *measured terminal velocities.* How can you explain any differences? [Various inaccuracies in measuring the elapsed time cause differences when computing the velocity.]
3. The *estimated* and *measured* terminal velocities should be in close agreement. Do you think *approximation* to be a useful measurement technique? Explain.
4. How might you determine if the paper skydiver were actually slightly speeding up or slowing down? [By measuring the time over shorter intervals, say each one-foot interval, average velocities for each interval could be computed and compared.]
5. Why does the paper skydiver reach terminal velocity so quickly? [The paper is so light that air resistance quickly balances its freefall weight.]
6. Compare the terminal velocity of the paper skydiver to the terminal velocity of a real skydiver (see *Fall-timeters*).

Extension
If you are at a school with a facility that allows you to hang a blue paper background like the one used in the video, then make your own video of your own experiments. For example, what is the terminal velocity of the paper skydivers in a 3-way formation?

3. Identify *"0"* as the *start* line and *"10"* as the *finish* line. Have students count the intervals to verify that there is a vertical distance of ten feet between the start and finish lines.
4. Teach students the one thousand one, one thousand two, one thousand three...method for approximating time in *seconds*. For intervals over ten seconds, teach students to count...one thousand nine...one thousand ten...two thousand one...two thousand two...and so on. Trying to say, even to one's self, ...one thousand thirty three...one thousand thirty four...destroys the rhythm and creates inaccuracy.

   A large wall clock with a second hand is useful for testing this counting system. Tell students they are going to test their ability to estimate a 30-second interval of time. Show them the clock and tell them that when the second hand reaches 12, they are to start quietly counting to 30. Hide the face of the clock. When 30 seconds have passed, show the clock face to students. They will then know where they are in their count and can compare their estimation with the clock's measurement.
5. Cue the *Estimating the Time* video sequence. Explain to students that the video will give a *Ready, Set, Go* cue. Tell the students they are to start measuring time on the *Go* cue. Instruct them to watch the paper skydiver fall in front of the background and use the quiet counting method to estimate — to the nearest second — the time it takes the paper skydiver to fall the ten vertical feet. Start the video. If necessary, rewind and repeat viewing the video. Tell the students to record their estimate.
6. Have students compute the average velocity using their estimated time and a distance of ten feet.

Terminal Velocity
Take Two

1. Label the vertical scale.
2. Use the one thousand one, one thousand two, one thousand three, quiet-counting method to estimate to the nearest second the time it takes the paper skydiver to fall through the vertical ten feet.

Estimated time = _____ seconds

Estimated terminal velocity $= \dfrac{\boxed{} \text{ feet}}{\boxed{} \text{ seconds}}$

Estimated terminal velocity $= \_\_\_\_\_ \dfrac{\text{feet}}{\text{second}}$

3. View the video three times. Each time, measure and record the elapsed time it takes the paper skydiver to fall through ten vertical feet.

Video Data Table		
Trial	Time (seconds)	Distance (feet)
1		10
2		10
3		10
Mean		10

4. Compute and record the mean (average) of the three time measurements.

5. Compute the average measured terminal velocity.

6. Compare the estimated terminal velocity to the measured terminal velocity.

Measured terminal velocity $= \dfrac{\boxed{} \text{ feet}}{\boxed{} \text{ seconds}}$

Measured terminal velocity $= \_\_\_\_\_ \dfrac{\text{feet}}{\text{second}}$

Video Companion
for
Terminal Velocity — TakeTwo

Note: Refer to the *Gravity Rules! Glossary* for definitions of skydiving words and phrases heard in the video.

Time = 45 minutes: 54 seconds

I. Labeling the Diagram
Narration:

> *"The horizontal lines on the blue paper are one foot apart. Label your diagram on your page titled 'Terminal Velocity — Take Two' like this ..."*

Time = 46 minutes: 14 seconds

II. Estimating Time

> "*A simple method for estimating one-second intervals of time is to quietly count to yourself like this, one thousand one, one thousand two, one thousand three, and so on. Use this method to estimate the time, to the nearest second, it takes the paper skydiver to fall ten feet.*"

Time = 46 minutes: 48 seconds

III Measuring Time

> *"Use a stopwatch to measure the time it takes the paper skydiver to fall ten feet."*

The video segment of the falling paper skydiver appears three times in succession. Use the *Pause* key between segments to allow students to record their measurement and get ready for the next measurement.

74

Canopy pilot

Topic
Aerodynamics

Key Questions
What is the glide ratio of a paper ram-air parachute?

Focus
Students will construct a paper model of a ram-air parachute. They will determine its glide ratio.

Guiding Documents
Project 2061 Benchmark
- *Numbers and shapes — and operations on them — help to describe and predict things about the world around us.*

NRC Standards
- *An object's motion can be described by tracing and measuring its position over time.*
- *The motion of an object can be described by its position, direction of motion, and speed. That motion can be represented on a graph.*

NCTM Standards
- *Represent and solve problems using geometric models*
- *Understand and apply geometric properties and relationships*
- *Develop the concepts of rates and other derived and indirect measurements*

Math
Measurement
    length
Ratio and proportion
Probability and statistics
    mean

Science
Physical science
    aerodynamics
        glide ratio

Integrated Processes
Observing
Collecting and recording data
Identifying and controlling variables
Interpreting data
Applying

Materials
Scissors
Glue sticks
Pennies, one per student
Gravity Rules! video
    Canopy Pilot sequence

Background Information
Model ram-air canopies cut from nylon fabric, expertly sewn and rigged, can be purchased from Parabatics™ Products. For a free brochure, write or call:

Parabatics™ Products
P. O. Box 757
Hamilton, MT 59840
1-800 821-4070

The paper pattern used in this activity to model a real ram-air parachute is, to the best of our knowledge, unique. Its paper construction makes it suitable for classroom use but also imposes limitations on its ability to duplicate the glide ratio of a real ram-air canopy. It is our hope that our paper ram-air canopy is just the first in a long string of improved designs. Challenge your students to identify its weaknesses and improve upon its construction and performance. The first person to fold and fly a paper glider never dreamed the extent to which paper gliders would be studied and improved.

Management
1. Do the activity beforehand. This allows you to familiarize yourself with how to construct and test fly the parachute.
2. Do this activity in three parts. *Part 1* provides detailed instructions for constructing a ram-air parachute from paper. You may choose to have your students construct their paper ram-air canopy as a model to be colored and hung from the classroom ceiling. *Part 2* provides instructions for fine-tuning the flight characteristics of the paper ram-air canopy, and *Part 3* measures the glide ratio of the paper ram-air.
3. This activity is best done indoors away from wind and air currents. If possible, use a large room. A

gymnasium or cafeteria is an ideal place to spread out and fly the ram-air parachute.

4. Instruct students to use a ruler and draw over any fold lines with a sharp pencil. This scores the lines and makes it easier to make straight folds.

Procedure

Show students the *Canopy Pilot* sequence of the video. Stop the video.

Discussion

1. Use the following *Did You See ...?* questions to facilitate further discussion.

   Did You See ...

   • **a tandem tumble out of the airplane?** [Jerry Cook and passenger *(Part I-2)*]

   • **two skydivers fly their canopies straight down?** [Members of a parachute demonstration team perform a downplane maneuver *(Part 1-4)*.]

   • **Mike dive the King Air straight towards the ground?** [The King Air can be clearly seen flying straight down, parallel to the tandem's drogue chute *(Part II-1)*.]

   • **an AFF student pull the ripcord and hold it as the parachute opens?** [The two AFF jumpmasters steadying the student are in the red jump suits. The ripcord can be clearly seen in the student's right hand *(Part II-4)*.]

   • **a skydiver do rapid left and right turns?** [Jumpmaster Vic Logan does rapid toggle turns with his high performance ram-air canopy *(Part -9)*.]

   • **a parachutist try to land on a house?** [A stunt man standing on the wing of a biplane jumps from a very low altitude *(Part II-15)*.]

   • **a smoke jumper?** [A smoke jumper prepares to land. Notice the big pocket on his leg. It contains a long rope in case he has to climb down out of a tree *(Part II-17)*.]

   • **another canopy pilot in the air with Shelly as she sashays above the clouds?** [Another canopy pilot can be seen in the background *(Part II-20)*.]

Procedure

Part 1 — Construction

1. Direct students to cut out the canopy and score along lines *a*, *b*, and *c*, folding them down.

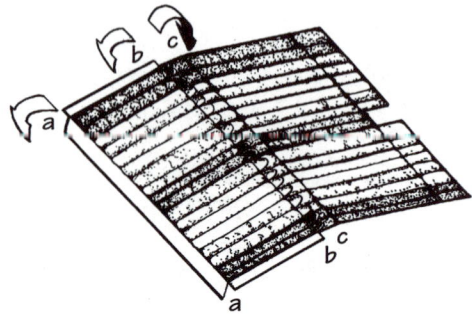

2. Have them glue the tab at *a* to the bottom of the canopy along line *f* but not across the notch. Instruct them to fold down along lines *d* and *e* to complete the canopy.

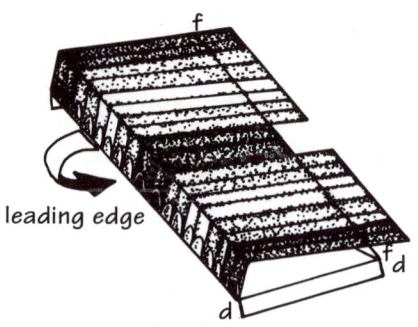

leading edge

3. Next, have students cut out the left and right suspension lines. (Note that the suspension lines can be cut in one of two ways, either thick or thin.)

4. Have them place the left suspension lines on top of the right suspension lines, carefully matching the two pieces. Direct them to glue **only** the bottom tips together. Note: Each suspension line is labled on its upper-right corner.

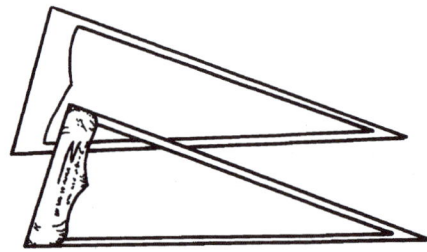

5. Have them glue the left and right suspension lines to the flaps on the sides of the canopy.

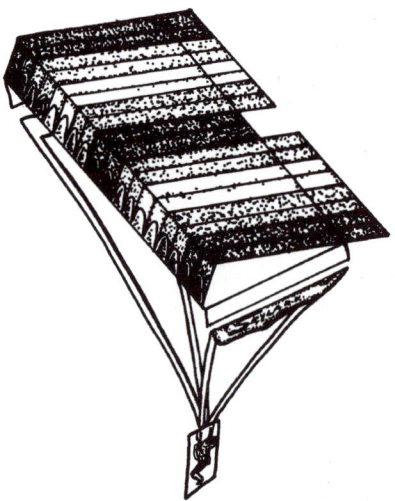

6. Tell students to cut out the skydiver figure of their choice. Have them vertically fold the figure along the line and tape a penny to the inside of the folded figure. Tape or glue the figure to the bottom of the suspension lines.

Part 2 — Flight Testing

1. Instruct the students to grip the parachute as shown in the diagram. Have them hold the parachute high over their heads and release their grips. The parachute should surge forward and glide straight and level to a smooth landing.

Problem-Solving Strategies

- If any parachute floats, inform the students to attach a paper clip to the skydiver figure.
- If any parachute falls rapidly, have them use a smaller paper clip or other weights.
- If any parachute doesn't fly straight, have students adjust the left or right brake by bending the brake slightly down. Caution students to make small adjustments, not large adjustments to the brakes.

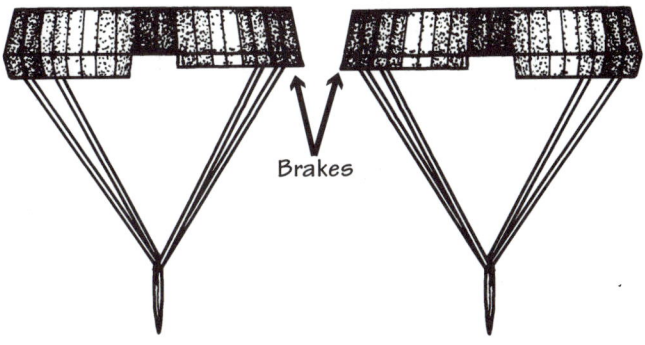

Brakes

- If the ram-air nose dives, direct students to bend both brakes up.
- If the ram-air still nose dives, have them add a paper clip.

Part 3 - Measuring the Glide Ratio

1. Do not attempt to measure the glide ratio of any ram-air that has not been trimmed to fly straight. Discuss with the class the parameters to be used to define *straight*. Use masking tape to lay out a course on the floor of a large room. (See illustration.) These guidelines might be helpful.
   - All canopy pilots will release their ram-air at a point above the release line.

- To qualify as a flight test, the ram-air must fly within the four-foot lane.

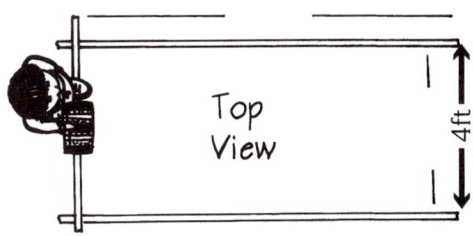

Top View

4ft

2. Have students complete three successful flight tests. For each test, direct them to measure the release height and the distance flown to the nearest centimeter. Have them determine the distance flown by measuring the straight line distance from the release point to the front edge of the canopy and record it in the data table.

3. Have them compute the glide ratio for each flight test by dividing the measure of the distance flown by the measure of the release height and record it in the data table.

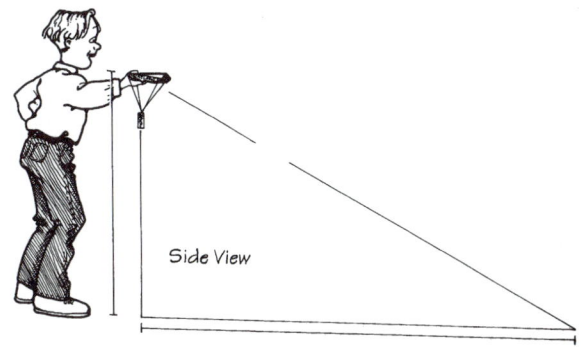

Side View

4. Lastly, have the students compute the mean glide ratio and record this computation in the test data table.

Discussion

1. How is your paper ram-air canopy like a real ram-air canopy? [The paper canopy, like a real canopy, is a wing.]
2. How is your paper ram-air canopy different from a real ram-air canopy? [The paper canopy doesn't actually inflate.]
3. Compare the glide ratio of your paper ram-air to the glide ratio of the real ram-air found in the *Glide Ratio* activity.

Extensions

1. What modifications could you make to your paper ram-air to increase its glide ratio and overall performance?
2. How would you design and test a different model of a paper ram-air canopy?

Canopy pilot

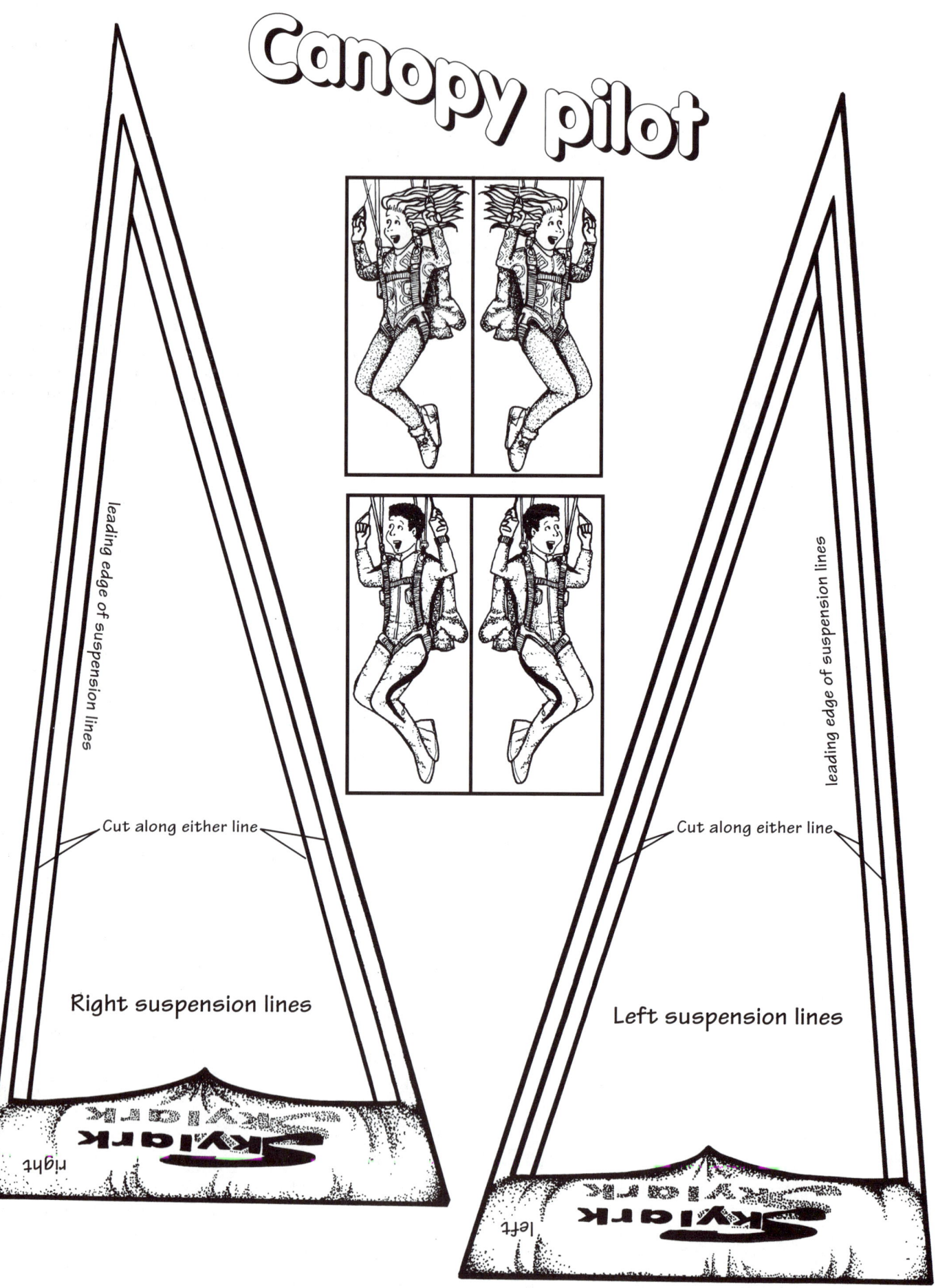

leading edge of suspension lines

leading edge of suspension lines

Cut along either line

Cut along either line

Right suspension lines

Left suspension lines

SKYLARK
right

SKYLARK
left

Canopy pilot

glue tab

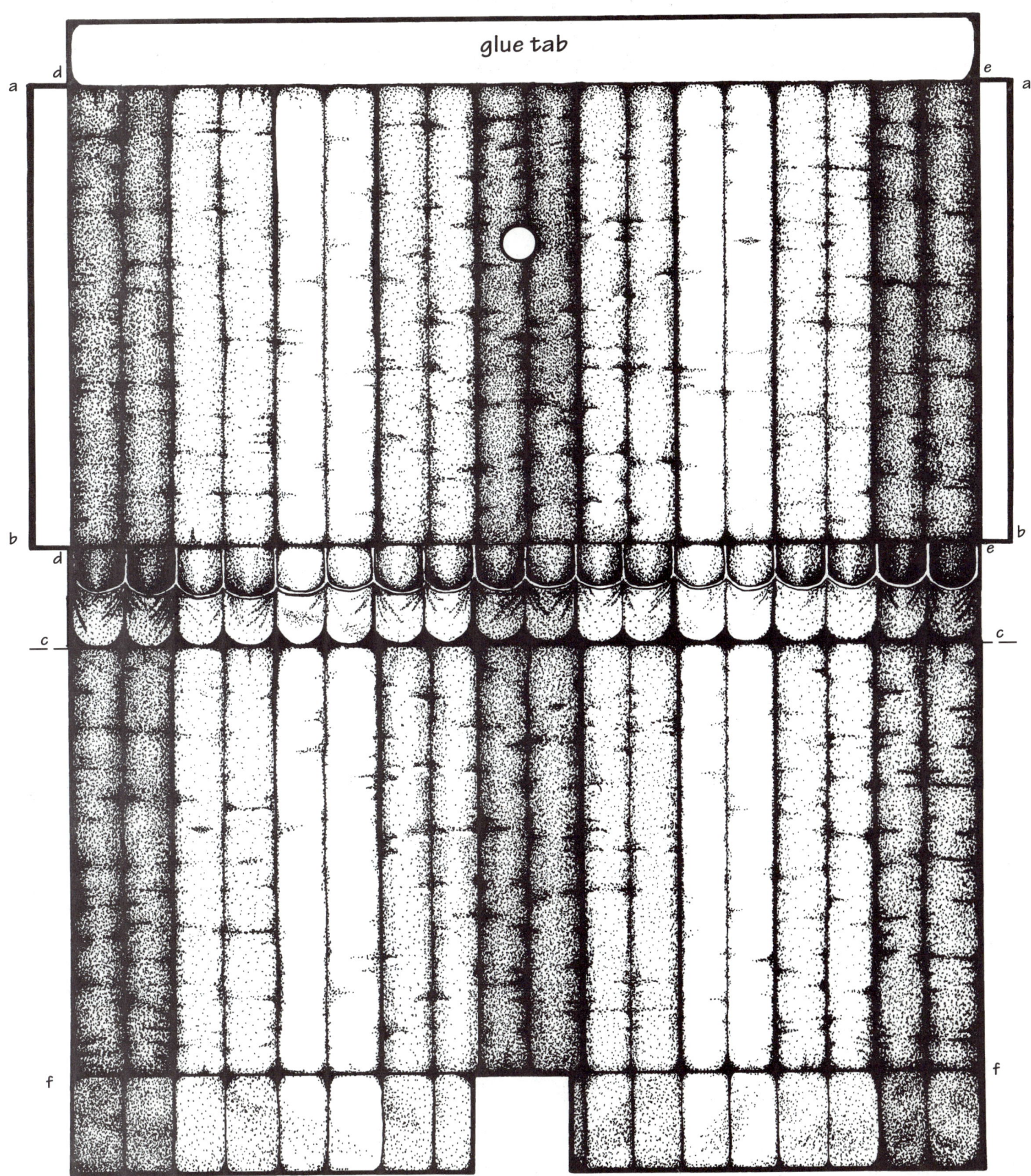

Canopy pilot

Glide Path / altitude / ground track

1. Trim your ram-air canopy
    to fly straight.
2. Measure release height and distance flown to the nearest
    centimeter. Retest any flights that don't stay within the flight
    test boundaries. Record *Flight Test Data* for three good flights
    of your ram-air canopy.
3. Compute the *Glide Ratio* for each
    flight test.
4. Compute the mean *Glide Ratio* from
    the *Flight Test Data*.

Flight Test Data			
Flight Test	Altitude (A)	Length of ground track (L)	Glide Ratio = $\dfrac{L}{A}$
1			
2			
3			
Totals			
Means			

5. Choose values for the axes of the graph that fit the *Flight Test Data*.
6. Graph the Glide Path for each flight test and the mean Glide Path of all three flight tests.

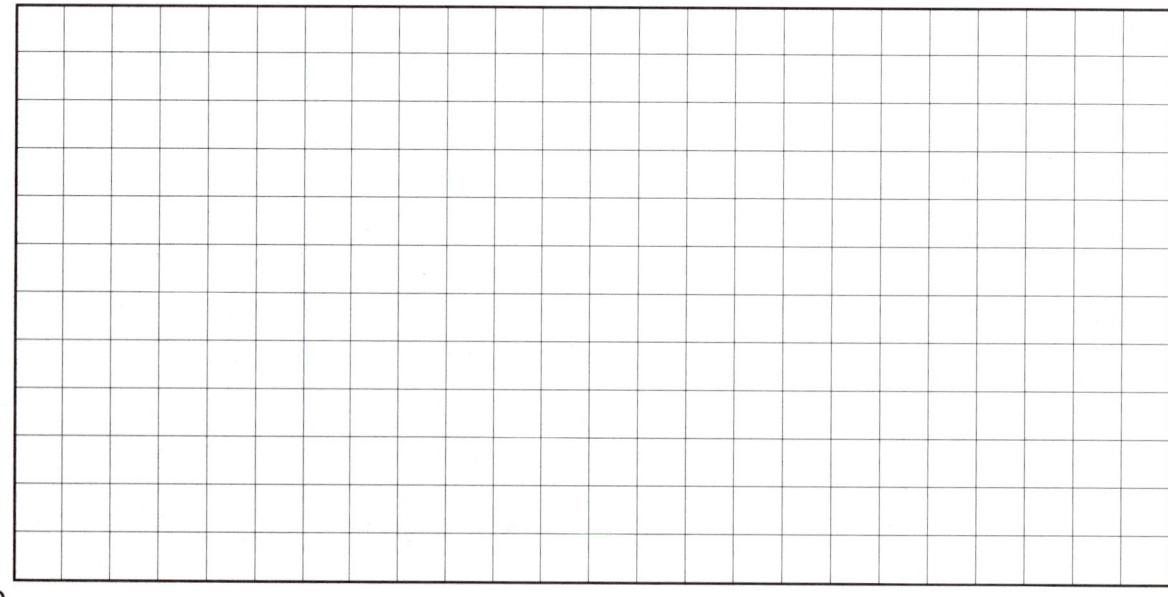

Altitude

0

Length of ground track

Video Companion
for
Canopy Pilot

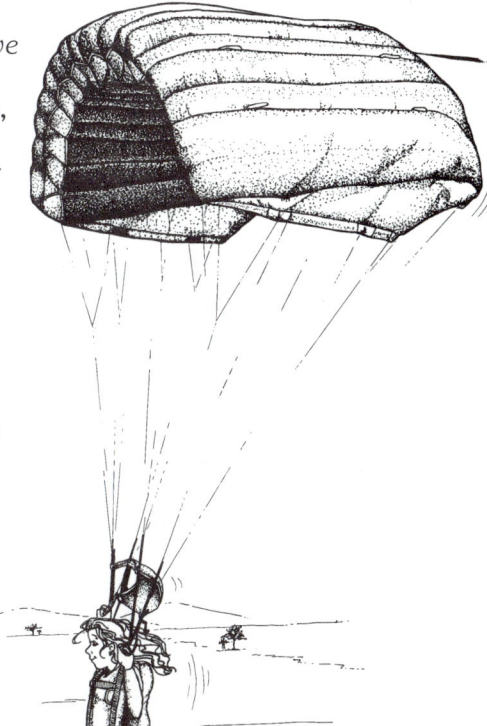

Note: Refer to the *Gravity Rules! Glossary* for definitions of skydiving words and phrases heard in the video.

Time = 47 minutes: 35 seconds

I. **Opening Sequence — A Montage of Skydiving Scenes**
   1. Skysurfer and videographer exit the airplane at an altitude of 13,500 feet.
   2. A young lady and her tandem jumpmaster exit the airplane at 13,500 feet.
   3. Tanya spins on her surfboard.
   4. Two skydivers lock their legs together to form what's called a down plane. Both canopies are flying straight down, towards the ground.
   5. Jumpmaster Vic Logan lands after an AFF skydive.

Time = 47 minutes: 51 seconds

II. **Narration**
   "A typical skydive has three distinct parts: First, a skydive begins with approximately one minute of freefall."
   1. **Tandem Master Jerry Cook and passenger are in the air. Notice, in the background, the airplane diving towards the ground.**
      "During this relatively short time span, a skydiver uses their [sic] arms and legs — like the controls of an airplane — to fly their [sic] body."
   2. **Shelly does left and right turns while in freefall.**
      "The high-speed, action-packed freefall ends — hopefully — with a quick and snappy opening of their [sic] ram-air parachute."
   3. **The tandem passenger opens the parachute.**
   4. **An AFF student opens the parachute as the jump masters turn and track away.**
      "In approximately two seconds, a skydiver slows down from 120 miles per hour to less than five miles per hour, and with an open canopy, a skydiver then 'flies their [sic] canopy' to a stand-up landing on the ground."
   5. **Two of Shelly's landings**
   6. **Two other skydivers land.**
      "The shape of a cross-section of a ram-air canopy is much like the cross-section of an airplane wing. This shape is called an airfoil."
   7. **The shape of an airfoil is drawn over a still picture of the tandem.**
      "Students and novices fly canopies that have an area of about 200 square feet."
   8. **A student lands.**
      "Experienced jumpers fly canopies with an area about 120 square feet."
   9. **Vic does fast and snappy left and right turns with his high performance canopy.**
      "An airfoil shape is cut from nylon fabric and sewn into a tube, open at the front, closed at the back. Two tubes make a cell; seven to nine cells make a canopy."

10. **The tubes and cells of a canopy are pointed out.**
    "The suspension lines attached to the front of the canopy are cut shorter than the suspension lines attached to the tail of the canopy. This gives the canopy a nose-down attitude."
11. **The suspension lines are drawn over a still picture of a canopy.**
    "A ram-air canopy slides down a gravity hill, converting gravitational potential energy for forward speed, like a Hot Wheels® car slides down the gravity ramp."
12. **A skydiver descends under canopy.**
13. **A Hot Wheels® car rolls down a ramp.**
    "The first parachutes were essentially circular, fabric umbrellas. When jumped, they filled with air to slow the jumper's descent rate."
14. **A jumper lands under a round canopy.**
15. **A low altitude stunt jump from the wing of an airplane into a house.**
    "They were not steerable, and went wherever the wind, if any, blew them. These canopies had no ability to glide, and therefore, had a zero glide ratio. The jumper is a passenger."
16. **A parachutist leaves the step of a Cessna. Her round canopy is opened by a line, called a static line, attached to the airplane.**
17. **A parachutist has a normal, round canopy landing.**
    "Modifications were eventually made to these 'round' canopies (see Derry Slots) that gave them some steerability. These changes vented air through slits in the canopy to provide a small amount of forward flight."
18. **A smoke jumper under a round canopy with Derry Slots**
19. **Looking up into a highly modified round canopy**
20. **Landing a highly modified round canopy**
    "The 'square-shaped' ram air canopy is essentially a fabric wing capable of generating lift. Like a glider, a ram-air canopy can be flown to the ground. The jumper is a pilot."
21. **Shelly enjoys flying her canopy above the clouds.**

The Father of the Ram-Air Canopy

Domina C. Jalbert
(1904-1991)

In the early 1960s Domina Jalbert, a balloon and kite-builder, was flying his twin engined airplane home to Florida. Idly gazing out the window at the left wing, thinking of the aerodynamic forces of lift, load, and drag acting on the wing, he had the inspiration for building a fabric, ram-air inflated wing.

The wing would consist of a series of tubes cut and sewn into the shape of the cross-section of a wing. The leading edge of the fabric wing would be open. The trailing edge would be sewn closed.

As the wing moved forward, ram-air would enter through the leading edge of each tube, pressurizing the fabric so that it would stiffen into a semi-rigid wing. The load would be suspended from beneath the wing on lines attached to the bottom of the wing.

> *M*y experience with kites, balloons, and parachutes, and the problems relating to their flight characteristics in all kinds of weather, involving problems of rigging, enabled me to design and patent an airfoil wing.
>
> *Domina C. Jalbert*

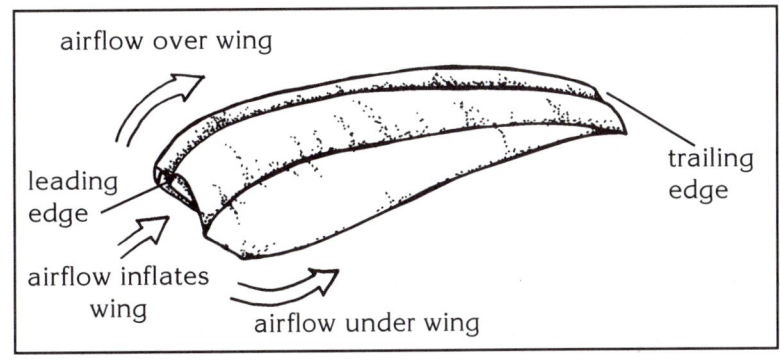

airflow over wing
leading edge
airflow inflates wing
airflow under wing
trailing edge

Jalbert didn't have the facilities to conduct aerodynamic research on his inflatable wing so he contacted J. D. Nicolaides, Chairman of the Aerospace Department at Notre Dame University. Dr. Nicolaides and his students spent several years testing the idea in a wind tunnel and eventually flew it on a tow line as a wing with a suspended load.

In 1968 aeronautical engineer and skydiver Steve Snyder purchased a parafoil from Dr. Nicolaides and modified it for use as a parachute. The major problems with the parafoil as a parachute were severe opening shock (12 times the force of gravity at 60 miles per hour) and line entanglements. Snyder's early developmental work eventually led to skydivers adopting the ram-canopy as the canopy of choice.

The modern ram-air canopy flown by today's skydiver represents the current stage in the evolution of canopy design and development. In the future, new ideas will merge with the development of lighter, stronger materials to produce canopies that are faster, easier to fly, and safer.

In recognition of a lifetime of innovation in parachutes, balloons, and kites in particular, his invention of the parafoil, ram-air wing, Jalbert was presented the 1986 American Institute of Aeronautics and Astronautics (AAIA) Aerodynamic Decelerator Systems Award.

Thirty skydivers wearing color-coordinated jumpsuits and parachutes form the five Olympic Rings over the Olympic stadium in Seoul, Korea, to open the 1988 Olympic games. An estimated one billion view the ceremonies on television.

Copy each page. Cut along the dashed line on this page. Align the two pages and glue or tape them together. Color each skydiver.

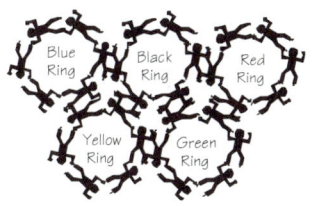

GLIDE RATIO

Topic
Aerodynamics: glide ratio

Key Question
What is the glide ratio of a ram-air parachute?

Focus
Students will observe a video sequence of a skydiver landing a ram-air canopy. At a known height, the skydiver drops a weighted streamer. After dropping the streamer, the skydiver continues to fly in a straight line, descending at a constant rate, until he lands. The line between the point where the skydiver dropped the weighted streamer and the point where it strikes the ground is taken to be the altitude of a right triangle. The skydiver's glide path is taken to be the hypotenuse of a right triangle. The line from the point where the weighted streamer hits the ground to the point the skydiver lands is taken to be the base of a right triangle. Students will then use information and measurements taken from the video to compute the *glide ratio* of the skydiver's canopy.

Guiding Documents
Project 2061 Benchmark
- *Numbers and shapes — and operations on them — help to describe and predict things about the world around us.*

NRC Standards
- *An object's motion can be described by tracing and measuring its position over time.*
- *The motion of an object can be described by its position, direction of motion, and speed. That motion can be represented on a graph.*
- *The position of an object can be described by locating it relative to another object or the background.*

NCTM Standards
- *Represent and solve problems using geometric models*
- *Understand and apply geometric properties and relationships*
- *Develop the concepts of rates and other derived and indirect measurements*

Math
Geometry and spatial sense
   right triangle
   cone
Ratio and proportion
Measurement
   length
   time

Science
Aerodynamics
   glide ratio

Integrated Processes
Observing
Collecting and recording data
Interpreting data
Generalizing

Materials
Gravity Rules! video
   Glide Ratio sequence
Per group:
   stopwatch or sports watch
   scissors
   transparent tape

Background Information
The landing area at the Taft drop zone consists of a large, square, grassy area for experienced jumpers and a rectangular gravel-filled pit for students. Typically, both experienced and student jumpers will adjust their flight paths so as to land on either the grass or gravel.

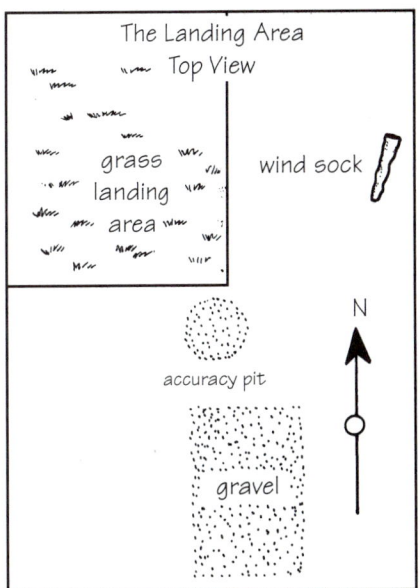

In order to measure the glide ratio of a ram-air canopy, the glide path — and therefore the ground track — had to be adjusted to make the ground track as long as possible. [The *ground track* is the projection of the glide path onto the ground.]

To maximize the length of the ground track, a southwest to northeast glide path was selected. The skydiver can (and often does) alter the angle of the glide path during the landing approach. To more accurately measure the glide ratio of the ram-air canopy, the skydiver purposely did not alter the angle of the glide path. The glide path needed to approximate as close as possible the hypotenuse of a right triangle. In the video the skydiver can be seen adjusting the direction, but not the angle of his glide path.

At the beginning of the video the skydiver is seen exiting the Cessna aircraft at an altitude of 4000 feet. He opens his parachute and flies his canopy to position himself near point *A* in the diagram, headed into the wind.

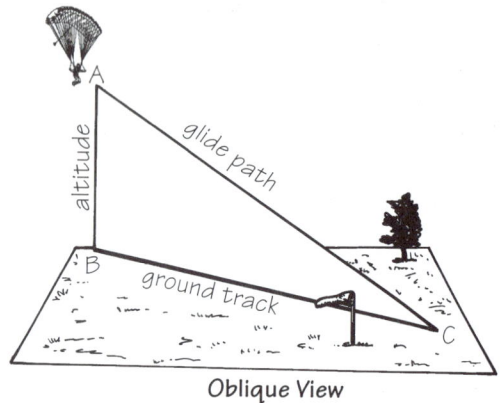

Oblique View

At point *A* he reads his altimeter and drops the weighted streamer. The streamer strikes the ground at point *B*. The skydiver flies in as straight a line as possible, without altering the glide angle, along the descending path to land at point *C*.

Computing the glide ratio of the ram-air canopy is predicated on triangle *ABC* being a close approximation to a *right triangle*.

In the activity, students will use the altimeter reading reported by the skydiver to determine the vertical leg *(AB)* of the right triangle *ABC*. The base leg *(BC)* of triangle *ABC*, called the ground track, is shown in the video being measured to the nearest hundred feet. Students take their own reading, from the video, to the nearest foot. The *glide ratio* of the ram-air canopy is computed by dividing the length of the ground track by the altitude.

A skydiver flies in three-dimensional space. Assume a no-wind condition. Upon opening, the skydiver can fly anywhere with the *cone* defined by the glide ratio of the canopy (see the *Glide Ratio Comparison* page).

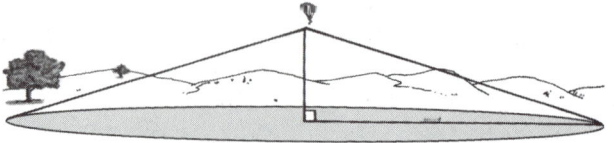

Any wind distorts the cone by moving the altitude of the cone *upwind*. The stronger the wind, the further upwind the altitude moves.

Students have too few opportunities to measure events in the real world. Unlike textbooks, the real world offers problems that have problems within problems. For example, if this were a textbook problem, the altitude, ground track, and glide path would form an exact right triangle. Because of its real-world context, each of the sides of the right triangle is approximated to varying degrees of accuracy (see *Discussion*).

Management

1. Preview the *Glide Ratio* episode of the video.
2. Refer to the Gravity Ru*les! Glossary* for answers to many of the questions you might have as a result of watching the video.
3. Groups students in pairs.
4. Make an overhead transparency of the *Wind Speed Indicator* and *Magnetic Compass* page.

Procedure

1. Distribute the *Glide Ratio* student page.
2. Distribute one right triangle and skydiver to each student (see the *Right Triangle Pattern* page).
3. Instruct the students to cut out the right triangle and skydiver. Have the students tape the tabs of the right triangle to the corresponding tabs on the *Landing Area* section of their *Glide Ratio* page. Tell them to adjust the triangle so it stands vertically on their page.
4. Have them cut out the small skydiver, fold back its upper right-hand corner, and then place it at point *A* on the paper triangle.
5. Tell the students that this three-dimensional model will help them visualize and understand what the skydiver in the video is doing.
6. Show the opening sections, *Glide Ratio Definition* and *Simulation*, of the *Glide Ratio* episode of the video. Stop the video. Have students compare their three-dimensional model with the animated video sequence. Be sure students understand the skydiver is trying to establish a right triangle.
7. Show the *Measuring the Glide Ratio* section of the video. Have students observe and record the altitude (approximately 400 feet) at which the skydiver drops the streamer. Stop the video.
8. Show the *Measuring the Ground Track* section of the video. Stop the video. Instruct the students to record, to the nearest foot, the length of the ground track.
9. Using the transparency of the *Wind Speed Indicator* and *Magnetic Compass* page, explain to students how to read the instruments.
10. Show the *Windsock Indicator* and *Wind Speed Indicator* sections of the video. Stop the video.

Have students record the wind data, both the direction and speed, from the video.

11. Have students use the data to compute and record the glide ratio.

12. Tell students to graph the glide path.

Discussion

1. Why do you think skydivers land *into* the wind? [Skydivers — like birds and airplanes — land into the wind to minimize their landing speed. Assume the skydiver is moving at a velocity of 20 miles per hour in the direction shown in the diagram.

20 miles per hour

Assume the wind is blowing in the opposite direction with a velocity of 10 miles per hour.

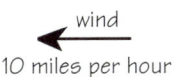
wind
10 miles per hour

By landing into the wind, the skydiver is moving, relative *to the ground*, at a velocity of only 10 miles per hour.

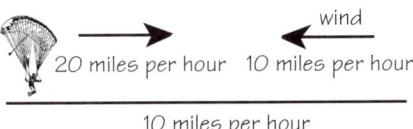
20 miles per hour   wind   10 miles per hour
10 miles per hour

Landing downwind (in the direction of the wind), the skydiver is moving, *relative to the ground*, with a velocity of 30 miles per hour.]

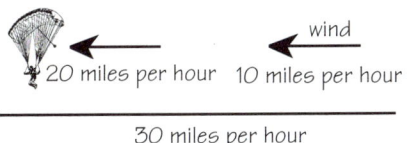
20 miles per hour   wind   10 miles per hour
30 miles per hour

2. Why does the wind data portion of the page report the *velocity* of the wind? [Both the direction and speed are known.]

3. Under what conditions would it be possible for a skydiver to be flying forwards, but *moving backwards* relative to the ground? [See diagram.]

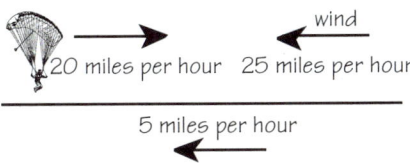
20 miles per hour   wind   25 miles per hour
5 miles per hour

4. Why is *ground track*, instead of *glide path*, used to compute the glide ratio? [It's the motion of the skydiver or airplane *relative to the ground*, that's important to know.]

Middle and Secondary School

1. How close do you think the skydiver and weighted streamer method approximates a mathematical right triangle?

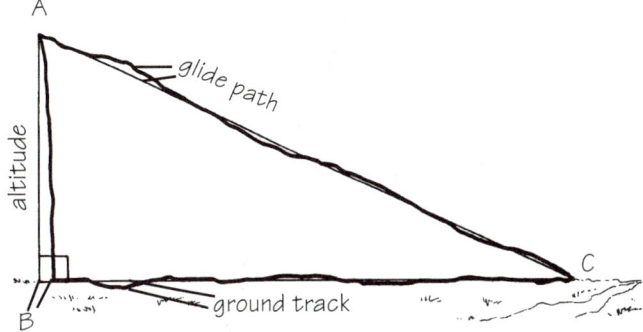

[The weighted streamer had a forward component of motion when it was dropped. As the streamer fell, it did not fall along a perfectly straight line. The skydiver had to use the steering toggles to descend along a straight line. This caused him to fly above and below the hypotenuse of the mathematical right triangle. The ground between the point where the weight landed and the point where the skydiver landed was not perfectly level.]

2. Assume the triangle formed from the data is a right triangle. Use the *Pythagorean Theorem* to compute the length of the *glide path*. [approximately 1054 feet]

3. Instruct students to use a stopwatch to measure the time it takes the skydiver to travel the hypotenuse of the right triangle. Have them use their computation of the length of the hypotenuse and their time measurement to compute the *average velocity* of the skydiver along the glide path.

4. Define the glide ratio of the skydiver seen in the video in terms of his horizontal velocity (v_x) and vertical velocity (v_y). [Glide ratio = $(v_x)/(v_y)$]

5. Use the average velocity of the skydiver to travel the glide path from point A to point C (computed in question three above). Knowing the time and the glide ratio, compute the average velocities for v_x, and v_y, and v (glide path). [Assume the time interval between the skydiver dropping the streamer and landing was 29 seconds. Then v_x is approximately 34 seconds and v_y is approximately 34 seconds.]

6. What glide ratio would you associate with the statement "Falls like a rock."

Extensions

1. The opening scene showing the skydiver falling away from the Cessna airplane has nothing to do with measuring the glide ratio of the jumper's ram-air canopy. Still, the opportunity to study this portion of the video should not be missed (see *Shelly Meets Galileo* in the *Appendix*). Time the

88

skydiver and compute how long he can be seen in freefall before the cut to the opening sequence is made. From this time, estimate the distance fallen.

2. This scene is also a very interesting example of *relative motion*. Ask students to describe what they observed. Have them illustrate their observations with diagrams showing what they perceive the relative motion between the skydiver, the airplane, and the ground to be.

3. Compare the motion of the falling skydiver relative to the airplane with the motion of the falling weighted streamer relative to the skydiver.

GLIDE RATIO

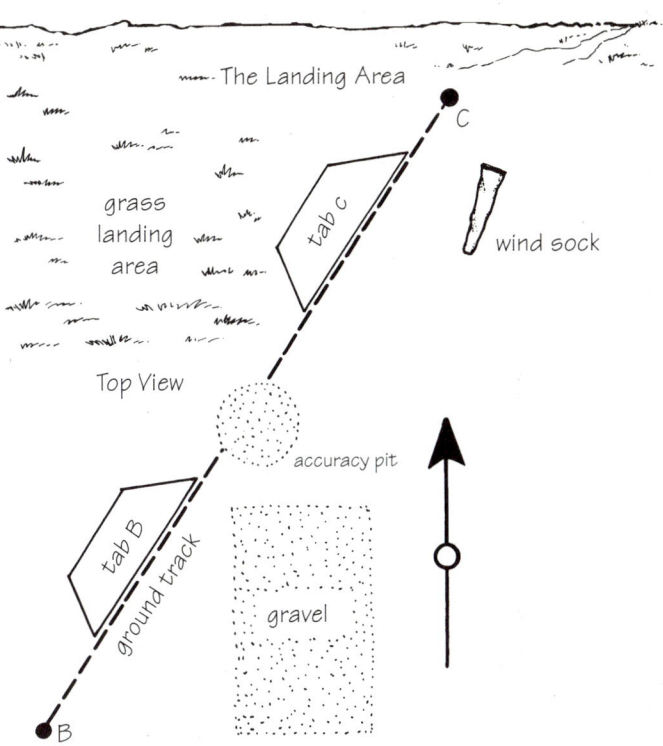

The Landing Area

grass landing area

Top View

tab C

wind sock

accuracy pit

gravel

tab B

ground track

B

1. Cut out the *Right Triangle Pattern*. Fold tab B and C.
2. Tape the tabs along the ground track line BC. Adjust the triangle so that it stands vertically.
3. Cut out the small skydiver figure. Fold the upper right corner along the line.
4. Place the skydiver at point A on the right triangle.
5. Record the *Altitude* as reported by the altimeter reading.
6. Record the *Length of Ground Track*.
7. Compute the *Glide Ratio*.
8. Record the *Wind Data*, direction and speed as measured by the wind sock and anemometer.
9. Graph the *Glide Path*.

Wind Data

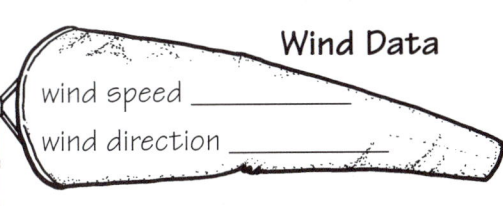

wind speed _____

wind direction _____

Flight Test Data

Altitude (feet)	Length of Ground Track (feet)	Glide Ratio = $\dfrac{\text{Length of Ground Track}}{\text{Altitude}}$

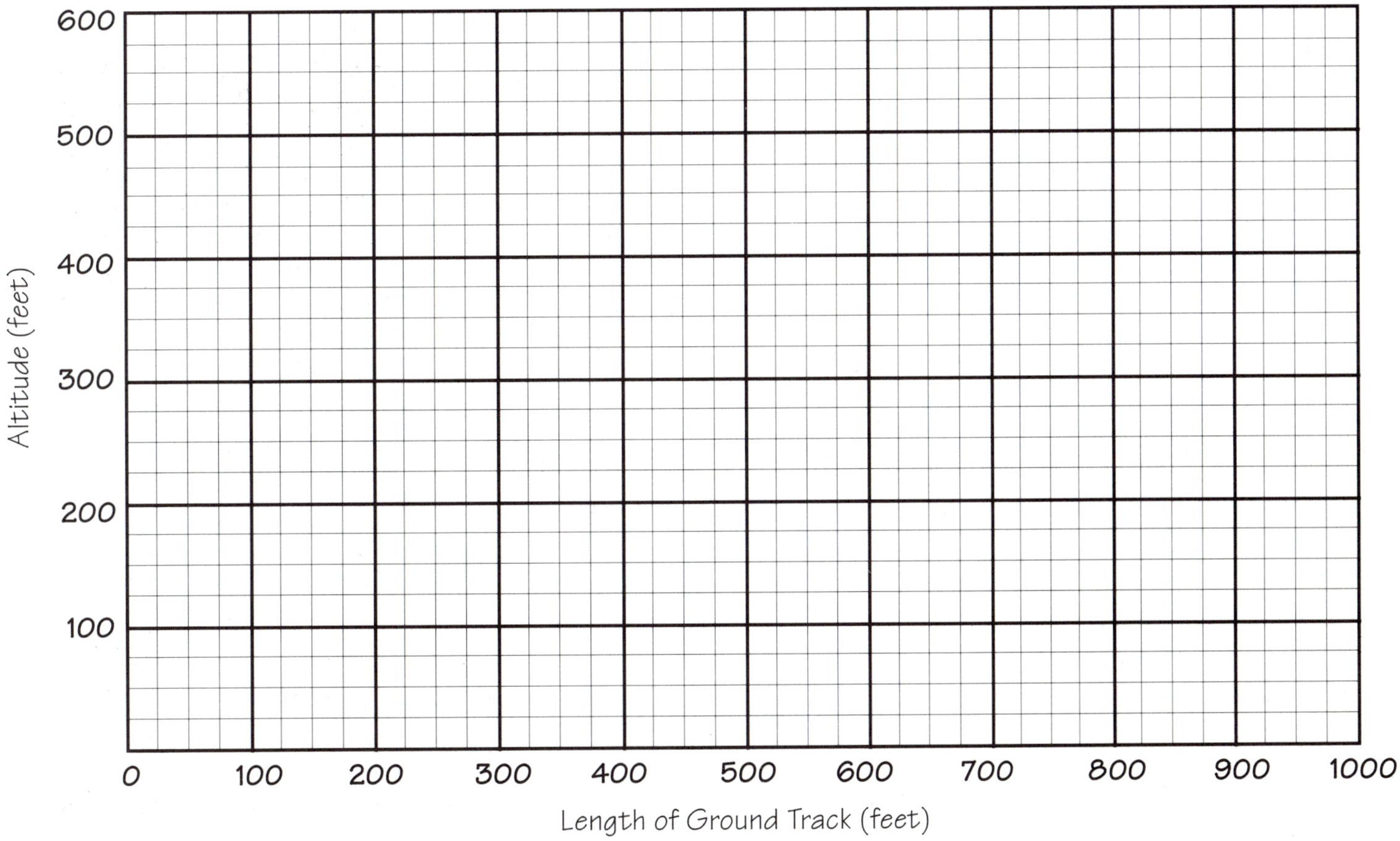

Altitude (feet)

600

500

400

300

200

100

0   100   200   300   400   500   600   700   800   900   1000

Length of Ground Track (feet)

GLIDE RATIO

Right Triangle Pattern

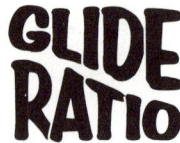

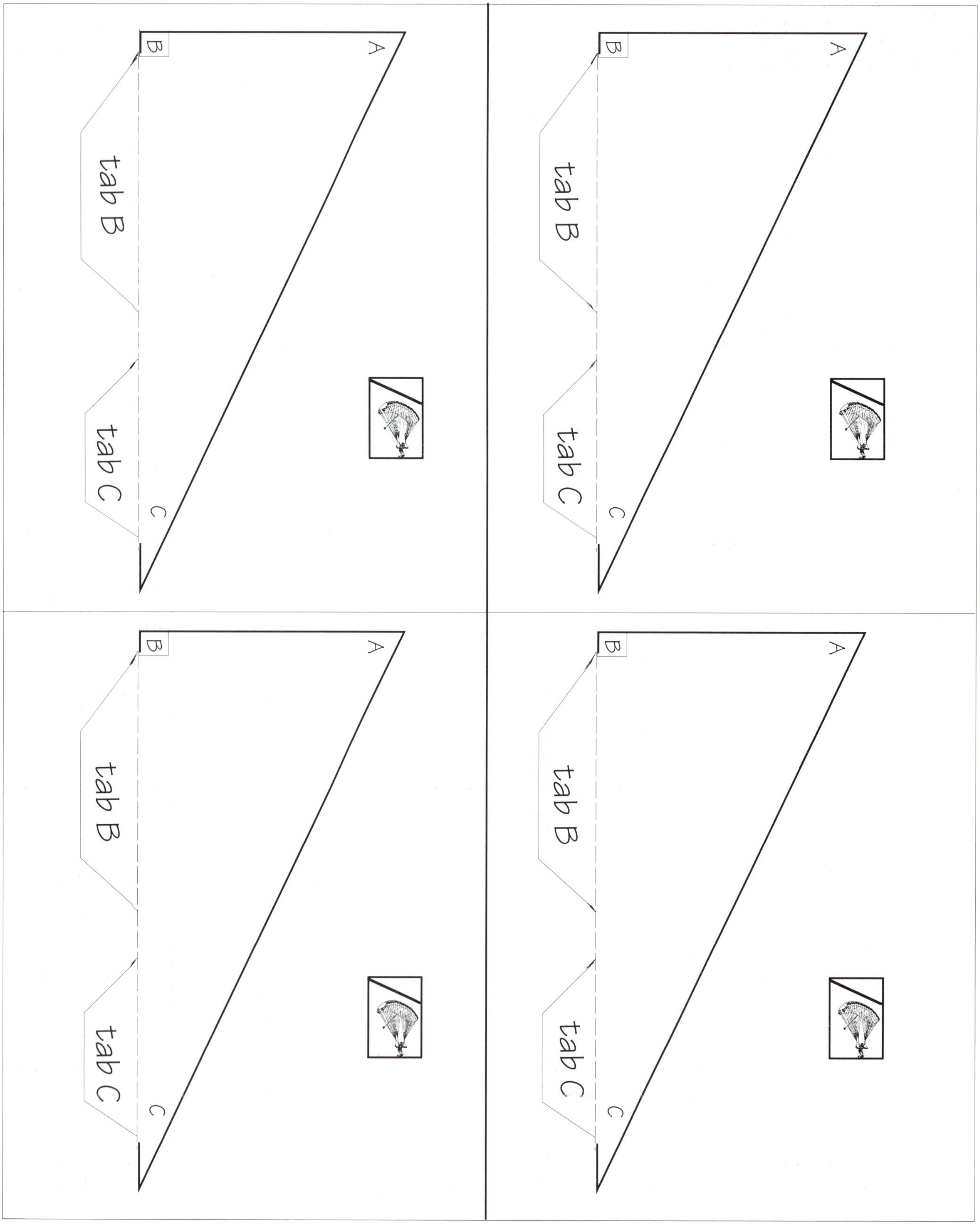

B
A
tab B
tab C
C
B
A
tab B
tab C
C
B
A
tab B
tab C
C
B
A
tab B
tab C
C

GLIDE RATIO

0 – 25 scale reading
_____ MPH

What would the needle do
if the scale knob were
turned to 0 – 100?

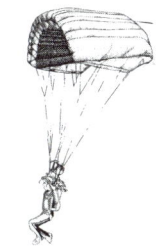

Wind Speed Indicator

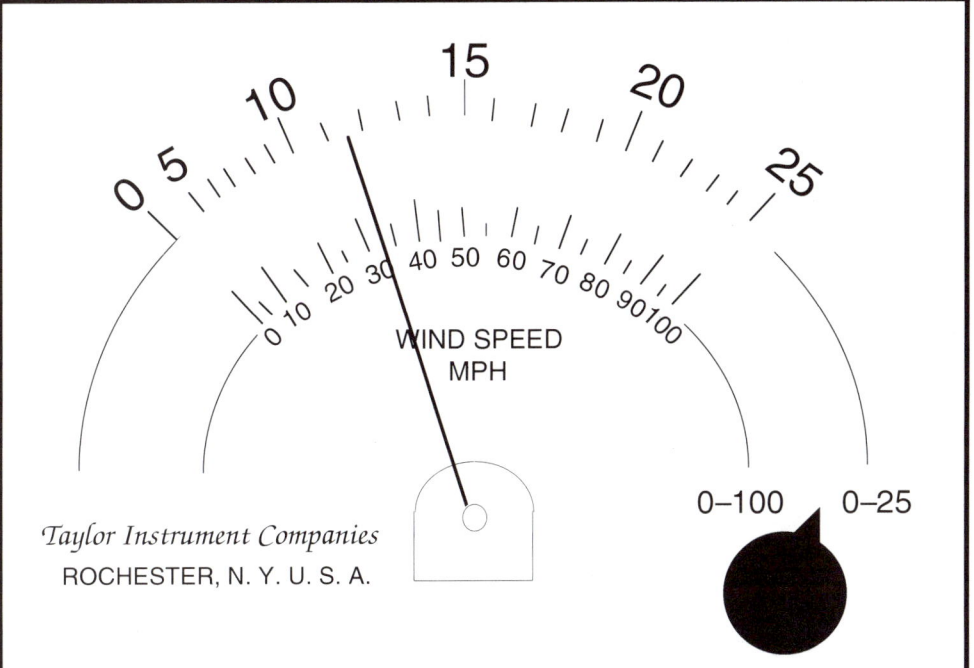

15
10
20
5
25
0

0 10 20 30 40 50 60 70 80 90 100

WIND SPEED
MPH

Taylor Instrument Companies
ROCHESTER, N. Y. U. S. A.

0–100   0–25

Magnetic Compass

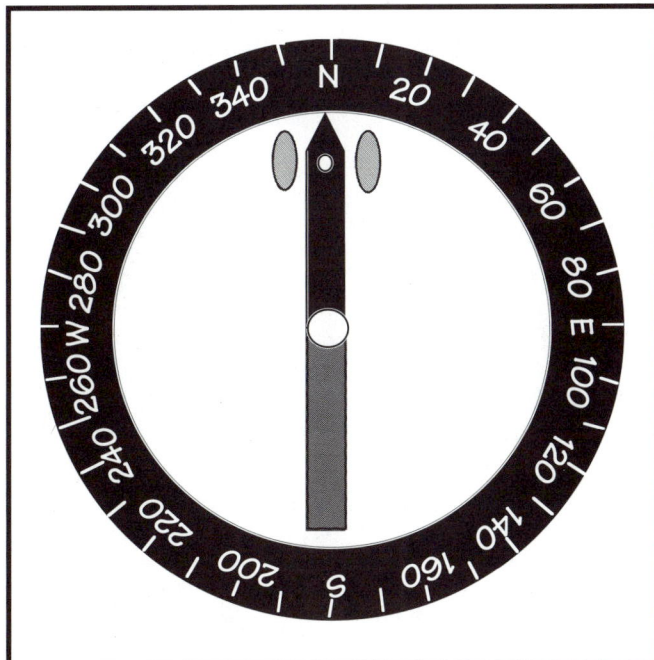

Glide Ratio Comparison

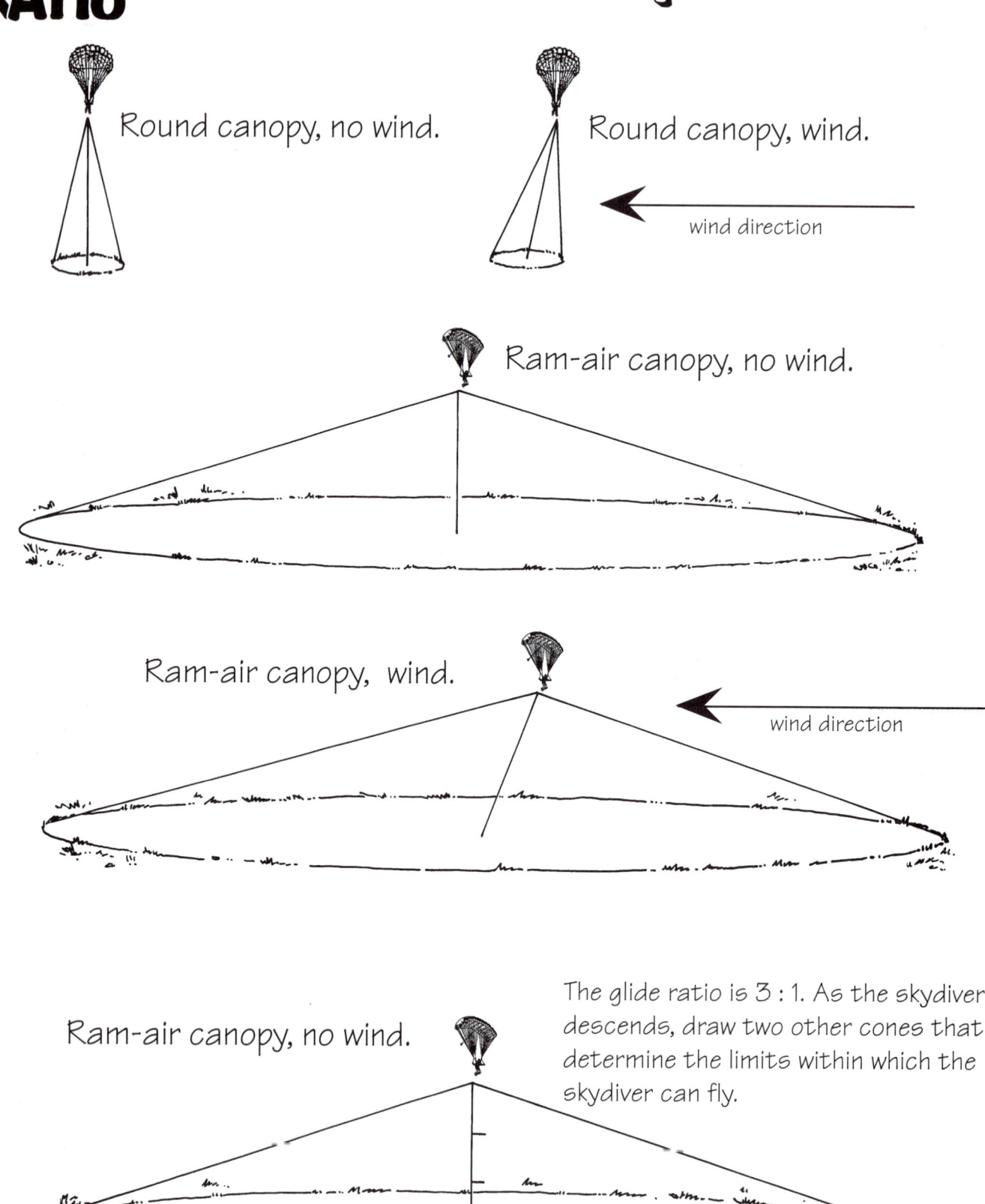

Round canopy, no wind.

Round canopy, wind.

wind direction

Ram-air canopy, no wind.

Ram-air canopy, wind.

wind direction

Ram-air canopy, no wind.

The glide ratio is 3 : 1. As the skydiver descends, draw two other cones that determine the limits within which the skydiver can fly.

Video Companion
for
Glide Ratio

Note: Refer to the *Gravity Rules! Glossary* for definitions of skydiving words and phrases heard in the video.

Time = 50 minutes: 35 seconds

Resource Section
I. Glide Ratio Definition

"The glide ratio of a ram-air canopy is defined as the horizontal distance flown over the ground, called the ground track, divided by the altitude above the ground. A ram-air canopy has a glide ratio, typically around 3 to 1. This gives the canopy pilot the capability to fly around in a large, cone-shaped volume of air."

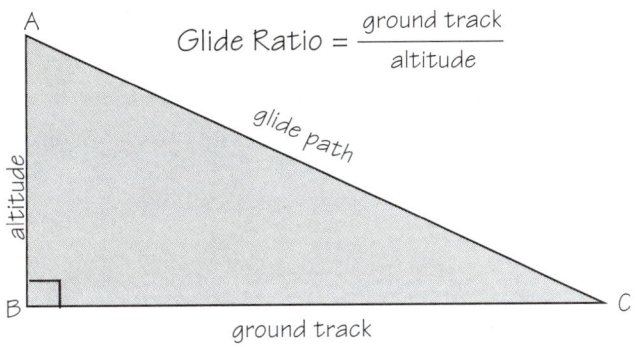

$$\text{Glide Ratio} = \frac{\text{ground track}}{\text{altitude}}$$

II. Glide Ratio Simulation

"Flying his canopy into the wind, the skydiver sets up for point A."

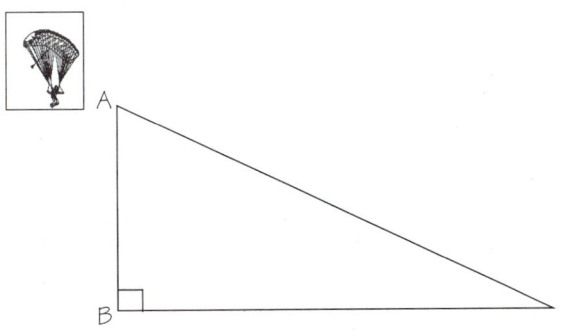

"At point A, the skydiver reads his altimeter and drops the weighted streamer."

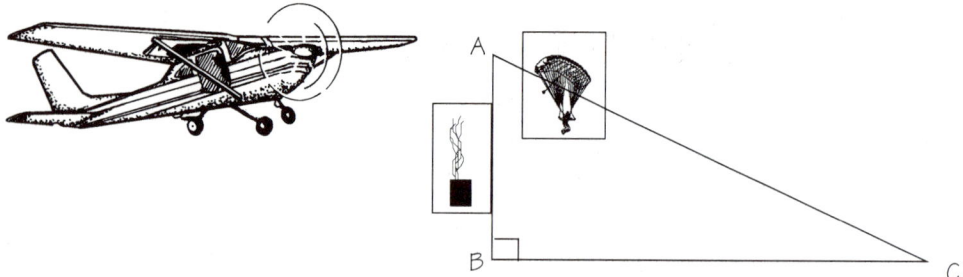

"The streamer strikes the ground at point B."

"The skydiver flies, in as straight a line as possible, landing at point C."

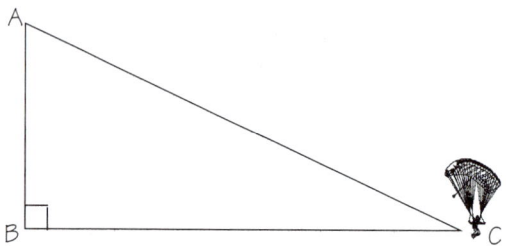

"The ground track is then measured with a 100-foot measuring tape."

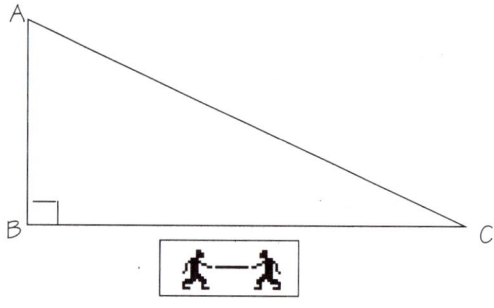

"Since the altitude and ground track are known, the glide ratio can be computed, from its definition, by dividing the length of the ground track by the altitude."

III. Measuring the Glide Ratio

"The skydiver exits the Cessna aircraft at an altitude of 4000 feet."
"He opens his parachute."
"The skydiver flies his canopy to position himself near point A, over the southwest corner of the landing area."

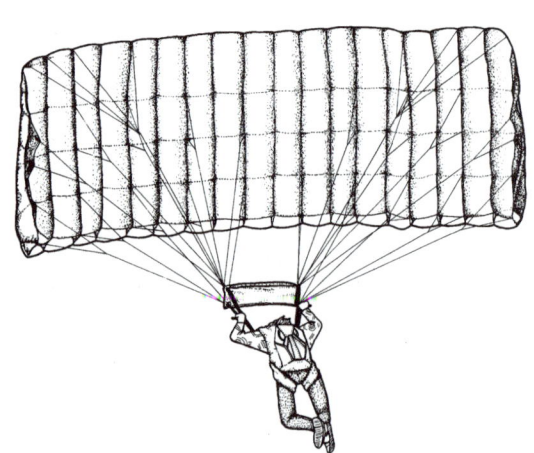

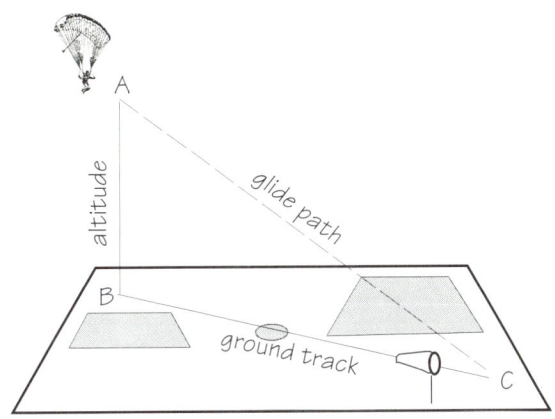

"He sets up for dropping the weight. Notice he has both steering toggles in one hand."
"He drops the weight and notes the altitude."
"He nears the circular gravel pit."
"He continues along the glide path to land near wind sock." (Note: Observe the "brakes" on rear of the canopy as he flares to land.)

IV. Measuring the Ground Track

"Johann and Ron start measuring, from point B, the ground track."
Jim asks Johann, "How many hundreds of feet did you measure?" Johann replies, "Nine hundred."
Jim says, "Nine hundred feet plus this measure equals the total horizontal feet flown."

V. Windsock Indicator

"A directional compass is used to determine from what direction the wind is blowing."

VI. Windspeed Indicator

"The drop zone's wind speed indicator is used to determine the wind speed."

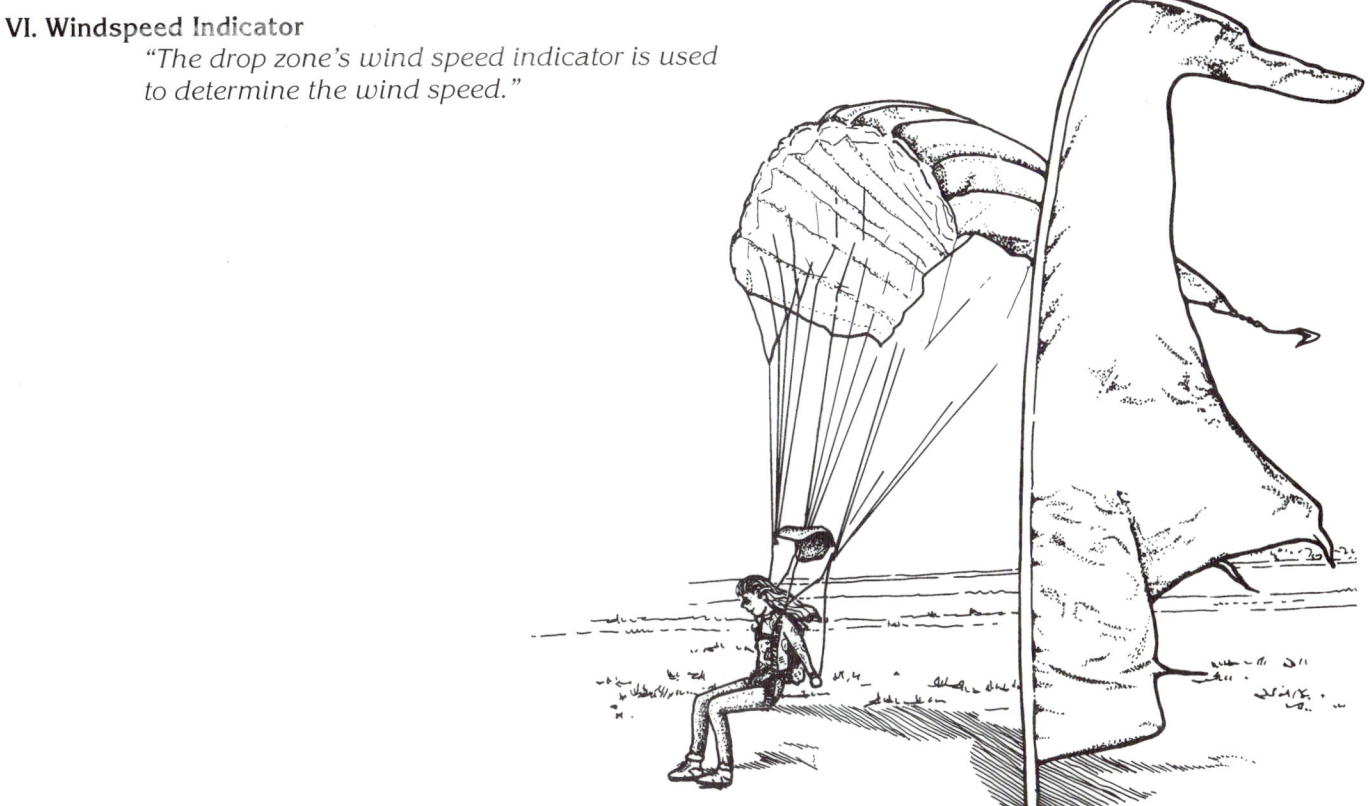

Rolling Rectangles

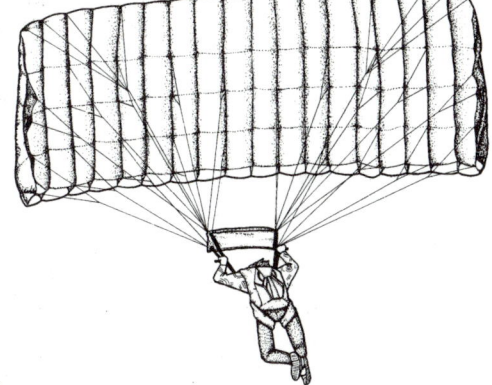

Topic
Aerodynamics: Aspect Ratio

Key Question
At what rate do paper rectangles fall?

Focus
Students will measure the fall rate of paper rectangles with different length-to-width ratios. Scientists and aeronautical engineers call the length-to-width ratio the *aspect* ratio.

Guiding Documents
Project 2061 Benchmark
- *Numbers and shapes — and operations on them — help to describe and predict things about the world around us.*

NRC Standard
- *The motion of an object can be described by its position, direction of motion, and speed.*

NCTM Standards
- *Understand and apply ratios, proportions, and percents in a wide variety of situations*
- *Understand and apply geometric properties and relationships*

Math
Measurement
   length
   time
Using rational numbers
   ratio
Finding area by formula

Science
Physical science
   gravity
   lift

Integrated Processes
Observing
Collecting and recording data
Identifying and controlling variables
Interpreting data
Applying

Materials
Per group:
   scissors
   ruler
   stopwatch or digital watch with timer
   calculator

Background Information
Parachute canopies are manufactured in two shapes, the round and the square.

The round canopy is used by paratroopers, National Forest Service smoke jumpers, and for dropping cargo. The square canopy is used by skydivers, Bureau of Land Management smoke jumpers, and special branches of the military.

Skydivers refer to their parachutes as *square* but the canopies are actually rectangular in shape when viewed from above or below. When viewed from the side, the canopy is shaped like an airfoil.

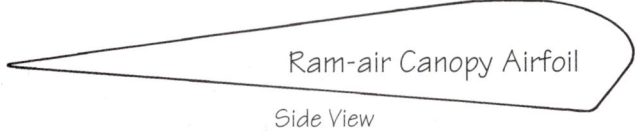

Ram-air Canopy Airfoil

Side View

An airfoil is the shape of a cross section of a wing. A *square* canopy is therefore a rectangular wing. The specific shape of an airfoil and the ratio of the length of the wing to its width are the major variables that determine how well the wing generates *lift*, the upward force needed to overcome gravity.

Aeronautical scientists call the length-to-width ratio of a wing its *aspect ratio* (AR). Scientists refer to the length of a wing as its *span* and the width of a wing as its *chord*. The span is measured tip to tip and the chord is defined as the perpendicular leading edge to trailing edge measurement.

> For a rectangle:
> Aspect Ratio = span : chord

For example, if the span of a rectangular shape is 3 units long and the chord of the same shape is 1 unit long then the aspect ratio of the shape is 3:1 or, simply 3.

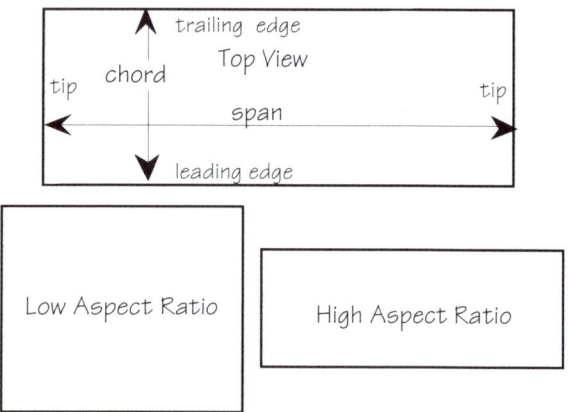

High aspect ratio shapes are said to have a high *lift-to-drag ratio L/D* (called *L over D*). The higher the aspect ratio (shorter chord, longer span), the greater the lift for the existing drag. That's why the wings of gliders and high-altitude reconnaissance aircraft — like the U-2 — have a long span and short chord.

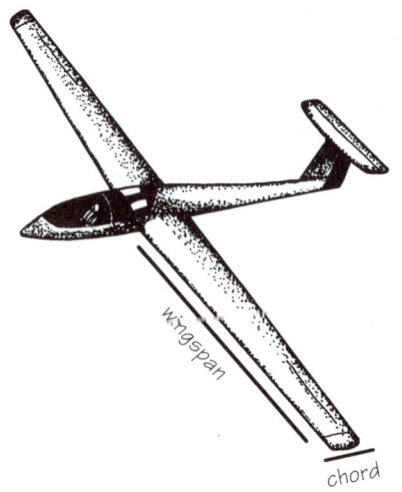

Cutting rectangles from a sheet of paper provides students the opportunity to explore the effects of varying the aspect ratio of a rectangle.

Management
1. Do the activity beforehand to familiarize yourself with how to cut, drop, time, and compute the aspect ratio for each paper shape.
2. This activity is best done indoors. If possible, use a large room such as a gymnasium or cafeteria.
3. Do not substitute heavy paper or tagboard for this activity. The heavier materials take longer to reach terminal velocity. The terminal velocity of a falling body is the speed at which the force of gravity is balanced by air resistance. At this point, the acceleration becomes zero, and the falling body continues to fall at a constant speed.
4. Group students in pairs. They can take turns timing each others drop-tests.
5. Review with students the method for naming rectangles.

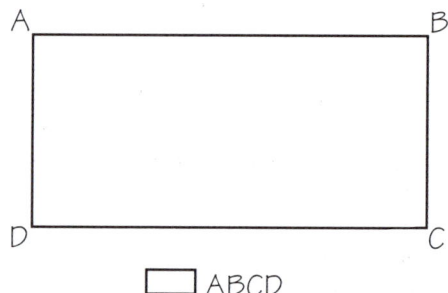

Procedure
1. Ask the *Key Question*.
2. Demonstrate to students the correct method for holding and releasing their paper shapes. To properly do this, grip the paper with the tips of forefinger and thumb along the center edge of the longest side of the shape, extend arm horizontally away from the body, and release the paper shape. Don't jump or move away as this can create an air current that will disrupt the falling shape.

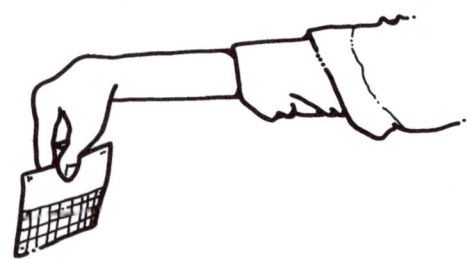

3. Distribute the *Rolling Rectangle Pattern* and *Data Table* pages. Instruct the students to follow the instructions.
4. Have students use a stopwatch (or a digital watch with timer) to measure descent times.

5. Students should make direct observations as to the manner in which the rectangles fell and how far they landed from the release position.
6. As an alternative, have students make direct comparisons by dropping two different shapes at the same time and observe which shape hits the ground first.

Discussion
1. Discuss the *Key Question*. [Descent rate appears to be related to the rectangle's aspect ratio.]
2. What relationship, if any, did you notice between *descent rate* and *glide ratio*? [The rectangles that take longer to reach the ground travel a longer horizontal distance. This indicates they have a *higher* glide ratio.]
3. What other observations did you make during the activity? What surprised you when you observed the rolling rectangles?
4. What questions arise because of this activity? What further investigating could you do to answer those questions?
5. The span of Shelly's canopy is 16.9 feet. Its chord is 6.3 feet. What is its aspect ratio? [2.68:1]
6. Show pictures of gliders, paragliders, and birds with long, thin wings. (Look under *Parachute, Glider,* and *Albatross* in an encyclopedia.) How are these things related to our rectangles?
7. Discuss what represents a workable *aspect ratio* for glider wings and ram-air canopies. [Extremely high aspect ratios are not used for canopies because of the problems associated with the packing, opening, and steering of ram-air canopies. Extremely high aspect ratios for glider wings create engineering problems associated with building long, rigid wings that won't bend from their own weight.]

Middle School and High School
1. The equation shown on the student page for the aspect ratio of a rectangle is a simplification of this more general formula.

$$\text{Aspect Ratio} = \frac{(\text{span})^2}{\text{area}}$$

Show that, for a rectangle where the length equals the span and the width equals the chord, this equation *reduces* to the equation shown on the student page, Aspect Ratio = span : chord. [Given a rectangle with *length* equal to *span* and *width* equal to *chord*,

$$\text{Aspect Ratio} = \frac{(\text{span})^2}{\text{span} \times \text{chord}}$$

$$= \frac{\text{span}}{\text{chord}}$$

which is just another form of span : chord.]

2. Distribute the *Rolling Rectangles Ratios* page. Have students compute the decimal equivalents and areas for each of the ratios. Tell students to circle and draw a connecting line between *equivalent ratios*. Ask students if *scale* makes a difference. That is, do similar rectangles have the same descent times?
3. Distribute the *Rolling Rectangles — Aspect Ratios of Various Geometric Wings* page. Challenge students to explore the algebraic expression for each shape.

Extensions
1. What happens to a paper rectangle when the aspect ratio gets too high?
2. A type of ram-air canopy often confused with a ram-air parachute canopy is called a *paraglider*. Research paragliding and compare a paraglider to a standard ram-air parachute.

Rolling Rectangles
Pattern Page

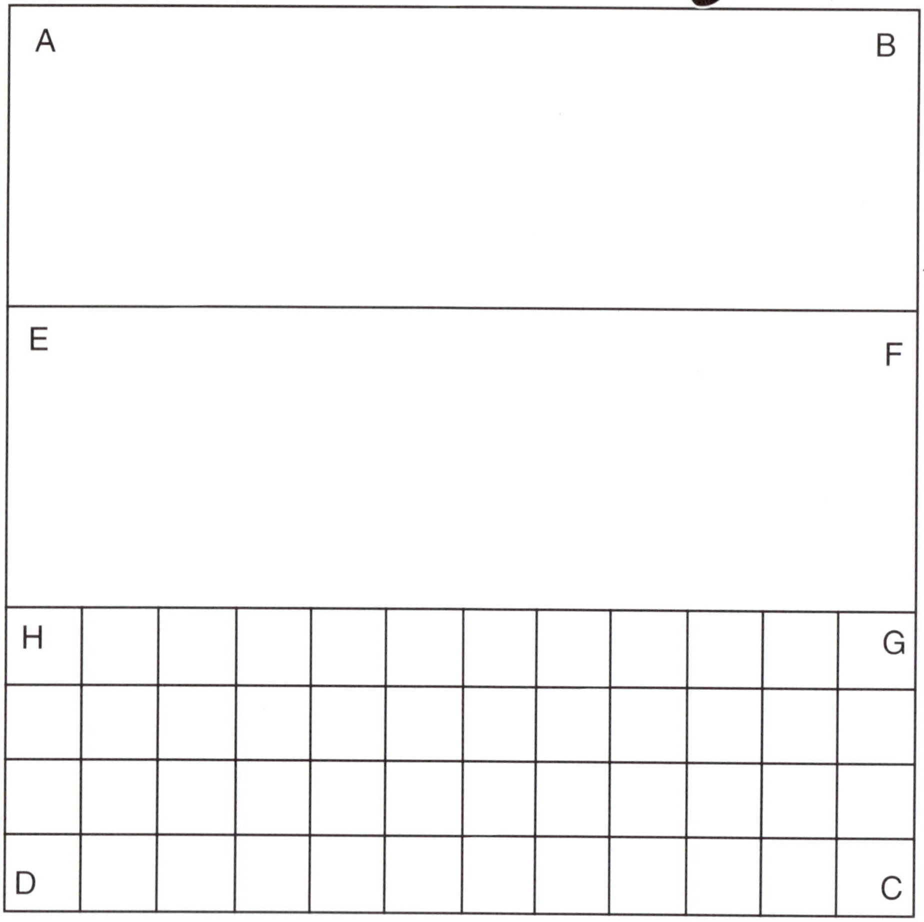

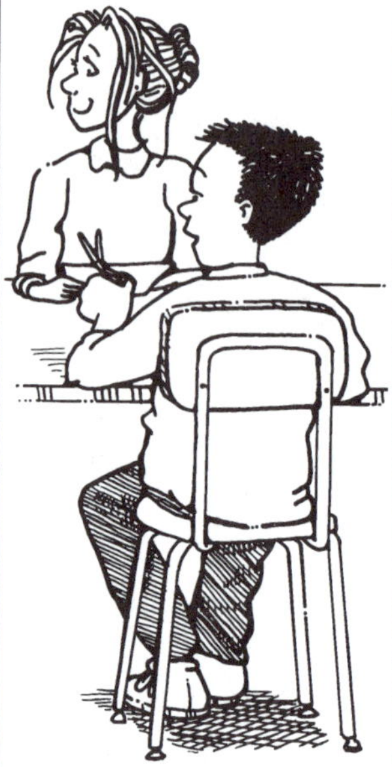

A   **B**

E   **F**

H   **G**

D   **C**

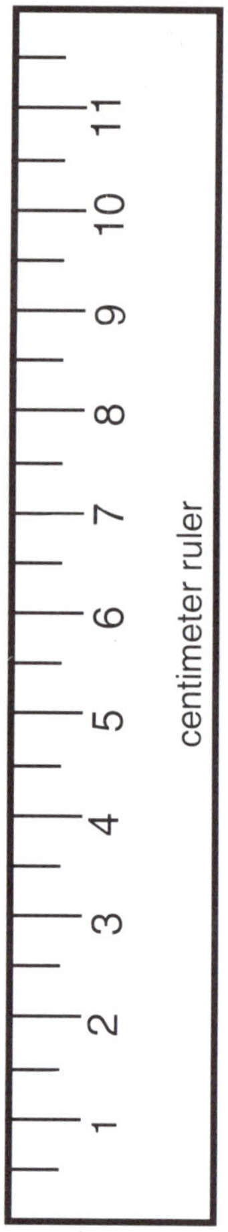

centimeter ruler

Instructions

1. Cut out the centimeter ruler and rectangle ABCD.
2. Use the ruler to find the measurements for the span and chord of rectangle ABCD. Record these measurements in the data table.
3. Compute and record the area and aspect ratio.
4. Drop-test and time the fall of rectangle ABCD. Do this three times. Record the times and average in the data table. Record other observations of the drops.
5. Cut the rectangle along EF. Throw away the smaller piece.
6. Repeat steps 2-4 for rectangle EFCD.
7. Cut the rectangle along HG. Keep rectangle HGCD. Throw away the other piece.
8. Repeat steps 2-4 for rectangle HGCD.

Rolling Rectangles
Data Table

Aspect ratio = span : chord
Span = length
Chord = width

Span and Chord Measurement Data

Rectangle	Span S (cm)	Chord C (cm)	Area S × C (sq cm)	Aspect Ratio S : C
☐ ABCD				
☐ EFCD				
☐ HGCD				

Time Measurement Data

Trial 1 (sec)	Trial 2 (sec)	Trial 3 (sec)	Average Time (sec)

Observation

Describe what you saw when you dropped the rectangle.

Rolling Rectangles

Ratios

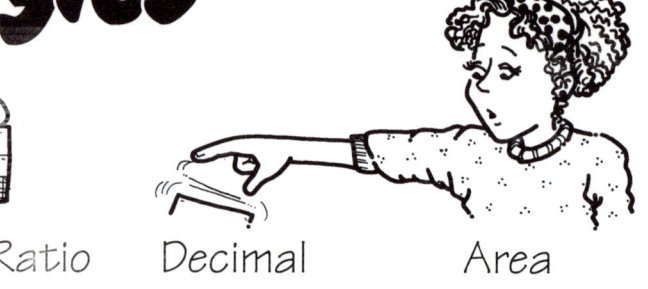

Ratio	Decimal Equivalent	Area	Ratio	Decimal Equivalent	Area
$\frac{12}{4}$			$\frac{12}{3}$		
$\frac{11}{4}$			$\frac{11}{3}$		
$\frac{10}{4}$			$\frac{10}{3}$		
$\frac{9}{4}$			$\frac{9}{3}$		
$\frac{8}{4}$			$\frac{8}{3}$		
$\frac{7}{4}$			$\frac{7}{3}$		
$\frac{6}{4}$			$\frac{6}{3}$		
$\frac{5}{4}$			$\frac{5}{3}$		
$\frac{4}{4}$			$\frac{4}{3}$		
$\frac{3}{4}$			$\frac{3}{3}$		
$\frac{2}{4}$			$\frac{2}{3}$		
$\frac{1}{4}$			$\frac{1}{3}$		

Rolling Rectangles

Ratios

Name_____

Ratio	Decimal Equivalent	Area		Ratio	Decimal Equivalent	Area
$\frac{12}{2}$	_____	_____		$\frac{12}{1}$	_____	_____
$\frac{11}{2}$	_____	_____		$\frac{11}{1}$	_____	_____
$\frac{10}{2}$	_____	_____		$\frac{10}{1}$	_____	_____
$\frac{9}{2}$	_____	_____		$\frac{9}{1}$	_____	_____
$\frac{8}{2}$	_____	_____		$\frac{8}{1}$	_____	_____
$\frac{7}{2}$	_____	_____		$\frac{7}{1}$	_____	_____
$\frac{6}{2}$	_____	_____		$\frac{6}{1}$	_____	_____
$\frac{5}{2}$	_____	_____		$\frac{5}{1}$	_____	_____
$\frac{4}{2}$	_____	_____		$\frac{4}{1}$	_____	_____
$\frac{3}{2}$	_____	_____		$\frac{3}{1}$	_____	_____
$\frac{2}{2}$	_____	_____		$\frac{2}{1}$	_____	_____
$\frac{1}{2}$	_____	_____		$\frac{1}{1}$	_____	_____

Rolling Rectangles
Aspect Ratios of Various Geometric Wings

Name _____

$$\text{Aspect Ratio} = \frac{(\text{span})^2}{\text{area}}$$

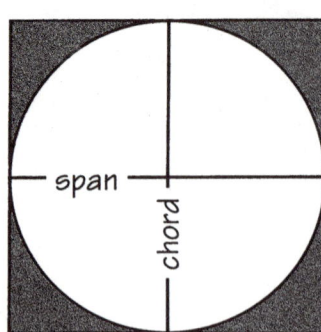

For wing shapes that are not rectangular, the aspect ratio equals the span of the wing squared divided by the area of the wing.

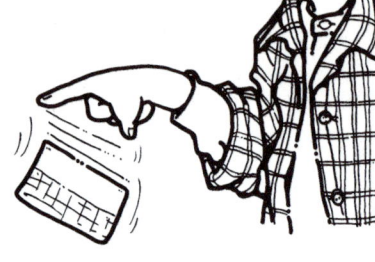

Drop test the shapes and compare their flight characteristics.

Compare the aspect ratio of the shaded rectangle to the aspect ratio of the smaller rectangle with semicircular tips. The span = 6 length units and the chord = 2 length units.

Drop test each shape and compare their flight characteristics.

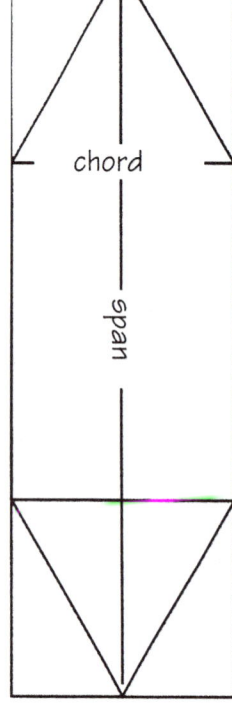

Compare the aspect ratio of the shaded rectangle to the aspect ratio of the smaller rectangle with equilateral triangle tips. The span = 6 length units and the chord = 2 length units.

Drop test each shape and compare their flight characteristics.

Rolling Rectangles
Pattern Page

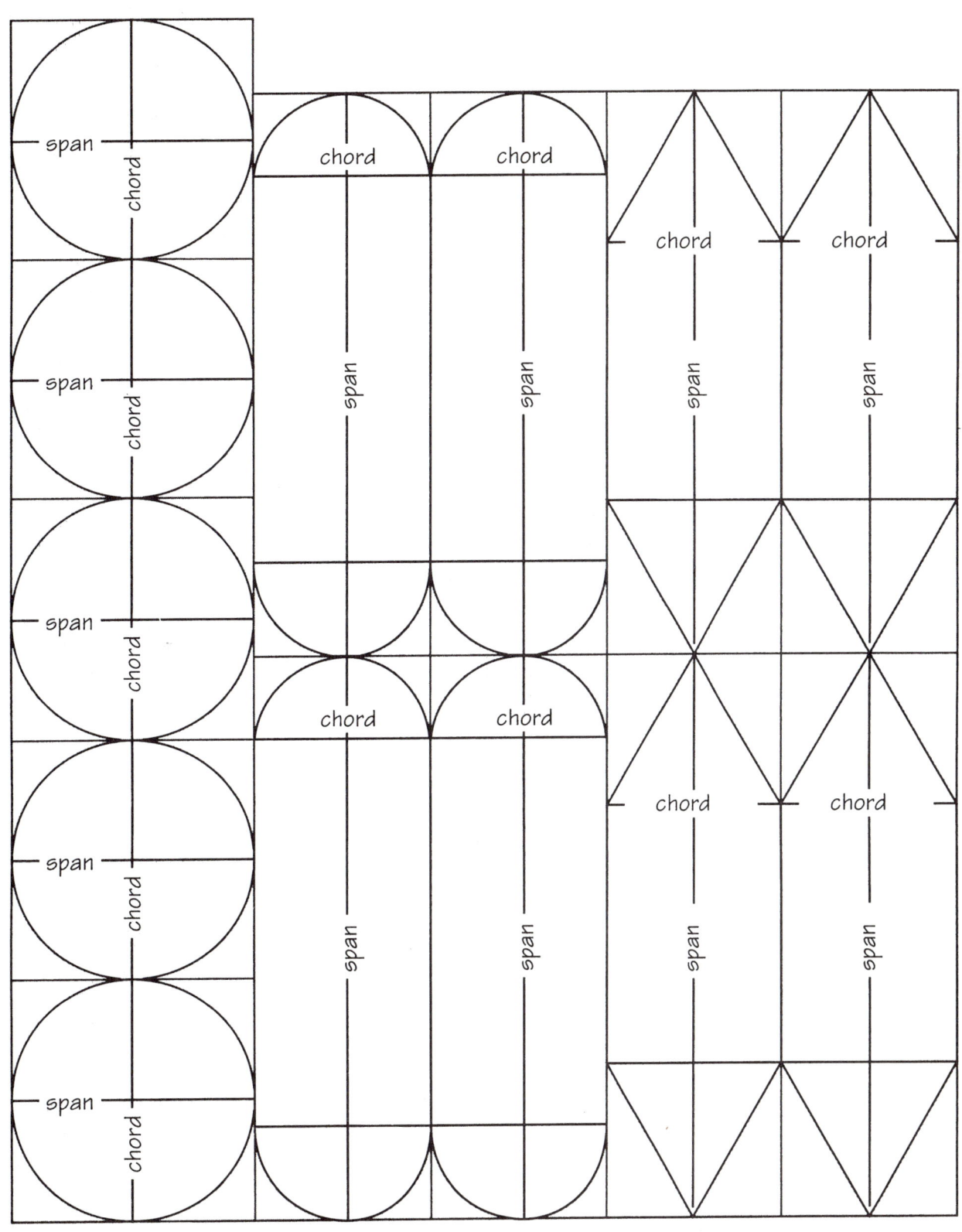

Topic
Force and motion
    motion along a straight line

Key Question
How do BASE jumpers determine how long they can safely freefall before opening the parachute?

Focus
Part 1
Students will graph and interpret the *distance-time* data contained in a *BASE Jumper Table*.

Part 2
Students will collect delay time data from a video segment showing BASE jumpers jumping off the New River Gorge Bridge. Students will then use delay times to compute altitudes.

Guiding Documents
Project 2061 Benchmarks
- *Mathematics is helpful in almost every kind of human endeavor — from laying bricks to prescribing medicine or drawing a face.*
- *In the absence of retarding forces such as friction, an object will keep its direction of motion and its speed. Whenever an object is seen to speed up, slow down, or change direction, it can be assumed that an unbalanced force is acting on it. [ed. Newton's first law of motion.]*

NRC Standards
- *An object's motion can be described by tracing and measuring its position over time.*
- *The motion of an object can be described by its position, direction of motion, and speed. That motion can be represented on a graph.*

NCTM Standards
- *Compute with whole numbers, fractions, decimals, integers, and rational numbers*
- *Describe and represent relationships with tables, graphs, and rules*
- *Develop the concepts of rates and other derived and indirect measurements*
- *Represent numerical relationships in one- and two-dimensional graphs*
- *Analyze functional relationships to explain how a change in one quantity results in a change in another*

- *Use patterns and functions to represent and solve problems*
- *Understand the concepts of variable, expression, and equation*
- *Represent situations and number patterns with tables, graphs, verbal rules, and equations and explore the interrelationships of these representations*
- *Analyze tables and graphs to identify properties and relationships*

Math
Number operations
Function
Graphs
Positive and negative integers
Absolute value
Finite differences
Sequence
Series

Science
Physical science
    linear motion

Integrated Processes
Observing
Collecting and recording data
Identifying and controlling variables
Interpreting data
Applying

Materials
Gravity Rules! video
    BASE Jumping sequence
Stopwatches, optional

Background Information
    Instead of jumping out of perfectly good airplanes, some skydivers enjoy jumping from fixed objects such as tall **b**uildings. They will also climb and then jump from radio and television **a**ntennas. Structures that **s**pan gorges and rivers are popular jump locations. Angel Falls, located in Venezuela, South America, is the world's highest waterfall. The edge of the rock cliff next to the top of the falls is 3212 feet above the base of the falls. The falls is a natural **e**arth formation. BASE jumpers, as these specialized skydivers call themselves, travel the world looking for new and exciting challenges. (BASE is an acronym for **b**uildings, **a**ntennas, **s**pans, and **e**arth.)
    BASE jumpers are especially careful packing their parachutes. The low altitudes from which they jump offer them little time to deal with equipment problems.
    Jumping from low altitudes is obviously a test of nerve and skill but it is not necessarily foolhardy. BASE jumpers study, plan, and prepare for each jump. In

particular, BASE jumpers know distance fallen as a function of time. The following table is one tool BASE jumpers use to gauge *delay time*, which is the time between jumping and throwing out the pilot chute to start the opening sequence.

BASE Jump Freefall Table	
Time (seconds)	Distance Fallen (feet)
1	16
2	62
3	138
4	242
5	366
6	504
7	652
8	808
9	971
10	1138
11	1309
12	1483

(reprinted with permission from the June 1991 issue of Skydiving magazine)

BASE jumpers are seldom in freefall long enough to reach terminal velocity. Terminal velocity is essentially reached after the twelfth second of freefall.

BASE jumping is becoming so popular among skydivers that special containers and canopies are being manufactured just for BASE jumping.

In this activity students have the opportunity to use several mathematical concepts, such as *directed numbers*, *absolute value*, and *congruent triangles*, to clarify their understanding of the science phenomenon of freefall with air resistance.

Management
1. Review the addition and subtraction of directed numbers.
2. Review the absolute value concept.
3. Allow flexible timing methods. BASE jumping is a real-time activity and BASE jumpers are not necessarily interested in measuring time to the third decimal place. There is a chronometer superimposed on the video of the BASE jumpers but feel free to use other timing methods. In fact, perhaps the *best* method for this activity is the silent counting method, one thousand one, one thousand two, one thousand three...and so on.
4. Remember, the video is a scientific record and, like most scientific data, is to be reviewed as many times as students request.

Procedure
Show students the *BASE Jumping* video sequence. Allow them to view the complete sequence even though jumps are repeated. Remember, a keen observer "sees" more than a casual observer.

Discussion
1. Use the following *Did You See ...?* questions to facilitate further discussion.
   Did You See ...
   - **a skydiver getting ready to land?** [During the first jumper's segment, the tops of two skydivers' canopies can be seen. One has just landed on the gravel beach. The other is crossing the river, in a right-hand turn, setting up to land on the same gravel beach.]
   - **a kayak and its owner sunning on a rock?** [During the second jump sequence, a kayak can be clearly seen on the left side of the triangular-shaped rock just below the two jumpers. The kayaker can be seen, laying down, on the right side of the rock.]
2. Ask students to determine, from viewing the video, which way, relative to the jumpers, the New River flows. In other words, if a jumper lands in the river, will the current carry him/her under the bridge or away from the bridge, in the direction of the landing area?
   Did You See ...
   - **one jumper delay much longer than another jumper?** [In the second jump sequence, the jumper on the right appears to take a much longer delay than the other.]
3. Ask the *Key Question*.

Procedure
Part 1
Analyzing the Data in the BASE Jumper Table
1. Distribute the student pages, the two *Analyzing the Data in the BASE Jumper Table* pages and the *Altitude-Time Graph* page.
2. Instruct student to complete column III. Remind them that the jumpers start at an altitude of 876 feet.
3. Ask students to interpret the negative numbers that appear as the last two entries in the column.
4. Tell the students to make a line graph of the altitude-time data (column I data on the horizontal axis, column III data on the vertical axis).
5. Have students estimate, from their line graph, the time at which the line graph meets the water.
6. Explain to students that the delta symbol (Δ) is used to indicate a *change* in a quantity. Instruct them to compute and record in column IV the change in distance (altitude) *between* successive seconds by subtracting the altitude at time *t* from the altitude at time *t-1*. (Note that Δd is used instead of Δa because Δa is commonly used to indicate a change in the acceleration of an object.)
7. Ask the students to describe in a sentence or two what's happening to the absolute value of Δd ($|\Delta d|$) as they look down column IV.
8. Tell the students to copy the column IV data from the first page of *Part 1* to the second page.

9. Instruct them to complete column VI by computing the ratio, Δd/Δt, for each one-second interval.

10. Have the students look at the diagram accompanying question 9. Instruct the students to shade the triangle formed by the *change in altitude* leg (Δd), the *change in time* base (Δt), and the line graph, for each one-second interval.

11. Have the students answer the remaining questions on the page.

Discussion

Part 1

1. Compare the values in your column III with these values.

2. The negative numbers that appear at the ninth and tenth second are interpreted as "being below ground level." Point out to the class the use of directed number computation, 876–971=-95, at the ninth second and 876–1138= -262 at the tenth second.

3. Compare your line graph to this one.

BASE Jumper Table

I Time (sec)	II Distance Fallen (ft)	III Altitude at Time t (ft)	IV Δd (ft)
0	0	876	
			-16
1	16	860	
			-46
2	62	814	
			-76
3	138	738	
			-104
4	242	634	
			-124
5	366	510	
			-138
6	504	372	
			-148
7	652	224	
			-156
8	808	68	
			-163
9	971	-95	
			-167

5. Compare the values in column IV with the values shown in the table (see the first *Discussion* question). Again point out to the class the use of directed number computation: 860–876=-16 for the interval between the first and zero second and -262–(-95)–167=-262 for the interval between the tenth and ninth second.

6. What's happening to the absolute value of Δd as you look down column IV? [The absolute value of Δd is increasing at a slower and slower rate per second.]

7. For question 8: Compare your column VI values with the ones in column VI in this table. Do you think one-second time intervals were purposely chosen and, if so, why?

IV Δd (ft)	V Δt (sec)	VI $\frac{\Delta d}{\Delta t}$ (ft) (sec)
-16	1	-16/1 = -16
-46	1	-46/1 = -46
-76	1	-76/1 = -76
-104	1	-104/1 = -104
-124	1	-124/1 = -124
-138	1	-138/1 = -138
-148	1	-148/1 = -148
-156	1	-156/1 = -156
-163	1	-163/1 = -163
-167	1	-167/1 = -167

8. For question 9: Compare the shaded triangles on your *Altitude-Time Graph* with this graph.

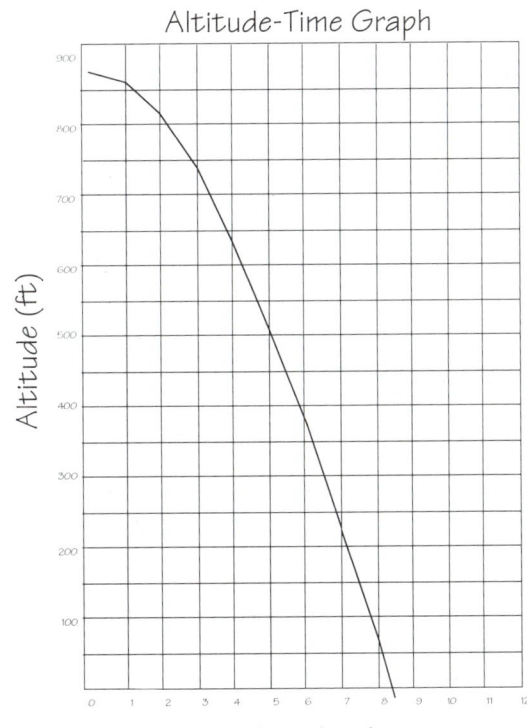

Altitude-Time Graph

Altitude (ft) / Time (sec)

4. Where did your line graph cross the horizontal (time) axis? [at approximately 8.4 seconds]

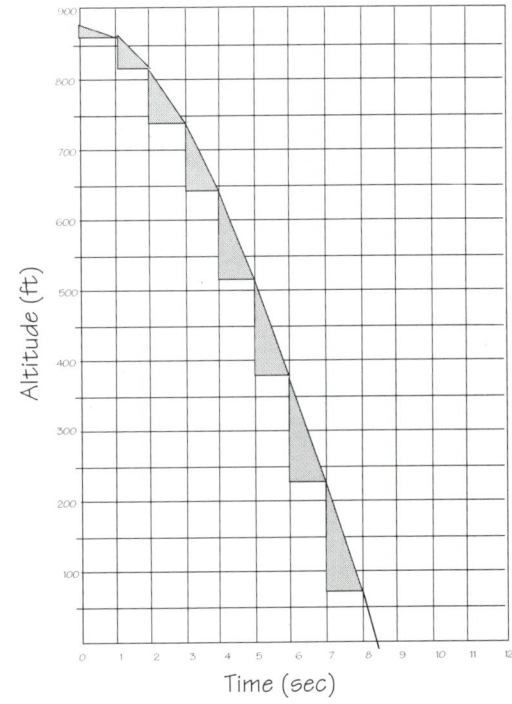

Altitude (ft) / Time (sec)

9. For question 10: What do the numbers in column VI represent? [The numbers in column VI represent *average* velocities. The negative sign indicates the motion is directed downwards.]
10. For question 11: What do the straight line segments connecting the data points in your line graph represent? [The straight line segments represent average velocities.]
11. Describe the sequence of shaded triangles in question 12. [The sequence of triangles appears to be converging to being congruent triangles.]
12. When do you think, if ever, the triangles become congruent triangles. [At terminal velocity, the triangles become congruent.]
13. Explain why you think a BASE jumper will, or will not, achieve terminal velocity, jumping from the New River Gorge Bridge. [The line graph should indicate that a BASE jumper, in freefall, would strike the river after approximately 8.4 seconds. Terminal velocity won't be reached until approximately the twelfth second. Also, the BASE jumper will have to slow down (decelerate) before the eighth second to survive the jump.]

Procedure

Part 2
Measuring the Delay Times of Real BASE Jumpers
1. Distribute the *Part 2* student pages.
2. Pair students. Assign one student to be responsible for measuring the time until the jumper throws the pilot chute and the other student to measuring the elapsed time before the parachute starts to inflate.

   Cue the video player to the beginning of the *BASE Jumping* sequence.
3. Instruct the students to view the young woman's three jumps, each time observing and recording the pilot chute throw out and parachute opening times. Have them average the data.

   Have the students record the altitudes corresponding to the average times. Instruct them to use their *Altitude-Time Graphs* to determine the altitude for each average time. Instruct the students to place the edge of a sheet of paper vertically along the time scale to help find the point of intersection.
4. Repeat this process for the two young men. Focus first on the young man on the right, then rewind the video and gather data on the young man on the left.
5. Have the students determine and record the altitudes corresponding to the average times for the two young men.
6. A video player that could step through the video, one frame at a time, was used to determine the following pilot chute throw-outs and parachute openings.

Young Woman	Throws Pilot Chute	Parachute Starts to Open
	1.7 seconds	3.3 seconds

Young Man (short delay)	Throws Pilot Chute	Parachute Starts to Open
	1.0 seconds	2.0 seconds

Young Man (long delay)	Throws Pilot Chute	Parachute Starts to Open
	4.00 seconds	4.7 seconds

7. The video camera which captured the BASE jumpers was on the bridge looking almost straight down. Ask students what someone on the ground, a distance away, looking from the side, would see. Instruct students to record the average pilot chute throw out and parachute opening times on the *New River Gorge Bridge Graph*. For each jumper, have the students draw a straight line connecting the edge of the bridge to the opening point.
8. Have students compare what's seen in the video with what a ground observer would see.
9. Have students compare the delay times of each jumper in safety terms.

Discussion

1. The points at which time measurements are taken may seem arbitrary. Why do you think these points were chosen? [The pilot chute throw out is a very good indicator that the BASE jumper is alert and has decided to end the freefall portion of the skydive. The pilot chute throw out is also the beginning of the all-important opening sequence. The point in time when the parachute starts to open is when the BASE jumper begins to slow down (decelerate). If the canopy is seen to be inflating, then the BASE jumper will probably reach the ground at a low enough speed, with enough control, to land safely.]
2. The straight-line, real-world, side view of the ground observer shows that all three jumpers were in the "safety zone." How does this compare to the third jumper? [The third jumper opened lower than the other two, but still opened safely.]
3. How do BASE jumpers determine how long they can safely freefall before opening the parachute? [BASE jumpers know that delay times depend upon the altitude of the object from which they're jumping. A BASE Jumper Table is probably something a BASE jumper would consult, especially for any jump less than 1000 feet.]

The following extensions provide a rich and varied resource of math explorations that connect freefall to the method of finite differences, formulas, functions, sequences and series, and number patterns.

Extensions

1. Distribute *Galileo Discovers Freefall*. Introduce or review the *method of finite differences* with students. The method works only if the second differences in a function table for y = f(x) are constant. If the second differences are constant, then it's easy to work backwards to the equation. The equation will be of the form y = ax² + bx + c. The dependent variable column (see following table), column y, is found by substituting zero and integer values of the independent variable x into the general equation. For example, if x =0, then y = c, the first entry in the dependent variable column. The other entries in the dependent variable column are obtained by substituting successive integers into the equation. The table is completed by taking, algebraically, successive differences.

	$y = ax^2 + bx + c$		
x	y	First Difference	Second Difference
0	c		
		a+b	
1	a+b+c		2a
		3a+b	
2	4a+2b+c		2a
		5a+b	
3	9a+3b+c		2a
		7a+b	
4	16a+4b+c		2a
		9a+b	
5	25a+5b+c		2a
		(2n-1)+b	
n	an² + bn + c		

Taking first and second differences in Galileo's hypothetical data table indicates that the method of finite differences could be applied to obtain an equation that fits the given data.

time	distance fallen	First Difference	Second Difference
0	0		
		16	
1	16		32
		48	
2	64		32
		80	
3	144		

By substitution, 2a = 32, therefore a = 16. And, a + b = 16. This means b = 0. Also, from the chart, it can be seen that c = 0.

Substituting the coefficients for a, b, and c into the general equation y = ax² + bx + c gives y = 16x².

Objects fall very fast so Galileo wasn't able to actually collect distance-time data by taking measurements on a falling cannonball. He slowed down the high-velocity motion of a falling cannonball by rolling a sphere (remember, the size and therefore the weight, of the sphere doesn't matter) down an inclined plane. A rolling sphere's motion was slow enough for Galileo to make the accurate measurements he needed in order to arrive at his law.

Galileo's Law of Falling Bodies is normally stated as

$$s = \frac{1}{2} gt^2$$

where *g* is the acceleration due to gravity. In the metric system, g = 9.8 meters per second per second. In the English system, g = 32 feet per second per second. Substituting the English system value for g, 32 feet per second per second, into the equation simplifies the equation to s = 16t².

2. Distribute the *Long Delays* page.

Students can compare their completed tables to this one.

	BASE Jumper Table		
Time	Distance Fallen(feet)	First Differences	Second Differences
0	0		
		16	
1	16		30
		46	
2	62		30
		76	
3	138		28
		104	
4	242		20
		124	
5	366		14
		138	
6	504		10
		148	
7	652		8
		156	
8	808		7
		163	
9	971		4
		167	
10	1138		4
		171	
11	1309		3
		174	
12	1483		2
		176	
13	1659		0
		176	
14	1835		0
		176	
15	2011		0
		176	
16	2187		0
		176	
17	2363		0
		176	
18	2539		0
		176	

The first differences are average velocities (Δd/Δt).

The second differences are *changes in velocities*, which are *accelerations!*

The column of first differences are getting close to some value in the 170 to 180 feet per second interval. Typically, terminal velocity is 120 miles per hour which is 176 feet per second. A well-educated guess for predicting the rest of the table would be to put 176 feet per second in the first difference column at the twelfth through eighteenth second. In other words, the jumper achieves terminal velocity at the thirteenth second.

Terminal velocity is defined as that velocity where the upwards directed force of air resistance balances the downward directed force of weight. Since the forces are balanced, the acceleration drops to zero. This is Newton's First Law of Motion.

An excellent discussion can be centered around the *Project 2061 Benchmark* (see the *Guiding Documents* section) reprinted below.

Project 2061 Benchmark
- *In the absence of retarding forces such as friction, an object will keep its direction of motion and its speed. Whenever an object is seen to speed up, slow down, or change direction, it can be assumed that an unbalanced force is acting on it. [ed. Newton's first law of motion.]*

Discussion

Is it *necessary* for any retarding force, such as air resistance, to be absent, for an object to keep its "direction of motion and its speed"?

[The retarding force of air resistance is built into the BASE Jumper Table. Still, a BASE jumper reaches a terminal velocity after approximately twelve seconds of freefall. It obviously isn't a necessary condition that retarding forces be absent for an object to keep its direction of motion and its speed, but any retarding forces do have to be *balanced* (see second sentence in the *Benchmark*).]

3. Distribute *Shelly Meets Galileo.*

When Shelly's freefall time of 50 seconds is substituted into Galileo's equation, x = 16t², a result of 40,000 feet is obtained. The reason the equation yields a value over four times the actual distance fallen is because the equation doesn't account for air resistance.

The cannonball and bullet hit the ground after approximately 3.32 seconds of freefall.

4. Distribute *Galileo at the Bridge.*

This extension gives students the opportunity to compare the BASE Jumper Table graph with the graph of s = 16t², Galileo's law.

Students can compare their computations to this completed table.

I	II	III
Time	$s = 16t^2$ (Distance Fallen)	$876 - s$
0	0	876
1	16	860
2	64	812
3	144	732
4	256	620
5	400	476
6	576	300
7	784	92
8	1024	-148
9	1296	-420
10	1600	-724

For the first three seconds of freefall (near the time it takes an object to hit the ground when dropped from the Leaning Tower of Pisa), Galileo's law gives results very close to those of the BASE Jumper Table. Students can compare their graph to this one.

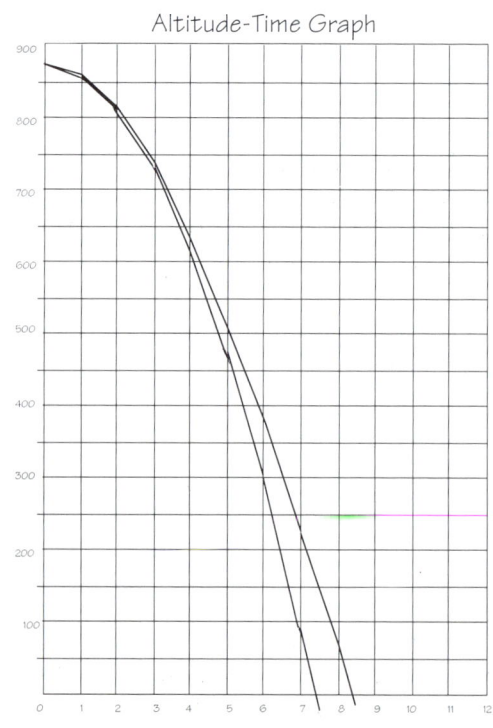

Altitude-Time Graph

One interesting comparison is to note that if a BASE jumper used Galileo's law to compute delay times, there would be almost a one second safety factor since Galileo's law computes ground level before the BASE Jumper Table does. In other words, to use Galileo's law is to err on safety's side.

Column III can be written as the equation, $y = 876 - 16t^2$.

5. Distribute *Isn't that Odd?*

There's a beautiful relationship between the set of odd numbers and Galileo's Law of Falling Bodies. Students can complete the table to discover that the square of any positive integer can be represented as a series of *odd numbers*. Galileo's law is a *square number* law. Have students compare their tables to this one.

I	II	III
n	n^2	For n ≥ 1, write n^2 as a series
0	0	0
1	1	1 + 3
2	4	1 + 3
3	9	1 + 3 + 5
4	16	1 + 3 + 5 + 7
5	25	1 + 3 + 5 + 7 + 9
6	36	1 + 3 + 5 + 7 + 9 + 11
7	49	1 + 3 + 5 + 7 + 9 + 11 + 13
8	64	1 + 3 + 5 + 7 + 9 + 11 + 13 + 15
9	81	1 + 3 + 5 + 7 + 9 + 11 + 13 + 15 + 17
10	100	1 + 3 + 5 + 7 + 9 + 11 + 13 + 15 + 17 + 19
11	121	1 + 3 + 5 + 7 + 9 + 11 + 13 + 15 + 17 + 19 + 21
n	n^2	1 + 3 + 5 + 7 + 9 + 11 + 13 ... + (2n-1) = n^2

Column I can be described as the set of *whole numbers*, which is the set of *natural numbers*, {1, 2, 3, 4, ...} plus the number zero.

Column II, beginning with 1, is the sequence of *square numbers*.

The nth odd number can be written as (2n-1).

Column III, beginning with 1, is the series of odd numbers.

The series 1 + 3 + 5 + 7 ... + (2n-1) in column III is equal to n^2, the sum of *n* successive odd numbers.

The computation of column II can be done mentally by noting that the square of any quarter-second will have 16 as a denominator. The numerators squared, in succession, are simply the square numbers. Students can compare their table with this one.

I	II		Δd
t	$16t^2$		
0	0		
			1
1/4	1		
			3
2/4	4		
			5
3/4	9		
			7
4/4	16		
			9
5/4	25		
			11
6/4	36		
			13
7/4	49		
			15
8/4	64		
			17
9/4	81		
			19
10/4	100		
			21
11/4	121		
12/4	144		

The Δd column is the set of odd numbers. This, by definition, is a sequence.

The odd numbers appear in column II of the previous graph as a *series* since summation is involved.

6. Distribute *Galileo Gets Even.*

The hint essentially gives the pattern away. Every value in the *d* column is an even number which means it's divisible by two. For each value for d, divide by two until two has been used as a factor four times. This holds true for all of the numbers in the d column (zero can also be written as 0 x 2 x 2 x 2 x 2 to keep the pattern alive), 2 x 2 x 2 x 2, or 16, is a factor of each of them. What's different for each d is the remaining factor. The remaining factor is simply the time, *t*, squared. There it is! Galileo's law, $16t^2$.

t (sec)	d (ft)	
0	0	0
1	16	8 x 2 = 4 x 2 x 2 = 2 x 2 x 2 x 2
2	64	32 x 2 = 16 x 2 x 2 = 8 x 2 x 2 x 2 = 4 x 2 x 2 x 2 x 2
3	144	72 x 2 = 36 x 2 x 2 = 18 x 2 x 2 x 2 = 9 x 2 x 2 x 2 x 2
4	256	128 x 2 = 64 x 2 x 2 = 32 x 2 x 2 x 2 = 16 x 2 x 2 x 2 x 2
5	400	200 x 2 = 100 x 2 x 2 = 50 x 2 x 2 x 2 = 25 x 2 x 2 x 2 x 2
6	576	288 x 2 = 144 x 2 x 2 = 72 x 2 x 2 x 2 = 36 x 2 x 2 x 2 x 2
7	784	392 x 2 = 196 x 2 x 2 = 98 x 2 x 2 x 2 = 49 x 2 x 2 x 2 x 2
8	1024	512 x 2 = 256 x 2 x 2 = 128 x 2 x 2 x 2 = 64 x 2 x 2 x 2 x 2
9	1296	648 x 2 = 324 x 2 x 2 = 162 x 2 x 2 x 2 = 81 x 2 x 2 x 2 x 2
10	1600	800 x 2 = 400 x 2 x 2 = 200 x 2 x 2 x 2 = 100 x 2 x 2 x 2 x 2
11	1936	968 x 2 = 484 x 2 x 2 = 242 x 2 x 2 x 2 = 121 x 2 x 2 x 2 x 2
12	2304	1152 x 2 = 576 x 2 x 2 = 288 x 2 x 2 x 2 = 144 x 2 x 2 x 2 x 2

Part 1

Analyzing the Data in the
BASE Jumper Table

Before jumping from a fixed object, a BASE jumper needs to know the "safe" delay times. Delay time is the time interval between jumping and opening the parachute. Safe delay times depend upon the altitude above ground level of the jump and the time it takes the jumper's parachute to open.

1. BASE jumpers leap from the bridge from a point 876 feet above the New River. Complete the third column of the chart by computing the altitude of a BASE jumper in freefall as a function of time.

2. Interpret the negative numbers that appear in the third column at the ninth and tenth second.

3. Make a line graph of altitude-time on the *Altitude-Time Graph.*

4. Estimate, from the graph, the time at which the line graph meets the water.

_____ seconds

5. Δd is the change in distance (altitude) per one second time interval. Compute column IV by subtracting the altitude at time t from the altitude at time t-1. Interpret the negative signs.

BASE Jumper Table

I	II	III	IV
Time (sec)	Distance Fallen (ft)	Altitude at Time t (ft)	Δd (ft)
0	0		
1	16		
2	62		
3	138		
4	242		
5	366		
6	504		
7	652		
8	808		
9	971		
10	1138		

Note: The data in this column is taken from a BASE Jumper's Freefall Table published in the June 1991 issue of *Skydiving* magazine.

6. Beginning at the top of column IV, describe on the back of this page, what's happening to the absolute value of Δd as you look down the column.

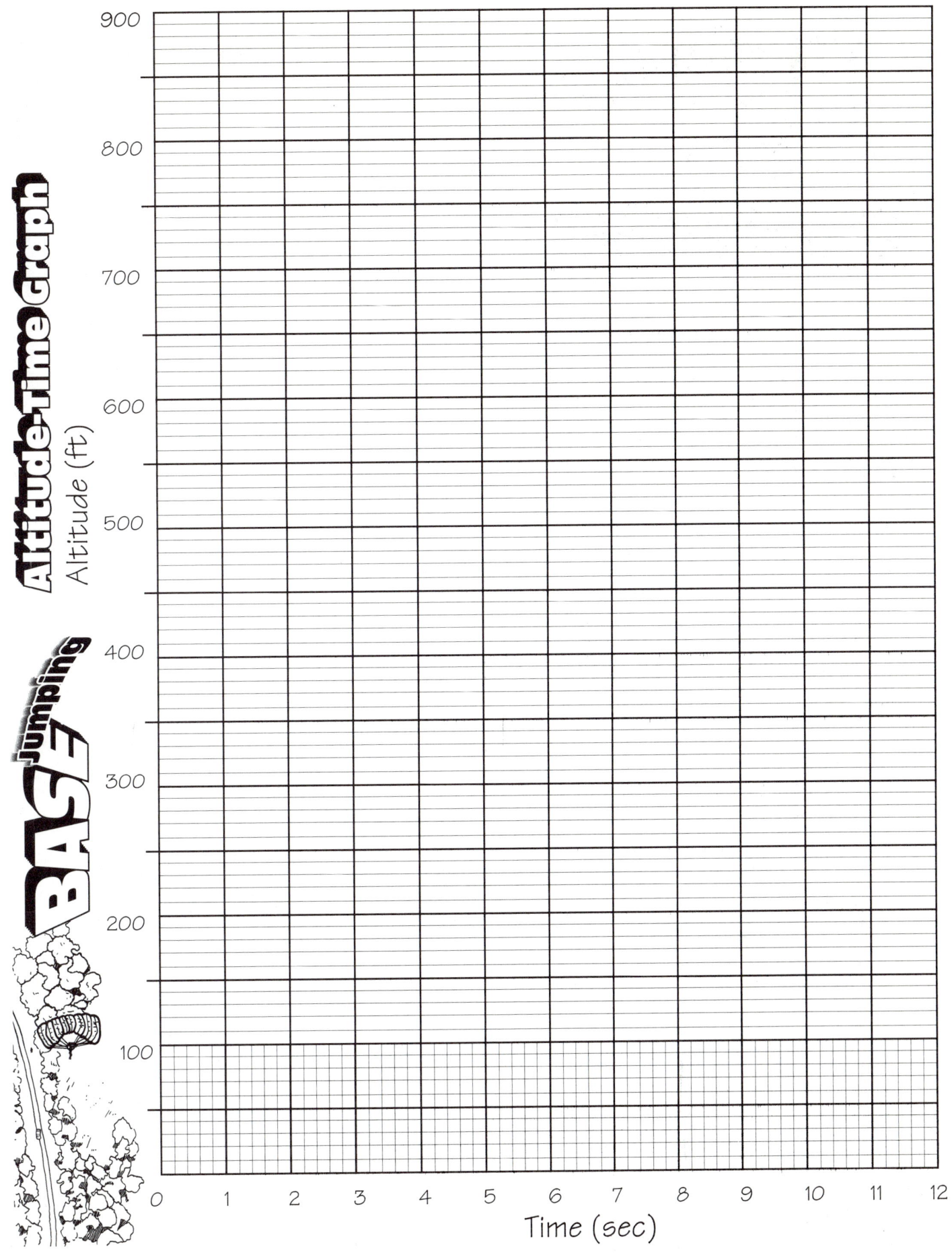

Altitude-Time Graph

Altitude (ft)

BASE Jumping

Time (sec)

Part 1, continued

7. Copy the column IV data from the previous page.

8. Complete column VI by computing the ratio, $\Delta d/\Delta t$, for each one second interval.

9. For each one-second interval on the altitude-time graph, shade the triangle formed by the change in altitude leg (Δd), the change in time base, and the line graph (see illustration).

IV	V	VI
Δd (ft)	Δt (sec)	$\dfrac{\Delta d}{\Delta t}$ (ft) (sec)
	1	
	1	
	1	
	1	
	1	
	1	
	1	
	1	
	1	
	1	

10. What is the physical interpretation of the numbers in column VI?

11. What is the physical meaning of the straight line segments connecting the data points on your *Altitude-Time Graph*?

12. Describe, in a general way, the sequence of shaded velocity triangles on your graph?

13. When will the triangles become congruent?

14. Will a BASE jumper reach terminal velocity jumping from the New River Gorge Bridge?

GRAVITY RULES!   115   © 1998 AIMS Education Foundation

Part 2

Measuring the Delay Times of
Real Jumpers

Young Woman	Throws Pilot Chute	Parachute Starts to Open
Trial # 1		
Trial # 2		
Trial # 3		
Average		

Altitude at which the pilot chute was thrown

_____ feet

Altitude at which the parachute started to open

_____ feet

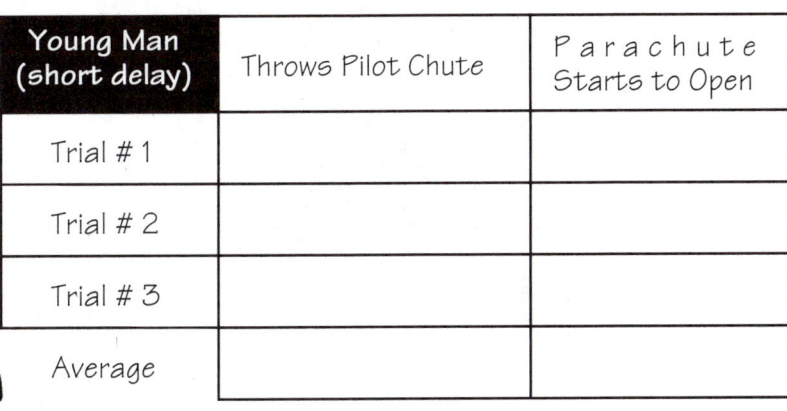

Young Man (short delay)	Throws Pilot Chute	Parachute Starts to Open
Trial # 1		
Trial # 2		
Trial # 3		
Average		

Altitude at which the pilot chute was thrown

_____ feet

Altitude at which the parachute started to open

_____ feet

Young Man (long delay)	Throws Pilot Chute	Parachute Starts to Open
Trial # 1		
Trial # 2		
Trial # 3		
Average		

Altitude at which the pilot chute was thrown

_____ feet

Altitude at which the parachute started to open

_____ feet

New River Gorge Bridge Graph

Jumpers 1 2 3

| | | | |
800
700
600
500
400
300
200
100
0

1. What would an observer, on the river, upstream next to the landing area see? To find out, plot the Delay Times data on this vertical line graph.

2. Compare what you saw in the video with what an observer on the ground would have seen.

3. Describe the delay time, in safety terms, of the young woman.

4. Describe the delay time, in safety terms, of the young man that threw his pilot chute second.

5. Compare this straight line graph with your Altitude-Time Graph.

Galileo Discovers Freefall

The story that Galileo dropped a cannonball and a bullet (sphere-shaped in those days) at the same time from the top of the Leaning Tower of Pisa to demonstrate that a lighter bullet falls just as fast as a heavier cannonball may or may not be true. It is true, however, that Galileo discovered that the distance an object falls is not a function of its weight, but it is a function of the time it is falling.

Imagine that Galileo was able to record the following distance-time data for a freely falling cannonball. The time is measured in seconds and the distance fallen, in feet.

time	distance fallen
0	0
1	16
2	64
3	144

$$y = ax^2 + bx + c$$

x	y	First Difference	Second Difference
0	c		
1	a+b+c		
2			
3			
4			
5			
n			

1. Complete the table of finite differences.

2. Apply the method of finite differences to the above distance-time data.

3. State Galileo's Law of Falling Bodies in the form of a function.

   y = _____

1. Look at the BASE Jumpers Data Table. Compute the first differences through the eleventh second. What do these first differences represent?

2. Compute the second differences through the eleventh second. What do these second differences represent?

3. Interpret the column of first differences.

4. Interpret the column of second differences.

88 feet per second = 60 miles per hour
Typical terminal velocity of a skydiver in a face-to-Earth position is 120 miles per hour.

120 miles per hour = _____ feet per second

5. Use this terminal velocity to complete the table.
6. Interpret the table.

BASE Jumper Table

Time	Distance Fallen(feet)	First Differences	Second Differences
0	0		
1	16		
2	62		
3	138		
4	242		
5	366		
6	504		
7	652		
8	808		
9	971		
10	1138		
11	1309		
12	1483		
13			
14			
15			
16			
17			
18			

Shelly Meets Galileo

BASE Jumping

According to popular legend, Galileo dropped a large cannonball and a small bullet from the Leaning Tower of Pisa to demonstrate that the lighter, smaller bullet falls at the same rate as the heavier cannonball. Whether or not this story is true, Galileo did formulate the laws that govern the motion of objects in freefall.

The distance, x, an object travels along a straight line, with a constant acceleration, a, as a function of its initial velocity, v_0, and time, t, is given by this equation.

$$x = v_0 t + \frac{at^2}{2}$$

Notice the equation does not contain a variable for mass and does not recognize the resistive force due to air resistance.

To apply the equation to both a cannonball, a bullet, and a skydiver, assume they all three start from a state of rest. Therefore, $v_0 = 0$ and the first term, $v_0 t = 0$

$$x = v_0 t + \frac{at^2}{2}, \quad x = 0 + \frac{at^2}{2}, \quad x = \frac{at^2}{2}$$

$$x = \frac{at^2}{2}, \quad x = \frac{32}{2}t^2, \quad x = 16\,t^2$$

The acceleration, a, is the acceleration due to gravity. The symbol for this special case of acceleration is g which is approximately equal to 32 feet per second per second. Substituting the value for g into the equation leads to another simplification.

The distance Shelly actually fell before opening her parachute, as measured from the real-time video viewed in the *Fall-timeters* activity, was 9250 feet. Her time of freefall was 50 seconds.

Use the formula, $x = 16t^2$, to compute the distance Shelly fell during the freefall portion of her skydive.

$$x = 16\,t^2$$
$$x = 16 \times t \times t$$
$$x = 16 \times \underline{\hspace{2cm}} \times \underline{\hspace{2cm}}$$
$$x = \underline{\hspace{2.5cm}} \text{ feet}$$

Why does Galileo's law give over four times the distance Shelly actual fell?

The Leaning Tower of Pisa is approximately 176 feet tall. Using Galileo's law, approximately how long did it take for the cannonball and bullet to hit the ground?

For low velocities, the resistive force of air resistance is proportional to the velocity of the object. For higher velocities, the resistive force is proportional to the square or even the cube of the velocity. Galileo's cannonball and bullet were in freefall for such a short time (and attained such low velocities) that air resistance didn't become an important factor. Shelly was in freefall long enough to reach terminal velocity, which puts a limit on her fall rate.

BASE Jumping Galileo at the Bridge

1. Substitute the time values in column I in Galileo's equation, $s = 16t^2$, and record the results in column II.

I	II	III
time	$s = 16t^2$ (distance fallen)	876 - s
0		
1		
2		
3		
4		
5		
6		
7		
8		
9		
10		

2. For column III, compute and record distance fallen relative to the New River Gorge Bridge.

3. Make a line graph of column I and column II on your original *Altitude-Time Graph*.

4. Compare the two line graphs.

5. Write an equation for column III of the table.

Isn't That Odd?

A mathematical sequence is a set of elements ordered in some specific way. For example, the set of even numbers is a sequence.

The set of even numbers = {0, 2, 4, 6, 8, 10, 12, …}

A mathematical series is the sum of a sequence.

The series formed from the sequence of even numbers is
0 + 2 + 4 + 6 + 8 + 10 + 12 + …

Describe column I as a sequence.

Describe column II, beginning with the number 1, as a sequence.

Express the nth odd number in terms of n.

Describe column III as a series.

Describe the relationship between columns II and III.

Complete the table.

I	II	III
n	n^2	For n ≥ 1, write n^2 as a series
0	0	0
1	1	1
2	4	1 + 3
3	9	
4		
5		
6		
7		
8		
9		
10		
11		
n	n^2	

Isn't That Odd?

BASE Jumping

Use Galileo's law, $s = 16t^2$, to compute the distance fallen after successive quarter-second intervals.

If you can, find a method for simplifying computing with fractions.

Compute the distance fallen (Δd) during each quarter-second interval.

I	II		Δd
t	$16t^2$		
0			
1/4			
2/4			
3/4			
4/4			
5/4			
6/4			
7/4			
8/4			
9/4			
10/4			
11/4			
12/4			

Describe the Δd column as a sequence.

Compare the Δd column of this table with column III of the previous table.

Galileo Gets Even

The story that Galileo dropped a cannonball and a bullet at the same time from the top of the Leaning Tower of Pisa to demonstrate that a lighter bullet falls just as fast as a heavier cannonball, may or may not be true. It is true that Galileo went on to discover his famous law of falling bodies.

The table below contains distance-time data for an object in freefall. Search for a pattern in the distance column of the table.

How are the numbers alike?

How are they different?

Hint: Getting even is the point!

t (sec)	d (ft)	
0	0	
1	16	
2	64	
3	144	
4	256	
5	400	
6	576	
7	784	
8	1024	
9	1296	
10	1600	
11		
12		

Video Companion

for
BASE Jumping

Note: Refer to the *Gravity Rules! Glossary* for definitions of skydiving words and phrases heard in the video.

Time = 56 minutes: 25 seconds

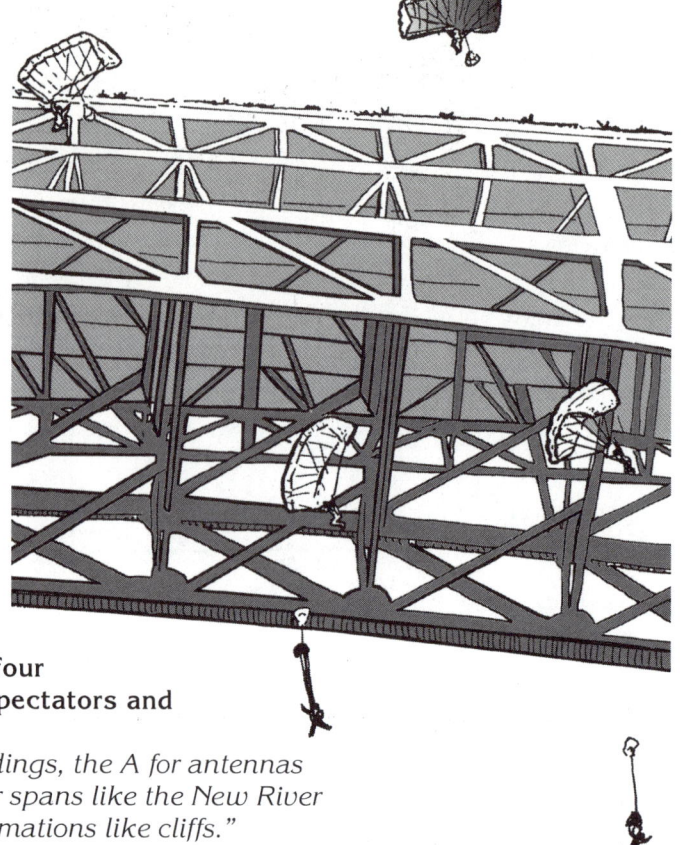

I. **Opening Sequence**

> *"Every year, on the third Saturday in October, skydivers are allowed to jump off West Virginia's New River Gorge Bridge."*

1. **A sweeping view of the New River valley and the New River Gorge Bridge.**

   > *"Skydivers that enjoy jumping from low altitudes are called BASE jumpers."*

2. **The view from a helicopter showing two of the four traffic lanes closed to vehicles and opened to spectators and BASE jumpers.**

   > *"BASE is an acronym. The B stands for buildings, the A for antennas such as radio and television towers, the S for spans like the New River Gorge Bridge, and the E for natural Earth formations like cliffs."*

3. **A closer view of vehicle and pedestrian traffic on the bridge**

4. **Two BASE jumpers check their pilot chutes before jumping together.**

   > *"Here a jumper stands on the railing near the center of the bridge."*

5. **An arrow superimposed on the video points to the Main Canopy Release Pin and Bridle.**

   > *"She waits for the jumpers that precede her to clear the area, and then jumps directly over the New River, 876 feet below."*

6. **A bird's-eye view of the jumper as she falls and then throws her pilot chute.**

   > *"After a delay of a few seconds, she throws the pilot chute to open the main canopy."*

7. **Her pilot chute fills with air, pulls the bag containing the main canopy from its container, and blossoms open.**

   > *"With a good parachute over her head, she sets ups to land on a small, tree-lined gravel beach next to the river."*

8. **The arrows indicate the positions of two previous jumpers. Their open canopies provide "scale" to the view.**

   > *"How long can a BASE jumper delay throwing the pilot chute?"*

9. **Eyeing each other, the two young men jump from the bridge.**

   > *"To answer that question, a BASE jumper needs to know distance fallen as a function of time."*

10. **One of the jumpers throws the pilot chute immediately as the other delays throwing the pilot chute. Notice the kayak and kayaker on the rock directly below the jumpers.**

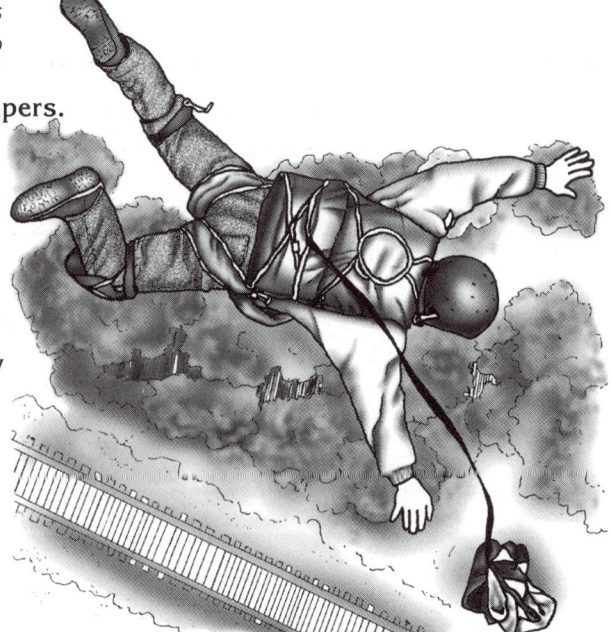

III. Get Ready to Measure Delay Times

1. A timer is superimposed on the video sequence of the young woman jumping from the bridge. (The sequence is repeated three times to save rewinding.)

Time = 57 minutes: 40 seconds

2. A timer is superimposed on the video sequence of the two young men jumping from the bridge. (The sequence is repeated three times to save rewinding.)

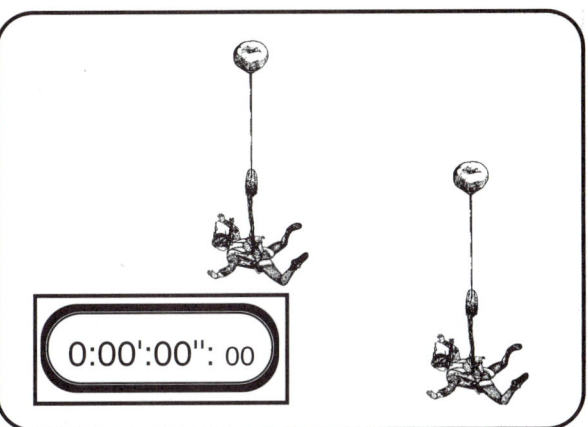

Time = 58 minutes: 14 seconds

3. A timer is superimposed on the video sequence of a jumper wearing a video camera on his chest. This provides a different perspective on a BASE jump from the bridge.

Time = 58 minutes: 44 seconds

THE RACE

Topic
Motion along a straight line

Key Question
Does the graph of an object's motion always look like the actual motion of the object?

Focus
Students will collect, record, and graph, in three different ways, the distance-time data of a race between a tortoise and a hare. They will then interpret each graph.

Guiding Documents
Project 2061 Benchmark
- *All motion is relative to whatever frame of reference is chosen, for there is no motionless frame from which to judge all motion.*

NRC Standards
- *An object's motion can be described by tracing and measuring its position over time.*
- *The motion of an object can be described by its position, direction of motion, and speed. That motion can be represented on a graph.*

NCTM Standards
- *Construct, read, and interpret tables, charts, and graphs*
- *Develop the concepts of rates and other derived and indirect measurements*

Math
Graphs
Ratio and proportion
Pythagorean triangle
    distance formula
Function

Science
Physical science
    motion
        average velocity
        displacement, Δd
        time interval, Δt

Integrated Processes
Observing
Collecting and recording data
Interpreting data

Materials
Cardboard
White glue

Background Information
Students have a difficult time *visualizing* physical situations (like the motion of an object) and *representing* physical situations mathematically. In this activity, a foot race between a tortoise and a hare, along a straight-line course, is used as a context for allowing conceptual difficulties to surface. Distance-time data for the race are collected and first graphed on a single-axis number line, then as a distance-distance graph, and finally, as a distance-time graph. It's during the discussion arising from interpreting all three graphs that the teacher has the opportunity to clarify students' conceptual difficulties.

If we ask students to visualize a race between a tortoise and a hare along a straight-line course laid out in the woods, they might visualize something like this.

As teachers, we probably visualize this setting and immediately abstract the race course to the number line. This is a *side view* of the race and, if we were standing at some point to the side of the race course, is what we would actually see. When the distance-time data of the race is graphed on the number line, we'll see that the graph fails to capture essential elements of the race.

Let's go back to the original visualization. If we gave students the x-y coordinate system as a reference frame, and some numbers for the coordinates of the starting and ending points of the race course, and then asked them to "graph" the race course in the woods, they would probably produce a distance-distance graph like this one.

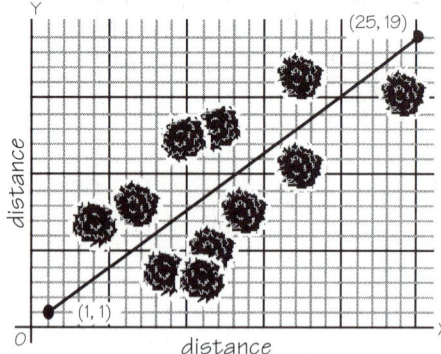

A distance-distance graph is a bird's-eye map view of the physical straight-line race course traversed by the tortoise and the hare. This graph locates the race course *relative* to the surrounding forest. In the activity, this is the second graph that students make. The *positions* of both the hare and the tortoise, for any time (*t*), can be graphed *on the line representing the actual course*. To do this, a tool for measuring distances *along* the course line will be needed. The advantage of this distance-distance graph is that it closely mathematically models the actual physical situation. The disadvantage of the graph is that, like the number line graph, information about the actual race cannot be interpreted from the graph. For example, during the race, the hare passes the tortoise at some point on the course. This point cannot be interpreted from the graph (see *Discussion, Part 3* for completed distance-distance graph).

Instead of a distance graph or a distance-distance graph, physicists use a distance-time graph to graph the motion of an object. The differences are subtle but important. In a distance-time graph, the race course is abstracted out of the forest, as in the distance graph, but with an important difference. The distance axis (x-axis) is switched from its natural, horizontal position to the vertical position. The horizontal axis then becomes the *time* axis.

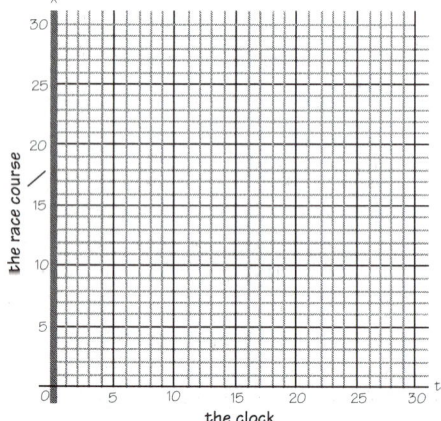

This is not an arbitrary change. Consider these two graphs.

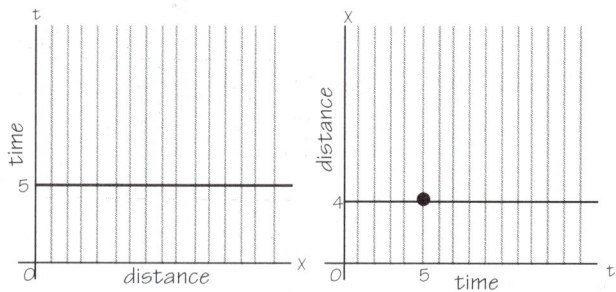

The first graph, the time-distance graph, tells us that at time t=5, the object is at every position along the line! But common sense tells us that it's impossible for the same object to occupy more than one position at the same time! The second graph, the distance-time graph, tells us that the object was at rest at a distance of four units from the origin throughout the time of observation. If the object represents the motion of say the hare, then the hare can be thought of as sitting under a tree, motionless, eating a carrot throughout the time period.

So, where the axes are placed makes a difference. The distance-time graph plots distance *x as a function of* time *t*. Time is the independent variable while distance is the dependent variable. The two-axes *distance-time* graph is therefore consistent with the function definition in mathematics.

The *distance-time* graph is a useful abstract tool because it embodies more information than a single-axis position graph or a two-axes distance-distance graph. It's natural for students to want to "see" a two-axes graph as a picture of an object's motion. Remember, the motion we're discussing is limited to motion along a *straight line*. You can anticipate that some students will be confused by distance-time graphs that are not straight lines. These students need additional time and practice to construct their understanding.

For motion along a straight line, average velocity is computed by dividing the distance traveled, from start to finish, (called the *displacement*, symbolized by Δd, read *delta d)* by the time interval, Δt (read *delta t)*. The use of the Δ symbol with a quantity such as distance, time, temperature, etc., means a *change* in that quantity.

$$\text{average velocity} = \Delta d / \Delta t$$

Management

1. Construct the race course. Either do it yourself or assign the task to a team of students. (Note: If you prefer not to construct the track at all, make a transparency of the *Announcer's Script* page. When using the transparency, cover the script page with a sheet of paper and reveal each position you want students to observe and record distance-time

data.) Follow the directions on the *Setting the Stage* page to make the race course.

2. Select a race announcer and race pacer (called the reporter) a day or two before doing the activity. Have them either write their own script, modify the script included in this activity (see *Announcer's Script*), or use the script as it stands.

3. Allow the race announcer and pace timer to practice announcing and simulating the race before doing the activity with the class.

4. Copy and cut out one *Distance Ruler* for every student.

Procedure
Part 1 — Collecting and Recording Data for the Race

1. Set up the cardboard race course and have the race pacer take his or her position behind the race course.

2. Distribute the student pages for *Parts 1, 2, 3, 4* and the *Distance Rulers*.

3. When everything is ready, tell the announcer to begin.

4. Instruct students to observe and record the displacement (distance) for both the tortoise and the hare at the times indicated by the announcer.

Discussion

1. What do you know about the motion of either the tortoise or the hare when it was hidden behind the trees? [Nothing, really. (In problems of this sort, we typically *assume* the motion between time data points to be smooth. It could be argued that the tortoise or the hare stopped to rest, or even went backwards, when hidden from view.)]

2. What can be *assumed* about the motion of the tortoise and the hare when they were hidden from view? [They continued to run *smoothly*, when hidden from view. (Each ran with a constant velocity).]

Procedure
Part 2 — A Distance Graph of the Race

1. Instruct the students to use the notation described in the first question and graph the distance-time data on the number line.

2. Using their *Distance Graph*, tell the students to answer questions two through seven.

Discussion

1. Have students compare their *Distance Graphs* with this one.

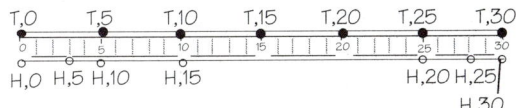

2. Which won the race, the tortoise or the hare? [The race ended in a tie.]

3. What's the geometric shape of the path the tortoise actually traveled during the race? [a straight line]

4. What's the geometric shape of the path the hare actually traveled during the race? [a straight line]

5. What's the geometric shape of the graph of the tortoise's motion? [a straight line]

6. What's the geometric shape of the graph of the hare's motion? [a straight line]

7. At what time and distance did the hare catch the tortoise? [The data indicate that the hare caught the tortoise at some point between 15 and 20 distance units and 15 and 20 time units. The graph does not show the exact point.]

Procedure
Part 3 — A Distance-Distance Graph of the Race

1. Instruct students to plot the starting and ending points for the race course on their *Distance-Distance Graph*.

2. For question two, have them draw the straight line between the two points and answer the two questions. For students that know the distance formula, $d = \sqrt{((x_2 - x_1)^2 + (y_2 - y_1)^2)}$, have them use the formula to compute the distance. [Let (x_2, y_2) = the point $(25,19)$ and (x_1, y_1) = the point $(1,1)$. Then $d = \sqrt{((25 - 1)^2 + (19 - 1)^2)}$, $d = \sqrt{((24^2 + 18^2))}$, $d = \sqrt{((576+324))}$, $d = \sqrt{(900)}$, $d = 30$ units.]

3. Direct the students to use their *Distance Ruler* to plot the distance data for both the tortoise and the hare on their *Distance-Distance Graph*. Instruct them to use a solid dot to represent the tortoise and to label each position of the tortoise with a T, and the time the tortoise was at that position. Likewise, instruct them to use a circle to represent the hare and to label each of the hare's positions with H, and the time the hare was at that position.

4. Using their *Distance-Distance Graph*, instruct the students to answer questions four through seven.

Discussion

1. Have students compare their *Distance-Distance Graphs* with this one.

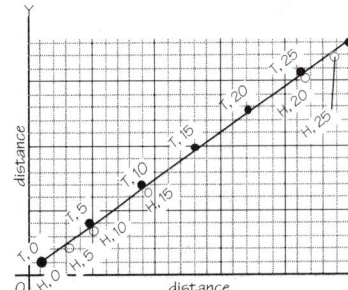

2. Draw the straight line between the two points $(1,1)$ and $(25,19)$. What does this line represent? [The straight line between the points represents the race course.] What is the length of the straight line? [The line (race course) is 30 units long.]

3. Which won the race, the tortoise or the hare? [The race ended in a tie.]
4. What's the geometric shape of the path the tortoise actually traveled during the race? [a straight line]
5. What's the geometric shape of the path the hare actually traveled during the race? [a straight line]
6. What's the geometric shape of the graph of the tortoise's motion? [a straight line]
7. What's the geometric shape of the graph of the hare's motion? [a straight line]
8. At what time and distance did the hare catch the tortoise? [The data indicate that the hare caught the tortoise at some point between 15 and 20 distance units and 15 and 20 time units. The graph does not show the exact point.]

Procedure
Part 4 — A Distance-Time Graph of the Race
1. Have the students graph the same data for the tortoise and the hare on their *Distance-Time Graphs*.
2. Instruct the students to use their graphs to answer the questions on their pages.

Discussion
1. Which won the race, the tortoise or the hare? [The race ended in a draw.]
2. What's the geometric shape of the path the tortoise actually traveled during the race? [a straight line]
3. What's the geometric shape of the path the hare actually traveled during the race? [a straight line]
4. What's the geometric shape of the graph of the tortoise's motion? [a straight line]
5. What's the geometric shape of the graph of the hare's motion? [a crooked line]
6. Shade in the portion of the hare's graph that shows the hare lagging behind the tortoise.

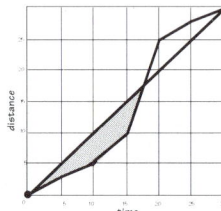

7. Shade in the portion of the hare's graph that shows the hare ahead of the tortoise.

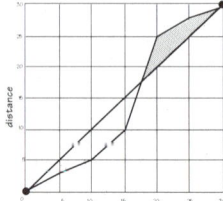

8. At what time and distance did the hare catch the tortoise? [17.5 time units, 17.5 distance units]

9. At the end of the race, what's the displacement, Δd, of the tortoise? [Δd = 30 distance units]
10. At the end of the race, what's the displacement, Δd, of the hare? [Δd = 30 distance units]
11. How long did it take the tortoise to complete the race? [Δt = 30 time units]
12. How long did it take the hare to complete the race? [Δt = 30 time units]
13. What was the average velocity, Δd/Δt, of the tortoise? [1 distance unit per time unit]
14. What was the average velocity, Δd/Δt, of the hare? [1 distance unit per time unit]
15. Did the tortoise run the race with a constant velocity? [yes]
16. Did the hare run the race with a constant velocity? [no]
17. What was the instantaneous velocity of the tortoise? [1 distance unit per time unit]
18. What was the instantaneous velocity of the hare? (When the velocity of an object is constant, its constant velocity and instantaneous velocity are the same. Connecting the distance-time points on the hare's *Distance-Time Graph* with straight lines makes the velocity of the hare between time intervals (every 5 units of time) an *average velocity*. Average velocities are constant velocities. Therefore, simply compute the average velocity for each 5 time unit interval. For example, between t = 15 and t = 20, the hare traveled 15 distance units. The hare's average velocity is 15/5 or 3 units of distance per unit of time. This is also the hare's *instantaneous* velocity for the same time interval. The following chart computes the average velocity which is equal to the instantaneous velocity.)

Time Interval	Average Velocity (Δd/Δt)	Instantaneous Velocity
0 - 5	3/5	0.6 velocity units
5 - 10	2/5	0.4 velocity units
10 - 15	5/5	1.0 velocity unit
15 - 20	15/5	3.0 velocity units
20 - 25	3/5	0.6 velocity units
25 - 30	2/5	0.4 velocity units

Extensions
1. On a copy of the *Announcer's Script* page, connect the successive positions for the tortoise and the hare. Compare this "graph" with your *Distance-Time Graph*.
2. The hare was hidden from view during the 15 – 20 time unit interval. One of the observers close to the race claims the hare ran in a circle, just to taunt the

tortoise, during this interval. This observer claims this is the graph of the hare's motion during this interval.

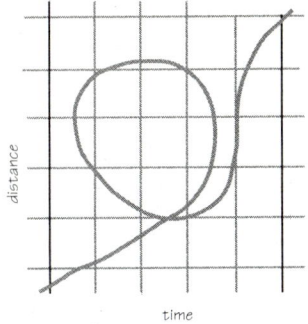

Attack or defend the observer's graph. [The observer may have accurately reported the hare's behavior but the graph is incorrect. Choose some time that intersects with the loop in the graph. This time line intersects the curve in three places, meaning, at that time, the hare was in three different places!]

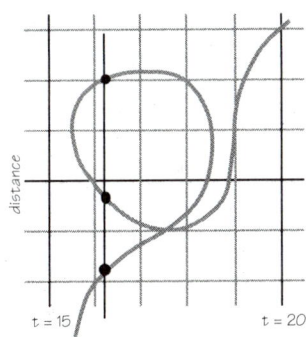

3. If you think the observer's graph is wrong but you can believe the hare would taunt the tortoise by running in a circle, what might the graph look like?

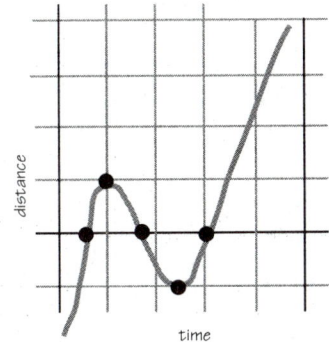

THE RACE

Setting the Stage

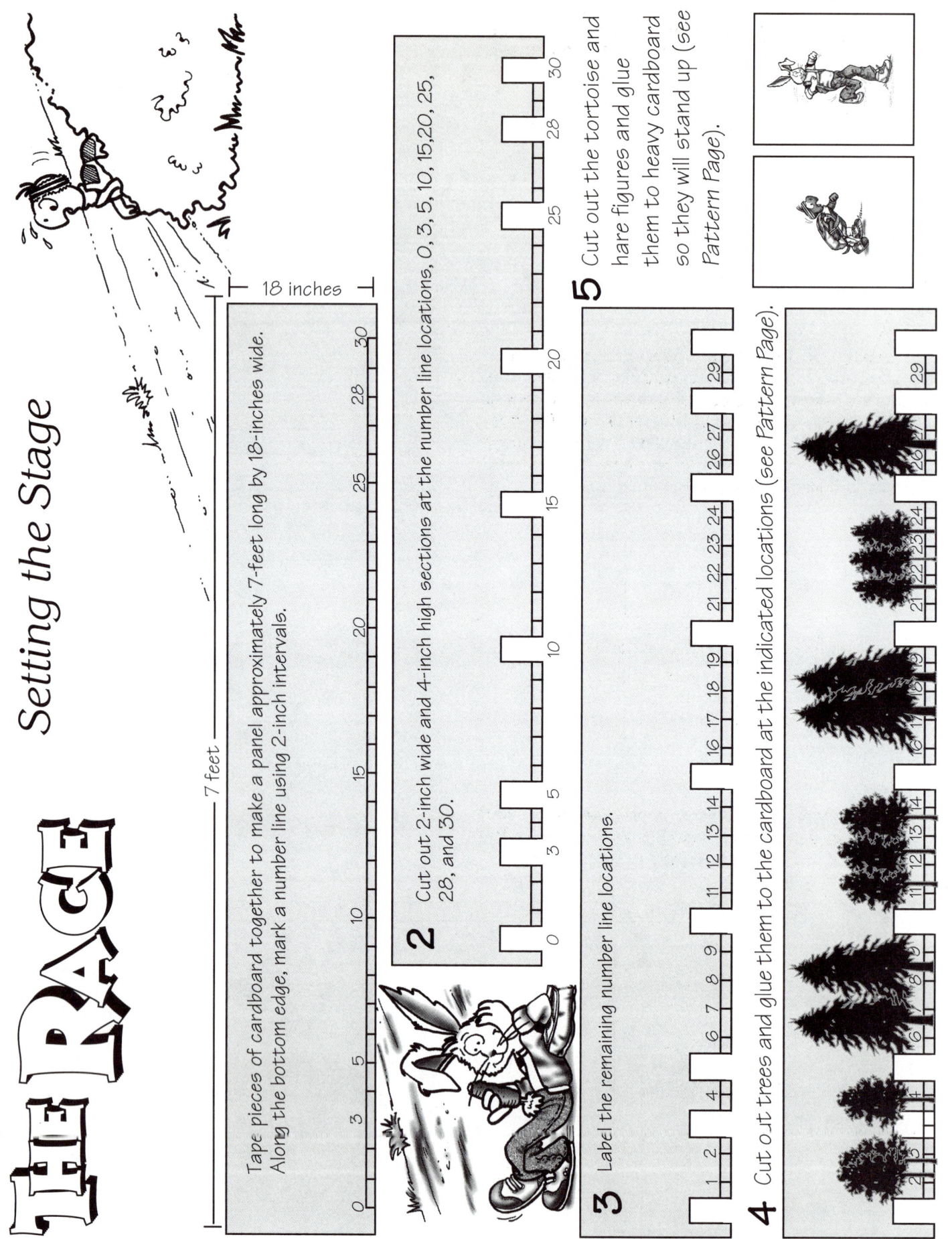

1. Tape pieces of cardboard together to make a panel approximately 7-feet long by 18-inches wide. Along the bottom edge, mark a number line using 2-inch intervals.

2. Cut out 2-inch wide and 4-inch high sections at the number line locations, 0, 3, 5, 10, 15, 20, 25, 28, and 30.

3. Label the remaining number line locations.

4. Cut out trees and glue them to the cardboard at the indicated locations (see Pattern Page).

5. Cut out the tortoise and hare figures and glue them to heavy cardboard so they will stand up (see Pattern Page).

Pattern Page

Announcer's Script

Welcome to the sporting event of the year. It's almost time for the race between...the tortoise and the hare! Unfortunately our cameras are not allowed near the race course so we'll be broadcasting the race from this vantage point. As you can see, trees hide portions of the course so we've stationed a reporter on the other side of the trees who will signal us by waving a flag when the tortoise and the hare reach open positions.

I see my reporter's flag waving. The race is about to start. Yes, they're off!

There's my reporter's signal. The tortoise has grabbed the lead and is at marker 5 with the hare at marker number 3. One has to wonder if the hare is confident of winning and is just toying with the tortoise.

I see my reporter's flag again. The tortoise has widened its lead! Can you believe it, sports fans? Those short legs must be really churning. The tortoise is now at marker 10 and the hare is at marker number 5.

There's the flag. Is there an upset in the making? At the half-way point the tortoise has managed to maintain its lead over the hare. The tortoise is at marker 15 with the hare at marker 10.

What legs! With an amazing burst of power the hare has zoomed past the tortoise to take the lead. The tortoise is at marker 20 and the hare is at marker 25.

There's the flag. The hare seems to have slowed down, with the tortoise closing the gap. The tortoise is at marker 25 and the hare is at marker 28.

It looks like the tortoise dug deep and found a second burst of energy to close the gap on the hare. Sports fans, it's a miracle performance of poise and determination. It's a drama seen once in a lifetime. But it's happened here, today, and you saw it. The tortoise has tied the hare!

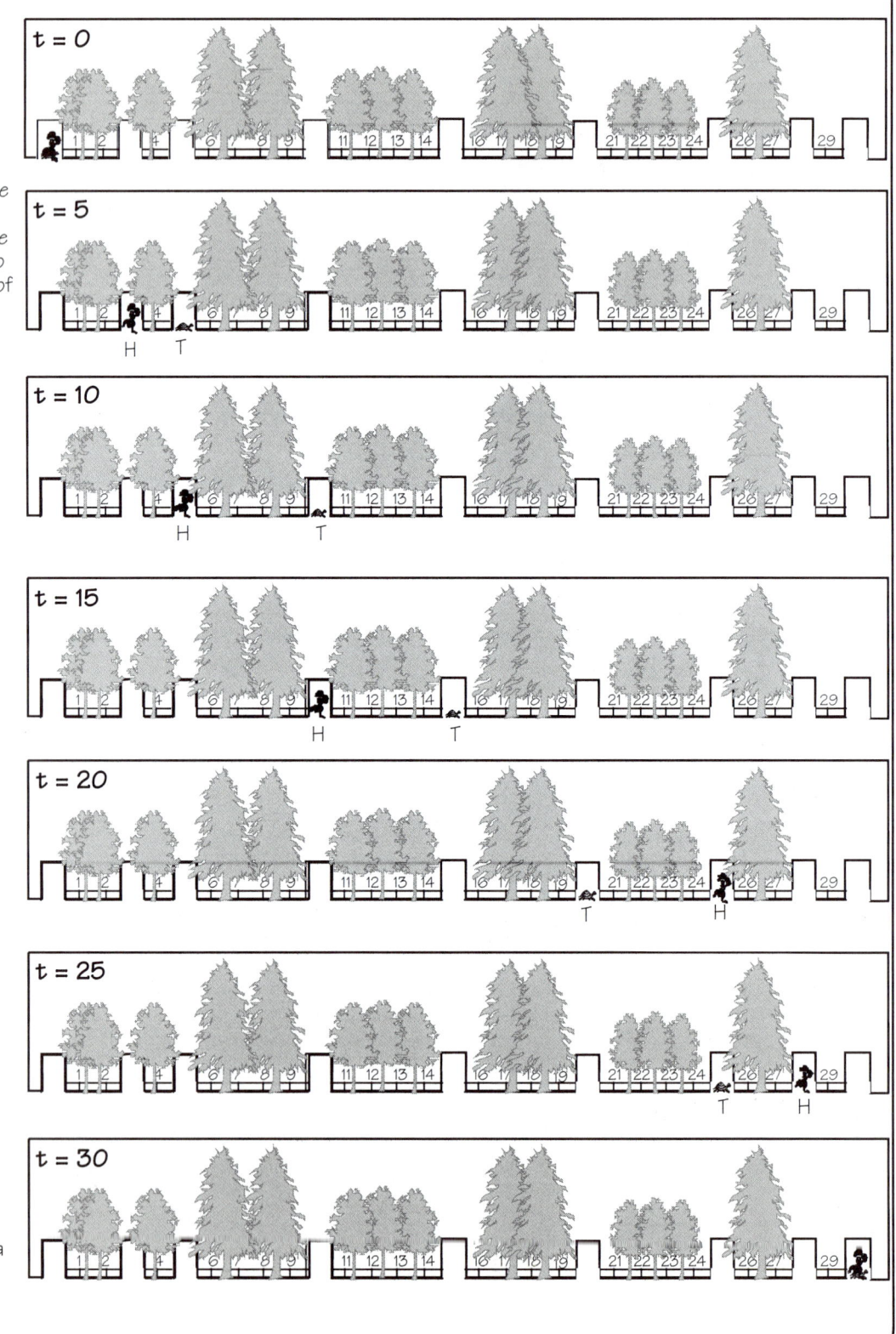

Distance Rulers

THE RACE

Part 1 - Collecting and Recording Data for the Race

Time	Distance		Time	Distance
0	0		0	0
5			5	
10			10	
15			15	
20			20	
25			25	
30			30	

Part 2 - A Distance Graph of the Race

T,O

0   5   10   15   20   25   30

H,O

1. Use a solid dot, just above the number line, to represent the position of the tortoise at time t. Label each position of the tortoise with a T, and the time the tortoise was at that position. Draw the line connecting each of the tortoise's position points. ●T,t

   Use a circle, just below the number line, to represent the position of the hare at time t. Label each of the hare's positions with a H, and the time the hare was at that position. Draw the line connecting each of the hare's position points. ○H,t

2. Which won the race, the tortoise or the hare?

3. What's the geometric shape of the path the hare actually traveled during the race?

4. What's the geometric shape of the path the tortoise actually traveled during the race?

5. What's the geometric shape of the graph of the tortoise's motion?

6. What's the geometric shape of the graph of the hare's motion?

7. At what *time* and *distance* did the hare catch the tortoise?

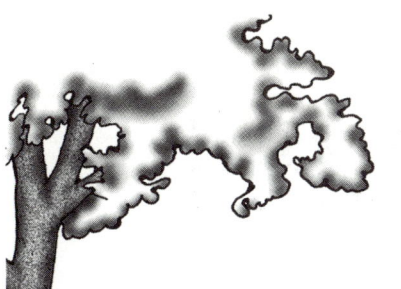

Part 3 - A Distance-Distance Graph of the Race

1. The coordinates of the starting point are (1,1). Plot the starting point on the *Distance-Distance Graph*.
   The coordinates of the finishing point are (25, 19). Plot this point on the graph.
2. Draw the straight line between the two points. What does this line represent? What is the length of the straight line?

3. Use the *Distance Ruler* to plot the distance data on the graph for both the tortoise and the hare.

   ●T,t Use a solid dot to represent the tortoise and label each position of the tortoise with a T, and the time the tortoise was at that position.

   ○H,t Use a circle to represent the hare and label each of the hare's positions with a H, and the time the hare was at that position.

4. Which won the race, the tortoise or the hare?
5. What's the geometric shape of the path the tortoise actually traveled during the race?
6. What's the geometric shape of the path the hare actually traveled during the race?
7. What's the geometric shape of the graph of the tortoise's motion?
8. What's the geometric shape of the graph of the hare's motion?
9. At what time and distance did the hare catch the tortoise?

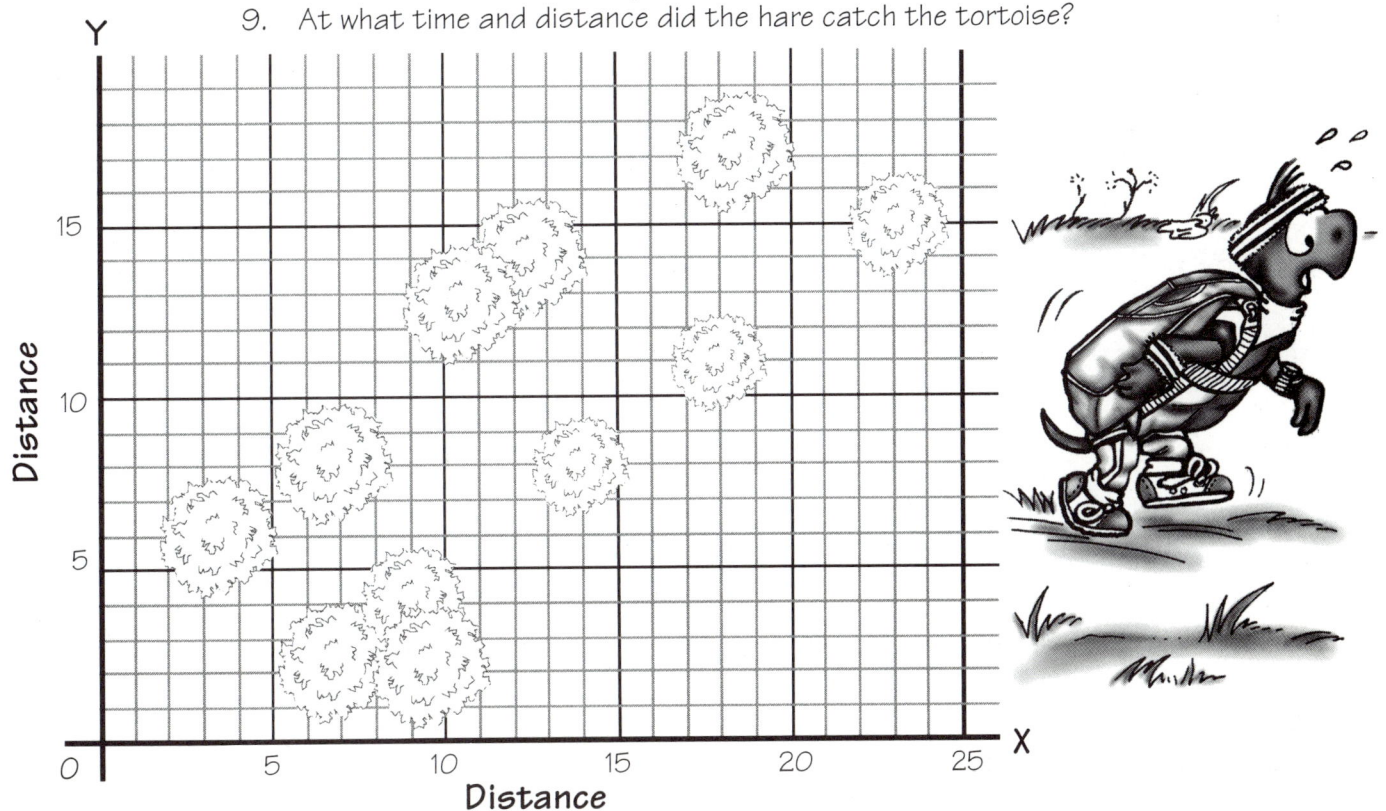

THE RACE

Part 4 - A Distance-Time Graph of the Race

Graph the distance-time data for both the tortoise and the hare on the *Distance-Time Graph*. Use a different color for each. Answer these questions about your *Distance-Time Graph*.

1. Which won the race, the tortoise or the hare?

2. What's the geometric shape of the path the tortoise actually traveled during the race?

3. What's the geometric shape of the path the hare actually traveled during the race?

4. What's the geometric shape of the graph of the tortoise's motion?

5. What's the geometric shape of the graph of the hare's motion?

6. Shade in the portion of the hare's graph that shows the hare lagging behind the tortoise.

7. Shade in the portion of the hare's graph that shows the hare ahead of the tortoise.

8. At what *time* and *distance* did the hare catch the tortoise?

9. At the end of the race, what's the displacement, Δd, of the tortoise?

10. At the end of the race, what's the displacement, Δd, of the hare?

11. How long did it take the tortoise to complete the race?

12. How long did it take the hare to complete the race?

THE RACE

What was the average velocity, $\Delta d/\Delta t$, of the tortoise?

What was the average velocity, $\Delta d/\Delta t$, of the hare?

Did the tortoise run the race with a constant velocity?

Did the hare run the race with a constant velocity?

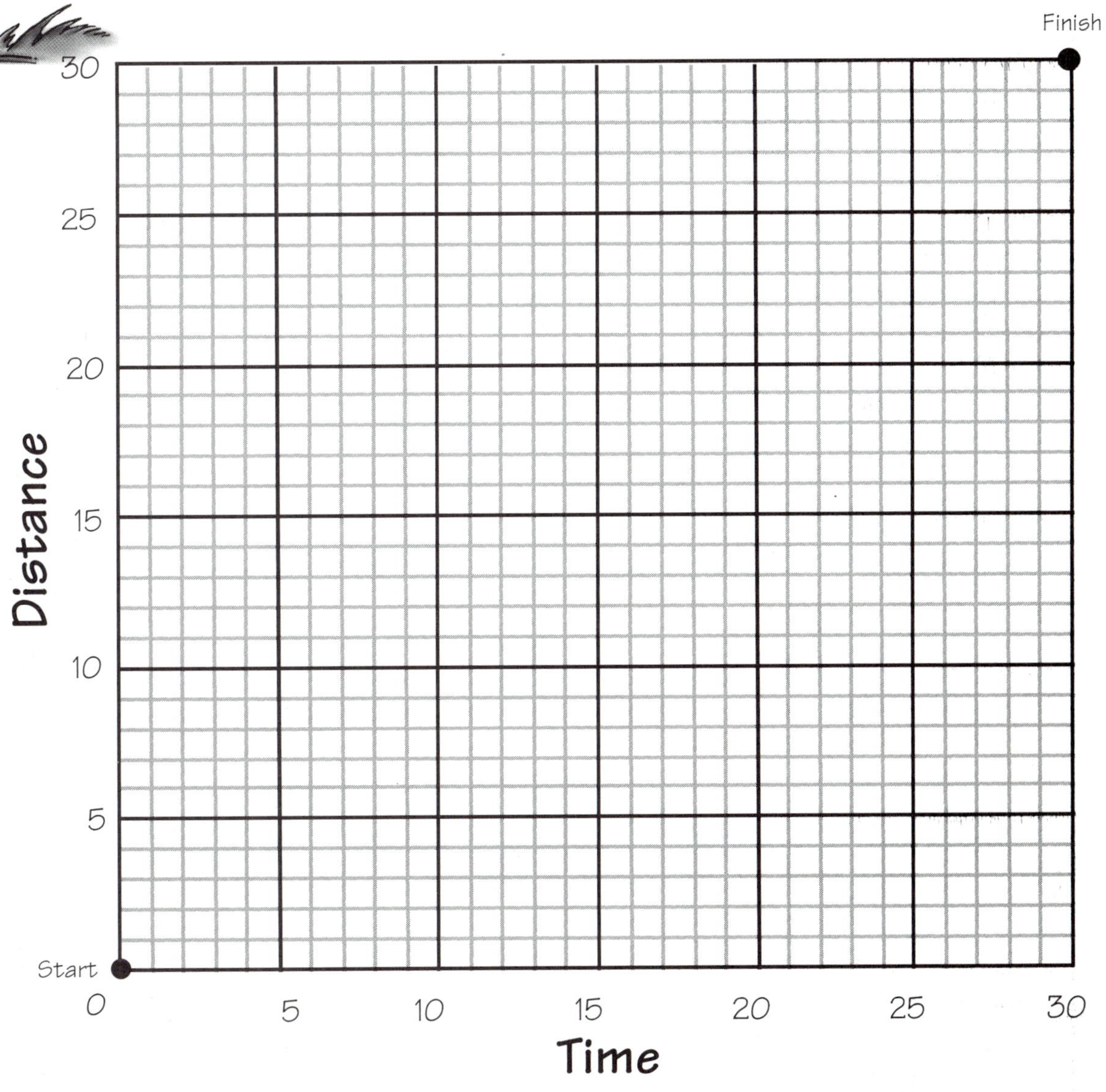

Finish

30

25

20

Distance

15

10

5

Start

0   5   10   15   20   25   30

Time

SKYDIVING
A GRAVITY POWERED SPORT

The easiest forces to understand are called *contact forces*. Contact forces always have a direct connection between the source of the force and the object on which the force is acting. For example, pushing on a box or pulling on a string attached to a box are contact forces.

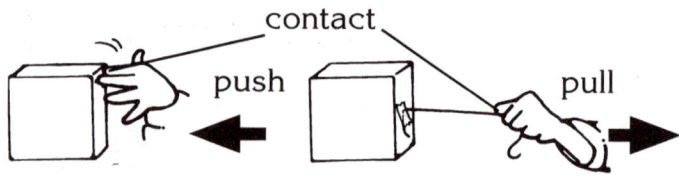

Not all forces are contact forces. Bring two magnets together and you can feel them pull or push on each other without the magnets actually contacting. Somehow, across the space separating them, a repulsive or attractive force exists between magnets. Electrical charges, like those generated by rubbing one object with another (a plastic comb through hair), also generate attractive or repulsive forces without directly contacting each other.

Magnets

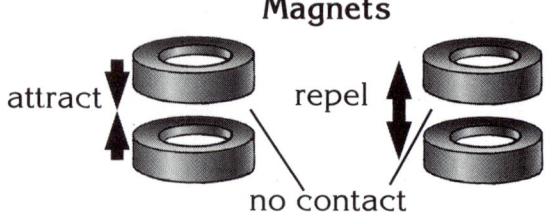

An important example of another non-contact force is the force due to gravity. An interesting characteristic of the force of gravity is that it's always an attractive force. (Antigravity, a repulsive force, is so far, just a dream of science fiction writers.) The great English scientist Sir Isaac Newton showed that the gravitational force between any two objects depends upon the mass of each of the objects and the distance separating the centers of the objects. For example, the gravitational force of attraction between the space shuttle in orbit and the Earth is determined by the mass of the shuttle, the mass of the Earth, and the distance between the center of mass of the shuttle and the center of mass of the Earth.

Near the surface of the Earth, the gravitational force of attraction is strong enough to cause an unsupported object (like a skydiver in freefall) to speed up (accelerate) at the rate of 32 feet per second, each second. This acceleration is called the *acceleration due to gravity* and *g* is its symbol. The speed of the object continues to increase unless some retarding force — like air resistance — limits its speed.

For an object in freefall — neglecting the retarding force of air resistance — the velocity (speed) at which the object is moving at the end of each of the first three seconds of freefall is given in the table below. Complete the table.

time [seconds]	0	1	2	3	4	5	6	7	8	9	10	11	12
velocity [ft/second]	0	32	64	96									

Questions:

1. Write an algebraic equation that expresses the relationship between t, time, and v, the velocity of an object in freefall (neglecting air resistance).

2. Why are you not afraid to jump off a three-foot high table?

3. Why should you be afraid to jump off a ten-story building?

Boy On A Raft — Newton's Third Law of Motion

Newton's third law of motion states:

If two objects interact, the force exerted on Object 1 by Object 2 is equal in magnitude and opposite in direction to the force exerted on Object 2 by Object 1.

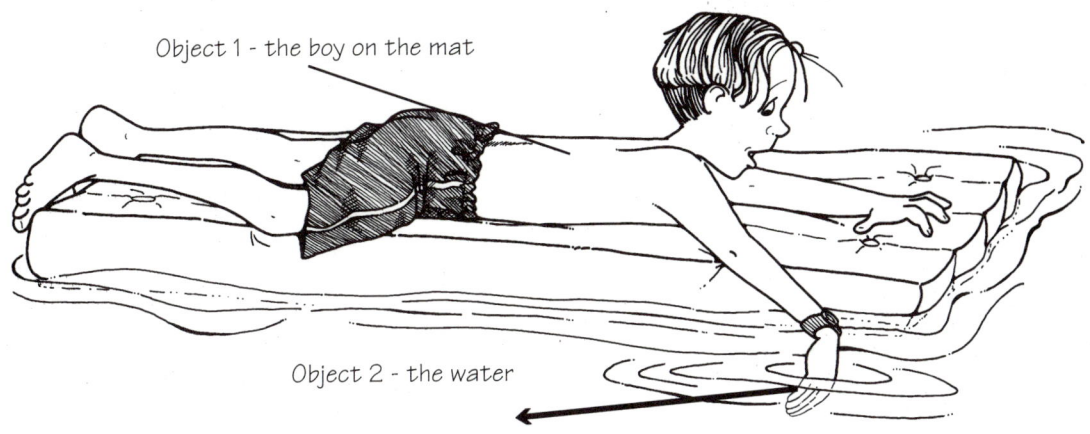

Object 1 - the boy on the mat

Object 2 - the water

If the boy on the floating mat is Object 1, and the water is Object 2, then, by Newton's third law of motion, when the boy exerts a force with his hand on the water, the water (Object 2) exerts an equal but opposite force on the boy's hand.

Newton's law is often stated this way: for every action there is an opposite but equal reaction. Stating the law this way hides the crucial fact that the *action force is on one object* while the *reaction force is on another object*. The action-reaction forces are not on the same object!

A boy floating on a mat is able to turn right or left, move forward or backward by exerting a force on the water.

Questions:

1. In the first picture the boy pushes water with his right hand in the direction shown by the arrow. In which direction will the floating mat and the boy move? [The boy and mat will turn to his left.]
2. In the second picture, the boy pushes water with his left hand in the direction shown by the arrow. In which direction will the floating mat and the boy move? [The boy and mat will turn to his right.]
3. What motions would the boy make with his hands to go forward? ... backward?

How A Skydiver "Flies"

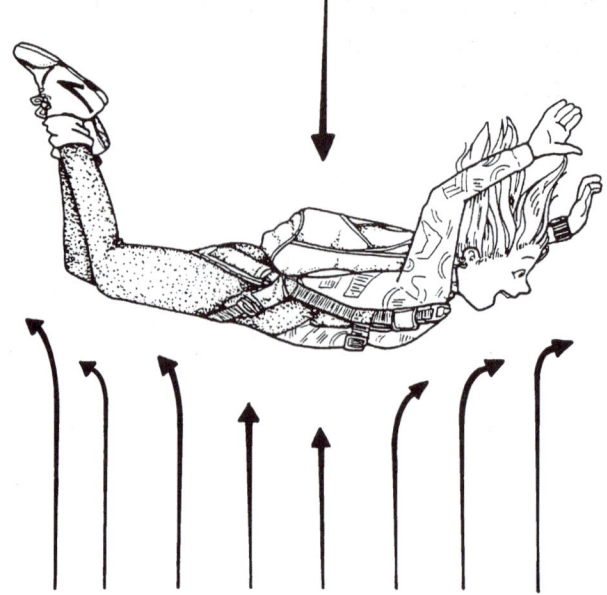

Newton's third law of motion states:

If two objects interact, the force exerted on Object 1 by Object 2 is equal in magnitude and opposite in direction to the force exerted on Object 2 by Object 1.

If the skydiver is Object 1, and the air passing over the skydiver is Object 2, then, by Newton's third law of motion, when the skydiver exerts a force on the air flowing past him/her, the air (Object 2) exerts an equal but opposite force on the skydiver.

A skydiver is able to fall straight down, turn left or right, move forward or backward by exerting a force (deflecting) on the air passing over his/her body. The reaction force on the skydiver then changes the direction of motion or position of the skydiver.

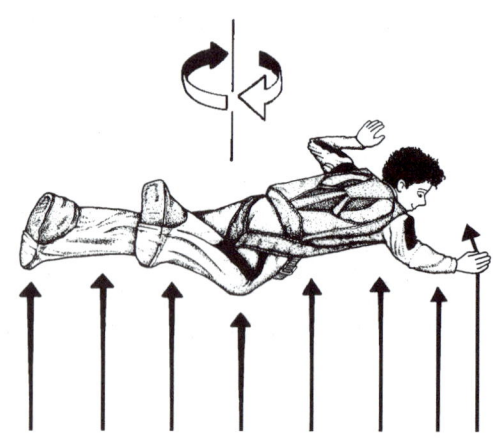

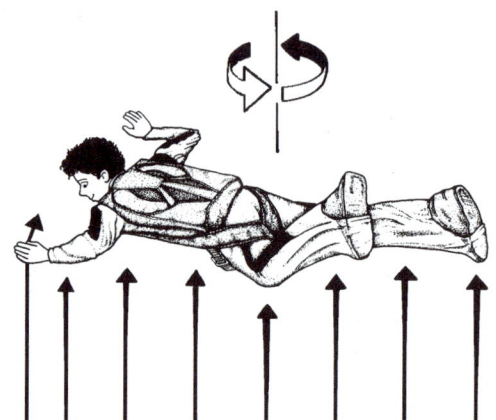

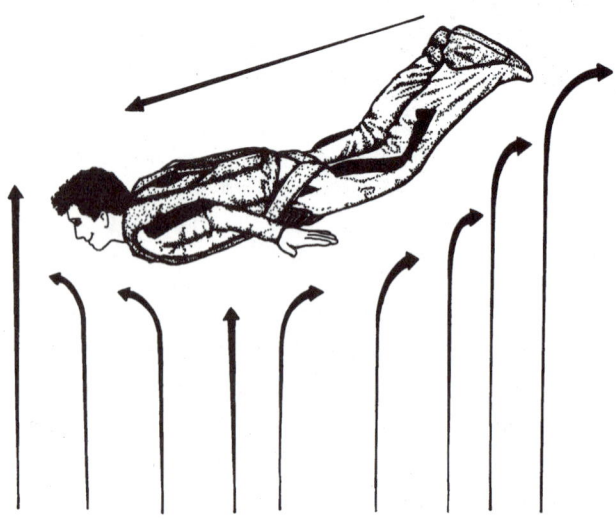

How Shelly's Parachute Opens

It takes two to four seconds for Shelly's parachute to open. Spreading the opening time over several seconds lessens the opening shock (the deceleration) she feels. It also gives time for the deployment bag, suspension lines, and risers to stretch out in a line before the canopy is pulled from its bag and begins to inflate. This helps minimize the possibility of the lines and bag getting tangled and causing a main canopy malfunction.

The Sequence of Events

See *Opening the Parachute*, video segment X, which includes a real-time and slow-motion replay of Shelly opening her parachute.

1. To start the opening sequence, Shelly pulls the pilot chute (a) from its pouch on the bottom of the container or the leg strap of the harness (b).
2. When she throws it into the air stream, the drag of the inflated pilot chute acts as an anchor as she continues to fall away. The bridle (c) stretches to its full length and pulls the main pin (d), opening the container. The bridle pulls the deployment bag (e) from the container.
4. As Shelly continues to fall, the risers (g) stretch to their full length and the suspension lines (h) are pulled from the rubber bands holding them to the deployment bag (see video segment II-3-c).
5. Once line stretch has been reached, the tension in the suspension lines pulls the main canopy from the deployment bag.
6. The slider, a small piece of fabric attached to the suspension lines and packed at the top of the suspension lines near the canopy, slows down the inflation of the canopy to further lessen opening shock (see *Opening the Parachute*, video segment X, 2, f).
7. The canopy fills with air and slows the descent of the skydiver.
8. Shelly is falling at approximately 176 feet per second (120 miles per hour) when she throws out the pilot chute. The opening sequence slows her to a speed of approximately 15 feet per second (10 miles per hour).
9. Shelly has been trained to follow a set of emergency procedures if, for whatever reason, something goes wrong with her parachute during this critical phase of her skydive. One procedure is to pull the cutaway handle to release a spinning or twisted main canopy and then pull the reserve handle to open her reserve parachute. She reviews and practices these emergency procedures on a regular basis.

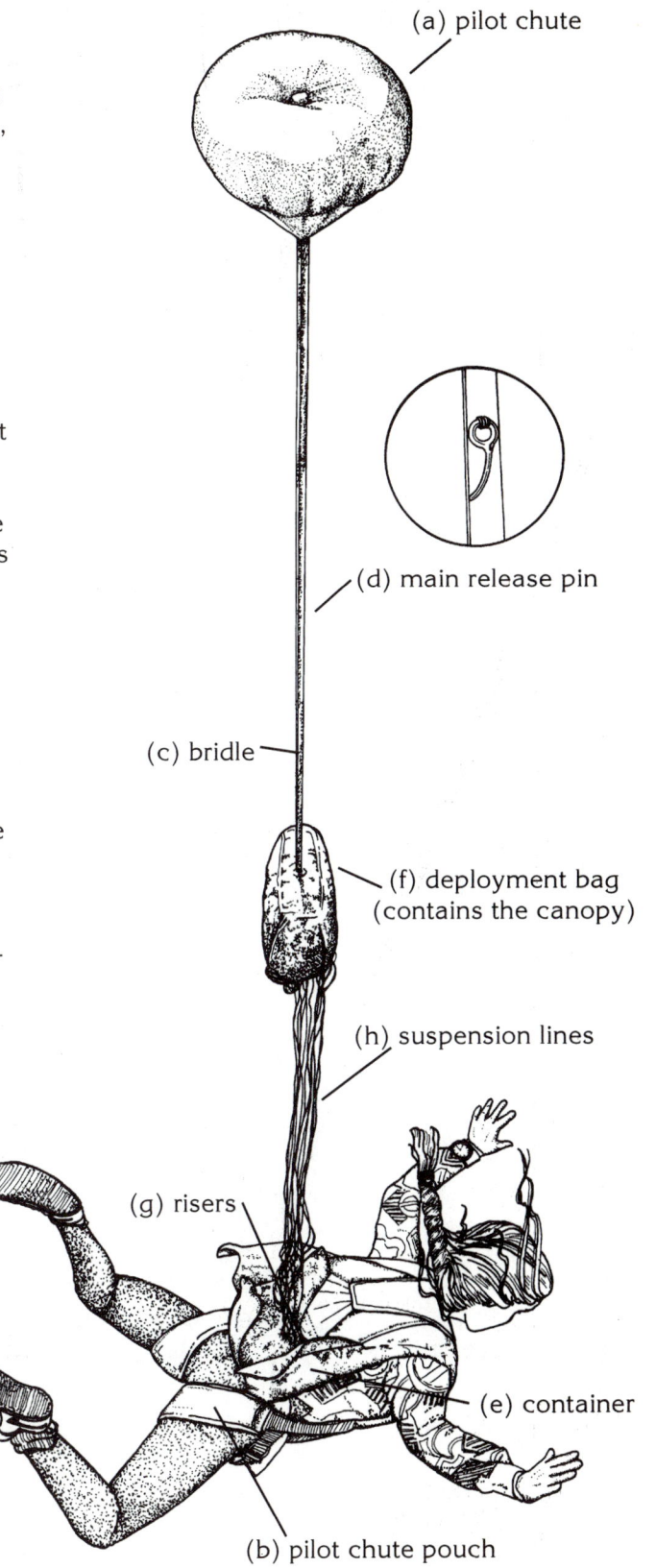

(a) pilot chute

(d) main release pin

(c) bridle

(f) deployment bag (contains the canopy)

(h) suspension lines

(g) risers

(e) container

(b) pilot chute pouch

A Close-Up Look at the Harness and Container

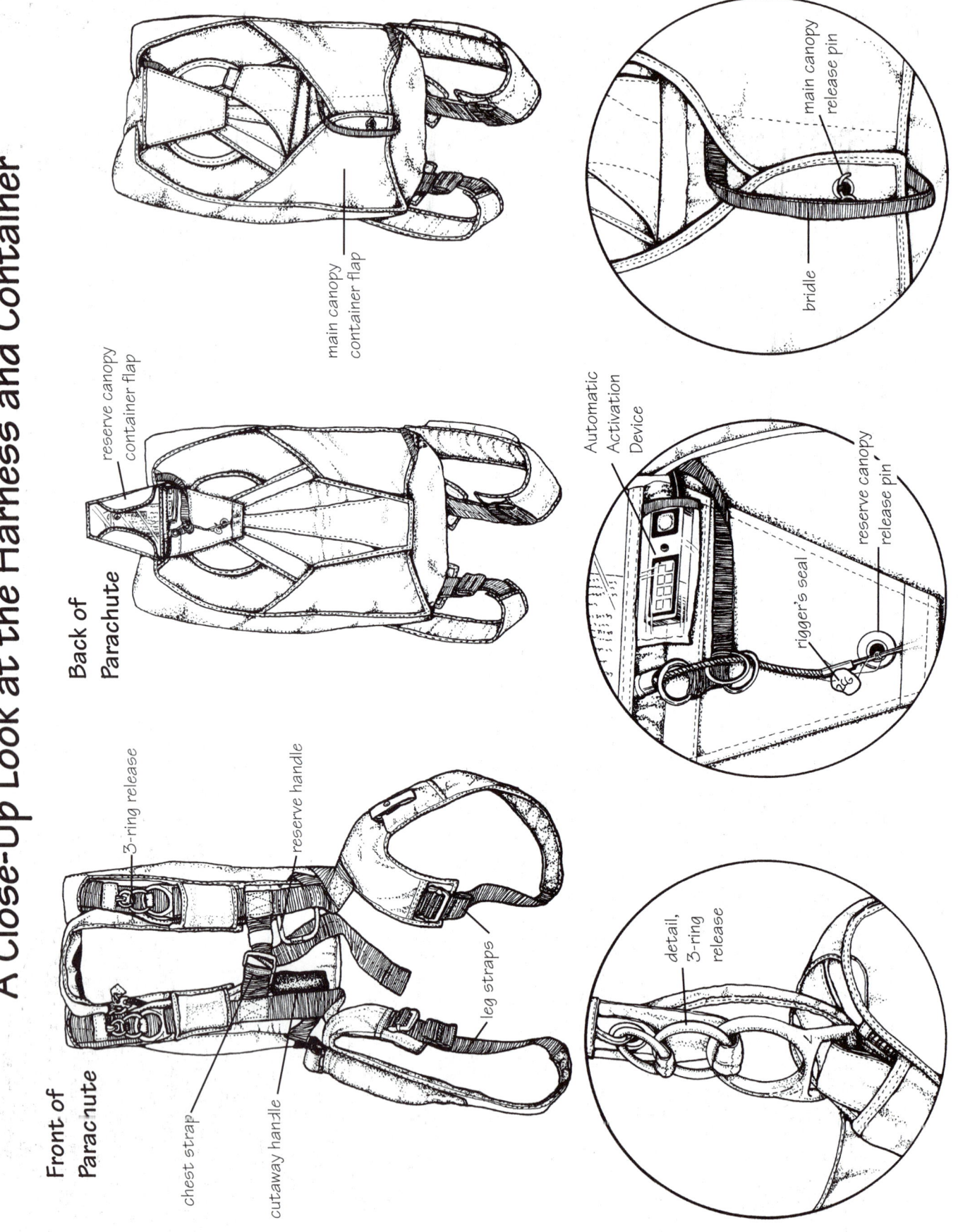

main canopy release pin

bridle

main canopy container flap

Back of Parachute

reserve canopy container flap

Automatic Activation Device

rigger's seal

reserve canopy release pin

Front of Parachute

3-ring release

reserve handle

chest strap

cutaway handle

leg straps

detail, 3-ring release

A Canopy Close Up

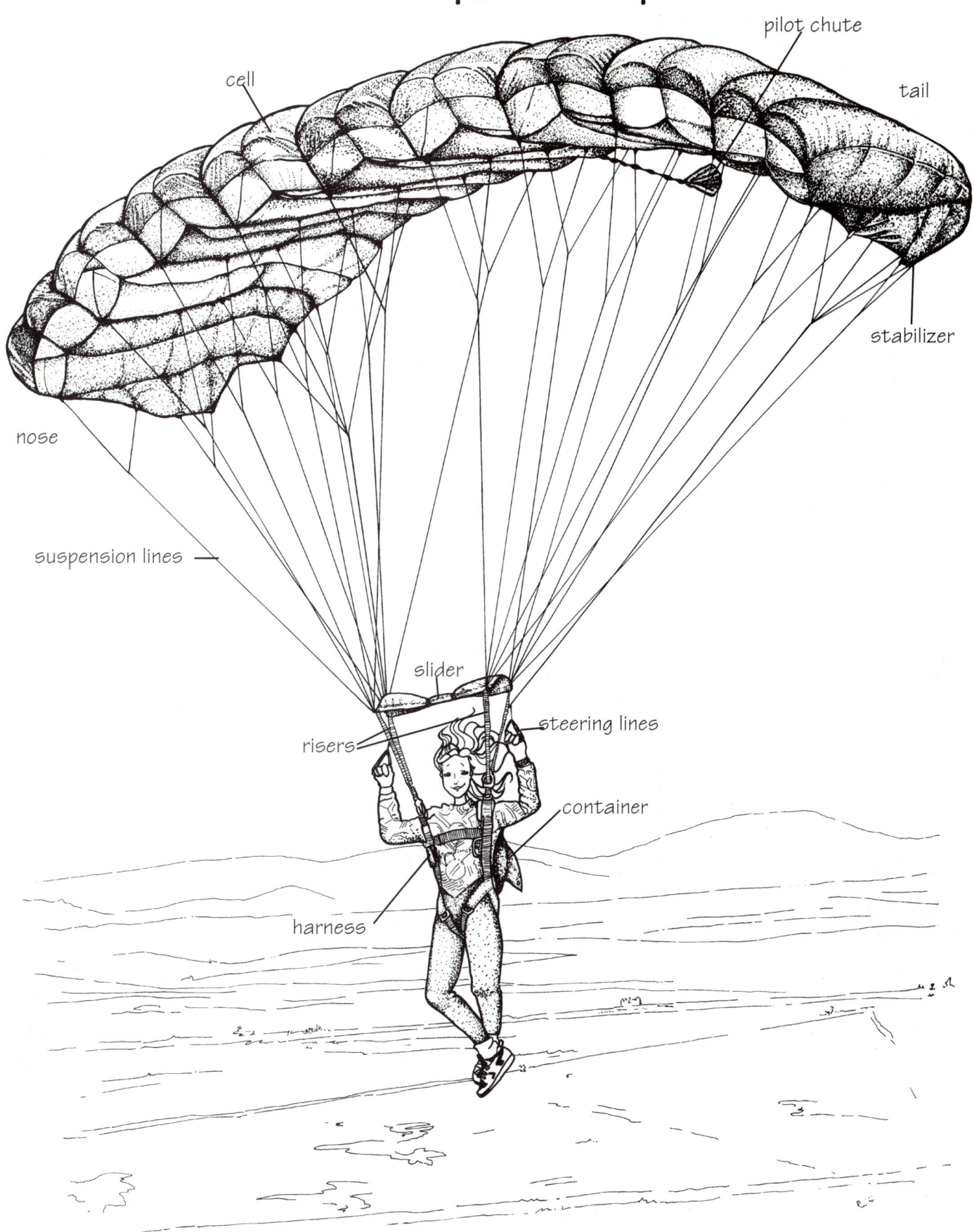

cell

pilot chute

tail

stabilizer

nose

suspension lines

slider

steering lines

risers

container

harness

WHAT IS TERMINAL VELOCITY?

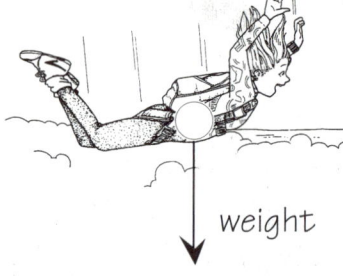

weight

The instant Shelly leaves the airplane and starts to fall, the attractive force of gravity pulling on her, called weight, causes her to fall faster.

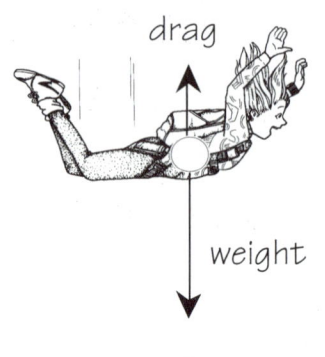

drag

weight

As her velocity increases, a resistive force (called *drag*) caused by air resistance, also begins to act on her in a direction opposite that of her weight.

At this point her weight is still greater than drag (weight > drag) so she continues to fall faster.

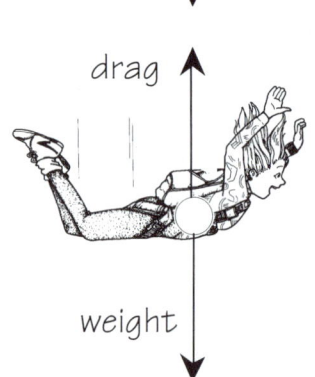

drag

weight

Her velocity continues to increase until she is falling fast enough for drag to equal her weight (weight = drag). When this balance is reached, she stops falling any faster but continues to fall at a constant rate called *terminal velocity*. This is an example of Newton's first law of motion.

Newton's first law of motion:

Consider a body on which no net force acts. If the body is at rest, it will remain at rest. If the body is moving with constant velocity, it will continue to do so.

The paper skydiver closely models Shelly's freefall motion because the forces acting on the paper skydiver are essentially the same as the forces acting on Shelly. The difference is that Shelly is able to control these forces to turn and move forward and backward during freefall whereas the paper skydiver cannot.

─────────────── **For the Physics Teacher** ───────────────

Newtons' second law of motion:

The acceleration (a) of a body is equal to the resultant of all forces acting on the body (f), divided by its mass (m). The acceleration has the same direction as the resultant force.

From Newton's second law, $a = \dfrac{f}{m}$: Substituting the forces acting on Shelly

(see the *Free-Body Diagram*) into the equation, $a = \dfrac{\text{weight - drag}}{m}$.

At terminal velocity, weight = drag and the equation simplifies to $a = \dfrac{0}{m}, = 0$.

Shelley continues to fall at the velocity she had when the forces acting on her became balanced.

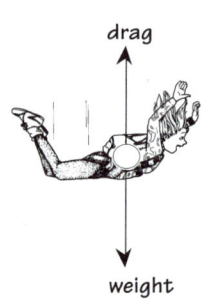

drag

weight

Free Body Diagram

Computing and Measuring the Terminal Velocity of a Hot Wheels® Car

Each car at the top of each track has a gravitational potential energy given by the expression *mgh* where *m* is the mass of the car, *g* is the acceleration due to gravity, and *h* is the vertical height. At the bottom of the track all of the gravitational potential energy has been converted to kinetic energy (the energy possessed by a moving object) given by the expression $\frac{mv^2}{2}$.

For this activity, it is assumed that all of the gravitational potential energy possessed by each car at the top of the track is converted into translational kinetic energy moving the car down the track. In reality, a portion of the gravitational potential energy is converted into rotational kinetic energy that turns the wheels. In any case, observe that the velocity of each car, when it reaches the bottom of the track, is at terminal velocity since the gravitational potential energy has reached zero and there is no longer any energy available to increase the velocity of each car.

The equations for the velocity of the cars is worked out below. These equations can be used to compute the terminal velocity for a car rolling down each track. The student pages containing the procedures for using the Texas Instruments Calculator Based Laboratory (CBL) system to measure the terminal velocities is found on pages A-11 through A-13 of the Appendix. If the Texas Instruments (or the equivalent) hardware and software is available, the computed values can be checked by comparing them to the measured values.

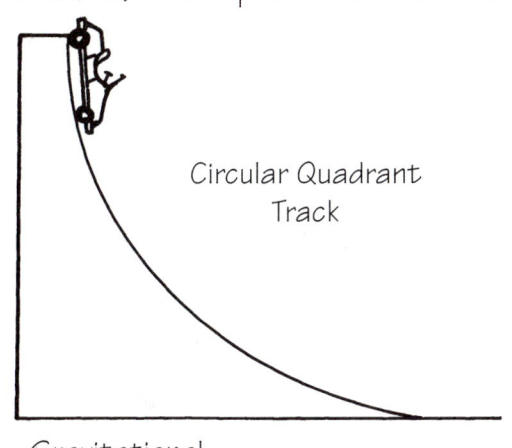

Circular Quadrant Track

Gravitational Potential Energy

Kinetic Energy

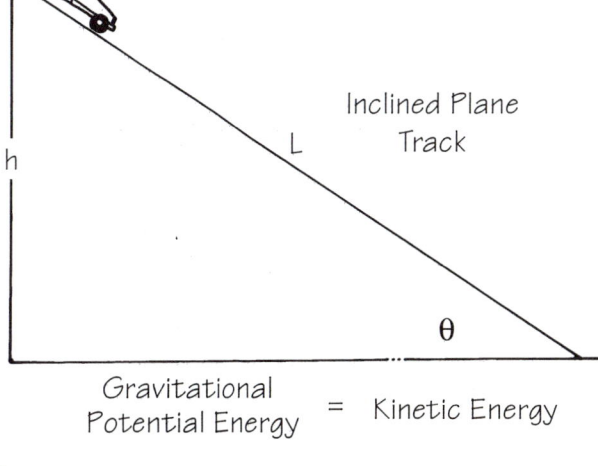

Inclined Plane Track

Gravitational Potential Energy = Kinetic Energy

Gravitational Potential Energy = Kinetic Energy

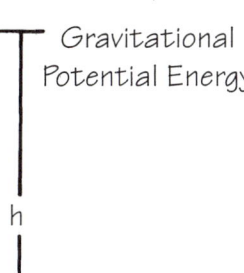

$$mgh = \frac{mv^2}{2}$$

$$2mgh = mv^2$$

$$v^2 = 2gh$$

$$v = \sqrt{2gh}$$

$g = 32$ feet per second per second

$$v = 8\sqrt{h} \quad \frac{ft}{sec}$$

$$mgh = \frac{mv^2}{2}$$

$$h = L\sin\theta$$

$$mgL\sin\theta = \frac{mv^2}{2}$$

$$v^2 = 2gL\sin\theta$$

$g = 32$ feet per second per second

$$v = 8\sqrt{L\sin\theta} \quad \frac{ft}{sec}$$

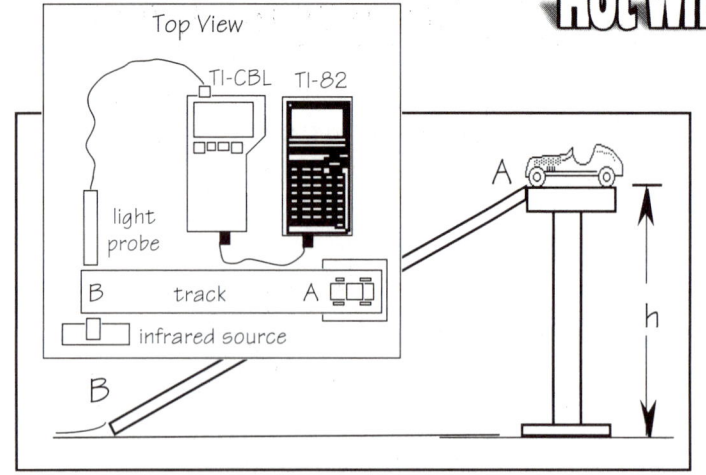

Measuring the Velocity of a Hot Wheels® Car

Procedure:

1. Make a infrared LED source (see A-11, *Constructing the Infrared Source for the Hot Wheels® Activity*). Set up track.
2. Measure and record the height, h, in inches.
3. Set up the light probe, infrared source, TI-82 and TI-CBL near the bottom of the track (point B).
4. Cut a rectangle from a business card equal to the length and height of the car. Tape the rectangle to the side of the car. The rectangle is a light shield that improves the accuracy of the time measurement made by the TI-CBL.
5. Measure and record D, the length of car in inches.
6. Use the TI-82 program STATUS to check the alignment of the light probe and infrared source. With the car between the probe and source, the TI-82 display should read BLOCKED. With the car removed, the display should read UNBLOCKED.
7. Start the program GATE on the TI-82. Place the car at the top of the track. Press ENTER to arm the gate and then release the car.
8. The time during which the car blocked the infrared beam is displayed at the top of the graph.

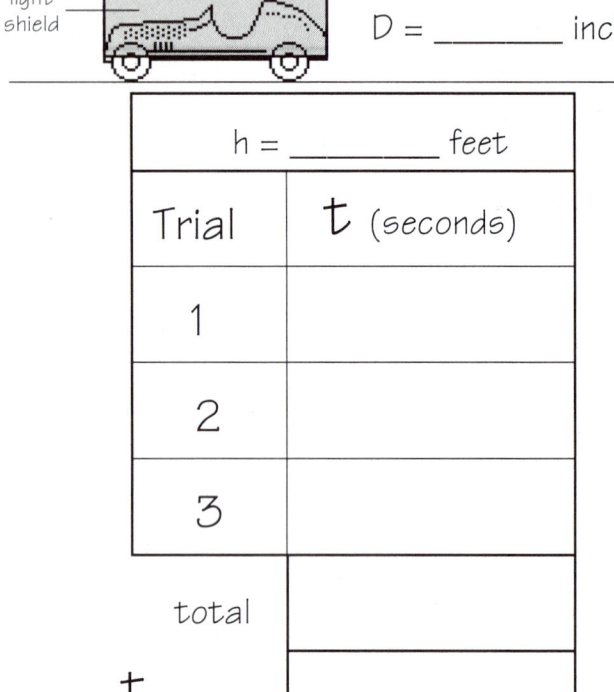

D = _____ inches

Trial	t (seconds)
h = _____ feet	
1	
2	
3	
total	
t average	

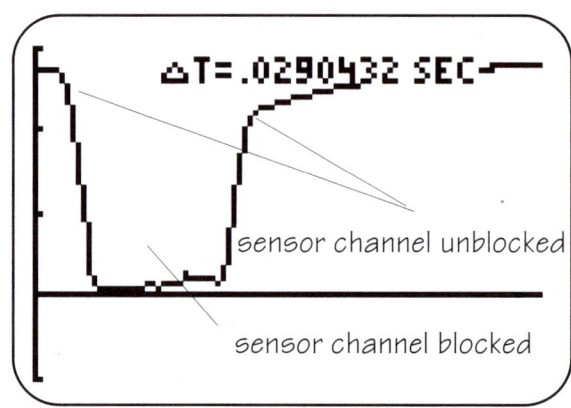

sensor channel unblocked

sensor channel blocked

9. Repeat the timing process two more times and then compute the average time .
10. Compute the velocity (feet per second) of the car, at point B, using the formula D = vt.

Distance = velocity X time. In symbols, D = vt. Divide both sides of the equation D = vt by t to obtain the equation, $v = \dfrac{D}{t}$

$$v \frac{feet}{second} = \frac{D \frac{feet}{second}}{t_{average}}$$

Convert the length of the light shield, D, from inches to feet.

$$\_\_\_\_ \text{ inches} \times \frac{1 \text{ foot}}{12 \text{ inches}} = \_\_\_\_\_ \text{ feet}$$

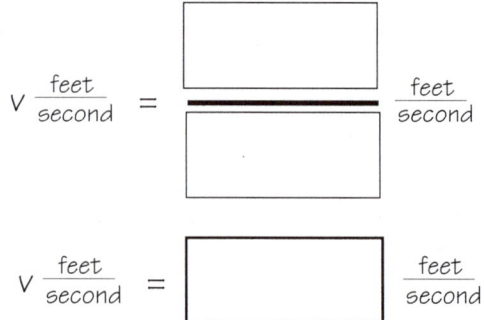

$$v \frac{feet}{second} = \frac{\rule{2cm}{0pt}}{\rule{2cm}{0pt}} \frac{feet}{second}$$

$$v \frac{feet}{second} = \boxed{} \frac{feet}{second}$$

A - 10

Procedure:

1. Purchase the required materials by part number at your local Radio Shack dealer.
2. Cut an 8 cm by 4 cm by 3 cm block of wood. Drill a five-sixteenths inch hole in one end of the block.
3. Use five-minute epoxy glue to permanently mount the LED holder in the hole.
4. Glue the switch to the block. Be careful not to get glue in the switch mechanism.
5. Solder the parts together according to the schematic. For this size block, you will not need additional hook-up wire.

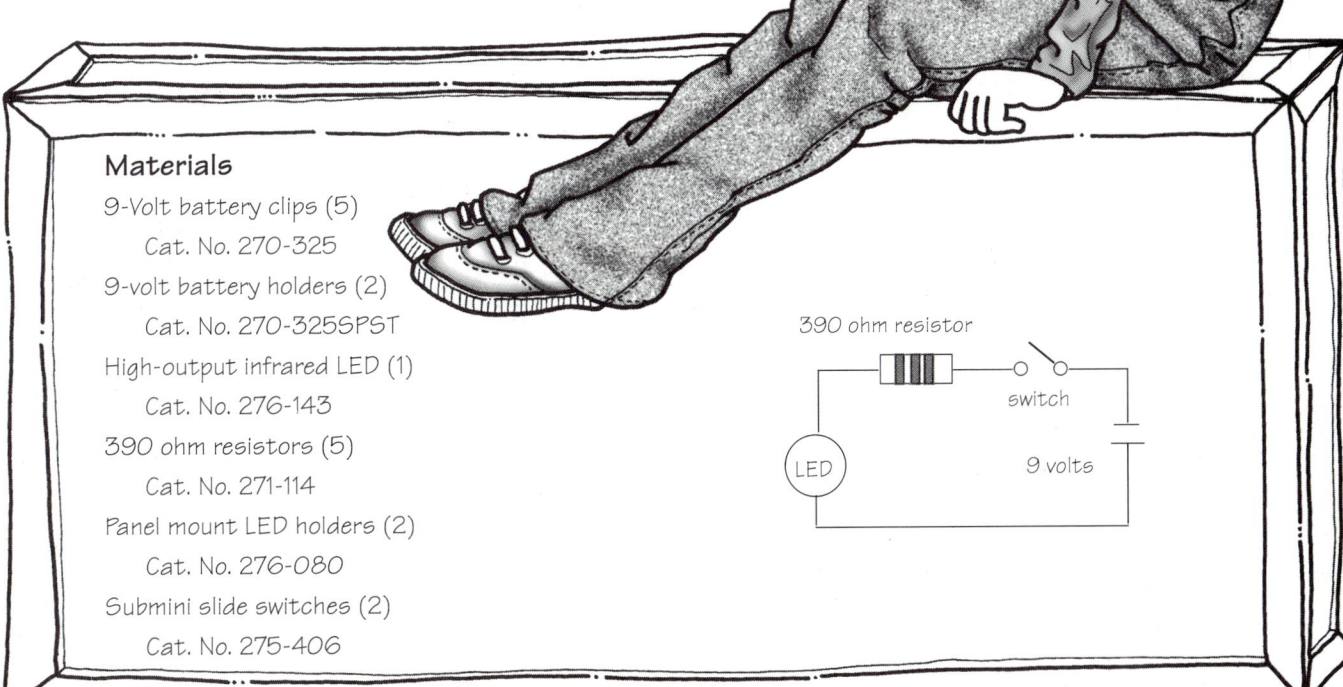

Materials

9-Volt battery clips (5)
  Cat. No. 270-325
9-volt battery holders (2)
  Cat. No. 270-325SPST
High-output infrared LED (1)
  Cat. No. 276-143
390 ohm resistors (5)
  Cat. No. 271-114
Panel mount LED holders (2)
  Cat. No. 276-080
Submini slide switches (2)
  Cat. No. 275-406

390 ohm resistor

switch

LED

9 volts

Computed

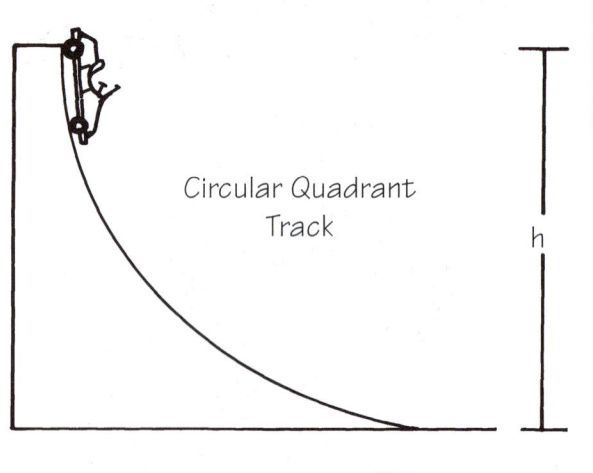

Circular Quadrant
Track

h

$$v = 8\sqrt{h}$$

h = 17 inches

$$17 \text{ inches} \times \frac{1 \text{ foot}}{12 \text{ inches}} = 1.42 \text{ feet}$$

$$v = 8\sqrt{1.42}$$

$$v = 9.53 \text{ feet per second}$$

Inclined Plane
Track

L = 2 feet

θ

$$v = 8\sqrt{L\sin\theta}$$

$$\theta = 30°$$

$$v = 8\sqrt{2 \times 0.5}$$

$$v = 8 \frac{\text{feet}}{\text{second}}$$

Measured

This is an actual display screen taken from a Texas Instruments graphing calculator. The CBL unit measures the time a car, of known length, blocks the light beam between a light detector and the CBL unit. Knowing the time interval and the length of the car, the student then computes the velocity.

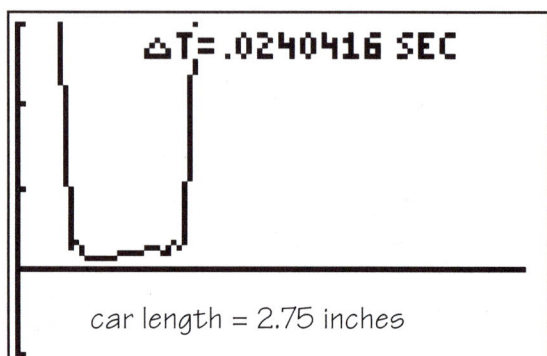

△T=.0240416 SEC

car length = 2.75 inches

$$2.75 \text{ inches} \times \frac{1 \text{ foot}}{12 \text{ inches}} = 0.23 \text{ feet}$$

$$v = \frac{\text{length}}{\text{time}} = \frac{0.23}{0.024} \frac{\text{feet}}{\text{second}}$$

$$v = 9.58 \frac{\text{feet}}{\text{second}}$$

△T=.0290432 SEC

$$2.75 \text{ inches} \times \frac{1 \text{ foot}}{12 \text{ inches}} = 0.23 \text{ feet}$$

$$v = \frac{\text{length}}{\text{time}} = \frac{0.23}{0.029} \frac{\text{feet}}{\text{second}}$$

$$v = 7.93 \frac{\text{feet}}{\text{second}}$$

TERMINAL VELOCITY
Teacher Page

Measuring the HEIGHT vs. TIME
Freefall of a Wiffle® Ball

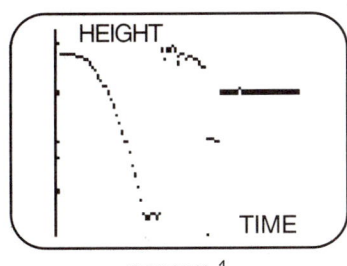

screen 1

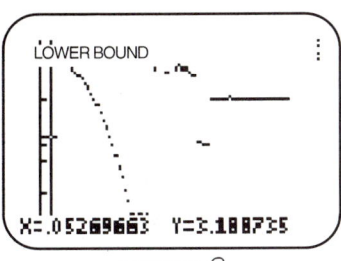

screen 2

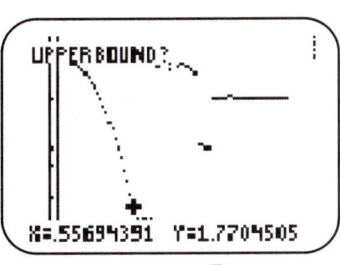

screen 3

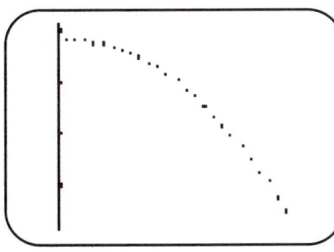

screen 4

screen 5

1. Load the BALLDROP and SELECT program into the calculator. Connect the calculator to the CBL.
2. Set up the same apparatus used to measure the terminal velocity of a paper skydiver. To protect the detector, stack books around it. Connect the detector to the SONIC port of the CBL. Turn on the CBL.
3. EXECute the BALLDROP program. The sonic detector should be emitting continuous audible clicks.
4. Hold the Wiffle® ball directly over the sonic window at a height of 5 to 6 feet.
5. Release the Wiffle® ball and press TRIGGER on the CBL at the same time.
6. After approximately 1.5 seconds, the CBL will send the data to the calculator. The message ANALYZING… will appear in the display. The HEIGHT vs. TIME graph will then be displayed on the calculator (screen 1). These are actual graphs copied (using the Graph Link™ hardware and software) from the calculator's screen.
7. From the program menu EXECute the SELECT program. Use the cursor left key to move the cursor to the lowest x-value (screen 2).
8. Use the cursor keys to move the cursor to the greatest x-value (screen 3). The ANALYZING… message will appear in the display screen as the selected data points are loaded into Lists L3 and L4.

Note: If a mistake is made, BREAK the SELECT program and start from the beginning. It may be necessary to use item 9, ZOOMSTAT, from the ZOOM menu to get the original graph.

9. The graph is then redrawn (screen 4) using the SELECTed points. This graph is obviously not the graph of a straight line.
10. Press the STAT key. From the EDIT CALC menu select number 6, QuadReg. Give L3, L4 as the lists so that the expression on the screen reads QuadReg L3,L4 and press the ENTER key.
11. The quadratic regression equation (screen 5) can be simplified to $y = -15x^2 + x + 5$. Of what famous law of falling bodies does this equation remind you? [Galileo's law for falling bodies, $s = 16t^2$]. What's the physical meaning of c? [The height from which the Wiffle® ball was dropped.]
12. Graph the regression equation and Galileo's law and compare the two graphs. What can you do to make the graphs closer in agreement?

Name _____

TERMINAL VELOCITY

Measuring the height vs. time Freefall of a Wiffle® Ball

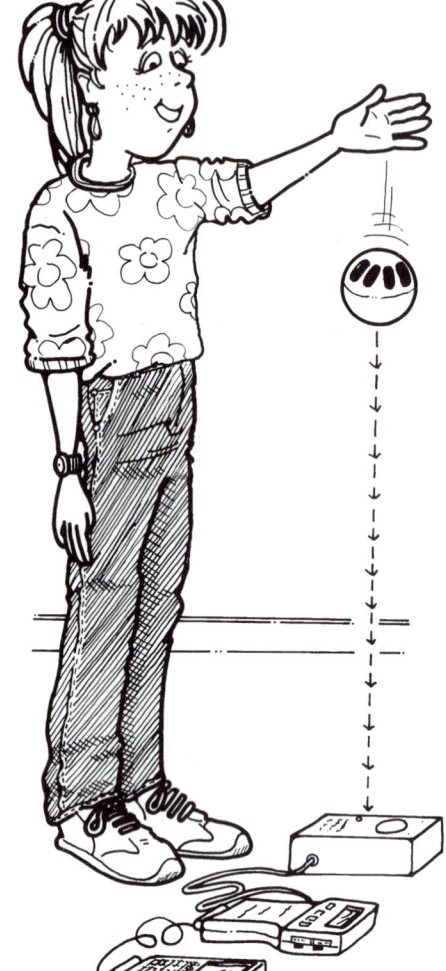

Procedure:

1. Load the BALLDROP and SELECT programs into the calculator.
2. Connect the sound detector cable to the SONIC port of the CBL. Connect the calculator to the CBL.
3. Turn on the CBL. EXECute the BALLDROP program. The sonic detector should be emitting continuous, audible clicks.
4. Hold the Wiffle® ball directly over the sonic detector window at a height of 5 to 6 feet.
5. Release the Wiffle® ball and press TRIGGER on the CBL at the same time. The CBL is now collecting HEIGHT and TIME data. After approximately 1.5 seconds the CBL will send the data to the calculator. The display screen on the calculator will show ANALYZING.... The HEIGHT vs. TIME graph will then be displayed on the calculator.
6. Copy the graph into display window 1 or use the Graph Link to get a hard copy and tape it into the window.

display window 1

display window 2

7. Use the SELECT program to capture the curved portion of the graph.
8. Copy the SELECTed graph into display window 2.
9. Press the STAT key. From the EDIT CALC menu select number 6, QuadReg. Give L3, L4 as the lists so that the expression on the screen reads QuadReg L3,L4 and press the ENTER key.
10. Copy the QuadReg equation into window 3.
    a. Of what famous law of falling bodies does this equation remind you?

    b. What's the physical meaning of c?

display window 3

11. Graph the regression equation and Galileo's law and compare the two graphs. What can you do to make the graphs closer in agreement?

MAKING A WIRE-FRAME SKYDIVER

1. Start with two four-inch pieces of unbraided wire.

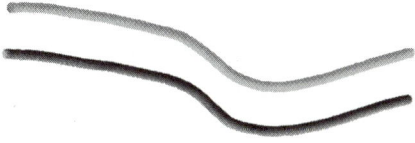

2. Cross the wires at their centers.

3. Tightly twist both wires several times.

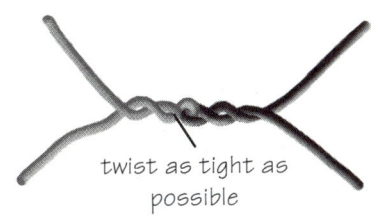

twist as tight as possible

4. Bend the arms and legs.

arms   legs

5. Bend the arch. Bend up the feet.

Side View

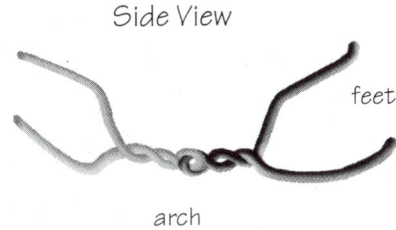

feet

arch

6. This step is optional. Bend a short piece of wire around a nail to make a loop. Twist the loop onto the shoulders to make the head.

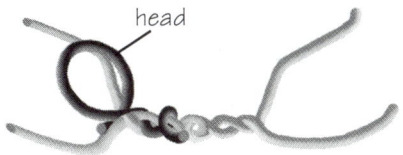

head

7. You may choose to add your own creative touches to the basic wire-frame skydiver. Just be sure that whatever you add to the wire-frame will not dissolve or weaken when submerged in fluids.

A real skydiver has to fall at a rate greater than 100 miles per hour in order to reach terminal velocity. A paper skydiver reaches terminal velocity very quickly because its weight is so small.

Both the real skydiver and paper skydiver fall through air. A wire-frame skydiver, like a real skydiver, will fall in air at a high rate of speed before it too reaches terminal velocity.

To decrease the wire-frame skydiver's terminal velocity, simply have it fall through a fluid like clear corn syrup.

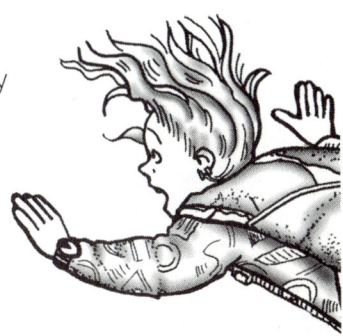

SKYDIVING IN A BOTTLE

1. Locate an empty glass or plastic bottle with at least a 12-ounce capacity. Test that your wire-frame skydiver will fit into the bottle.
2. Fill the bottle with water. Insert your wire frame skydiver into the bottle. (It should rapidly fall to the bottom of the bottle.) Fill the bottle to overflowing and cap tightly.
3. Turn the bottle upside down and observe the fall-rate of the wire-frame skydiver.
4. Empty the bottle and dry both the inside and outside of the bottle. Fill the bottle with light corn syrup. Insert your wire-frame skydiver, fill the bottle to the brim (to minimize air bubbles) and cap the bottle.
5. Now turn the bottle upside down and observe the fall-rate of the wire-frame skydiver.
6. Cut out one of the centimeter scales and tape it to the bottle in a vertical position.
7. Use a watch with a seconds hand and measure the time it takes the wire-frame skydiver to fall a given number of centimeters. Compute the terminal velocity of the wire-frame skydiver.
8. Try different fluids. Any fluid you use in this experiment should be very dense and flow slowly. Substitute one or more of these fluids for corn syrup and determine the terminal velocity of your wire-frame skydiver in each fluid.
   - cooking oil
   - different weights of motor oil
   - molasses
   - honey
9. The terminal velocity that a solid metal sphere reaches in a fluid is related to the viscosity of the fluid. To explore the concept of viscosity do the *Skydiving In A Test Tube* extension activity on the next page.

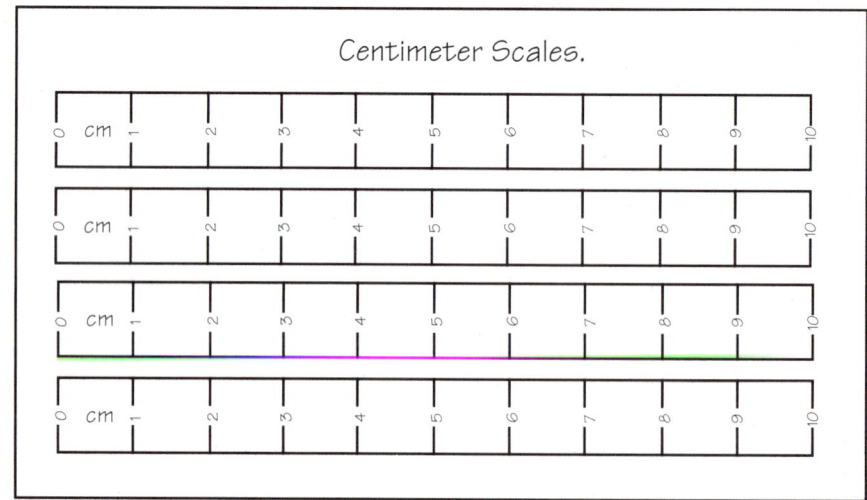

Centimeter Scales.

SKYDIVING IN A TEST TUBE

Terminal Velocity and Stokes Law

In 1845 the English scientist George Stokes studied the motion of a sphere falling through a viscous fluid. He found that the viscous force F acting on a sphere of radius r, falling through a fluid of viscosity η, with velocity v, is given by the equation

$$F = 6\pi\eta rv.$$

This equation is known as Stoke's Law

Stoke's law provides a method for determining the viscosity of a fluid if the following variables can be measured or computed.

F = resistive viscous force of fluid
B = buoyant force (equals the weight of the fluid displaced by the sphere)
w = weight of sphere
ρ = density of sphere
ρ′ = density of fluid

At terminal velocity, $v = v_t$, F + b + W.

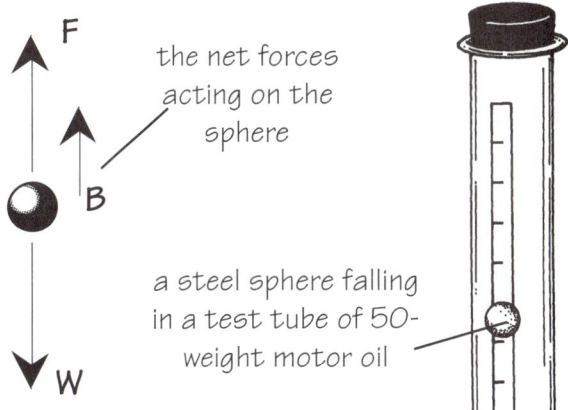

the net forces acting on the sphere

a steel sphere falling in a test tube of 50-weight motor oil

$$F + B = w$$
$$6\pi\eta rv_t + (4/3)\pi r^3\rho′g = (4/3)\pi r^3\rho g$$

1. Solve this equation for the terminal velocity, vt.

$$6\pi\eta rv_t + (4/3)\pi r^3\rho′g = (4/3)\pi r^3\rho g$$

2. Solve this equation for the viscosity, η.

$$v_t = \frac{2r^2 g\,(\rho - \rho′)}{9\eta}$$

$$\eta = \frac{2r^2 g\,(\rho - \rho′)}{9v_t}$$

This equation is a common method for measuring the viscosity of fluids. That's the next activity!

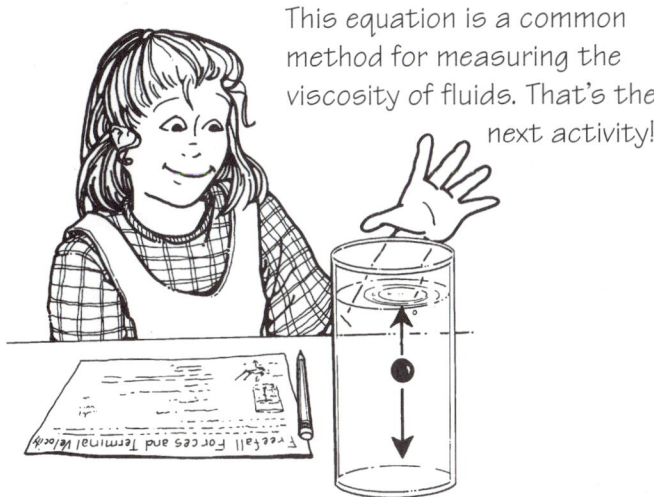

$$v_t = \frac{2r^2 g\,(\rho - \rho′)}{9\eta}$$

Measuring the Viscosity of a Fluid

 Sphere _____

Fluid _____

m = mass of sphere = _____ g

r = radius of sphere = _____ cm

v = volume of sphere = $(4/3)\pi r^3$ = _____ cm^3

ρ = density of sphere = _____ g/cm^3

m_f = mass of fluid = _____ g

v = volume of fluid = _____ cm^3

ρ' = density of fluid = _____ g/cm^3

$(\rho - \rho')$ = _____ − _____ g/cm^3

$(\rho - \rho')$ = _____ g/cm^3

g = 980 cm per sec^2

Materials:

One test tube with tight cork
Metal sphere that fits in test tube
Viscous fluid such as light corn syrup
Timer

Procedure:

1. Find the mass of the sphere.
2. Measure the radius of the sphere.
3. Compute the volume of the sphere.
4. Compute the density of the sphere.
5. Find the mass of the fluid.
6. Measure the volume of the fluid.
7. Compute the density of the fluid.
8. Fill the tube with the fluid until the fluid overflows. Drop the sphere into the container, top off the tube and seal as tightly as possible.
9. Cut out and attach a cm scale along the vertical axis of the tube.
10. Measure the terminal velocity of the sphere (cm per sec).
11. Compute the viscosity of the fluid.

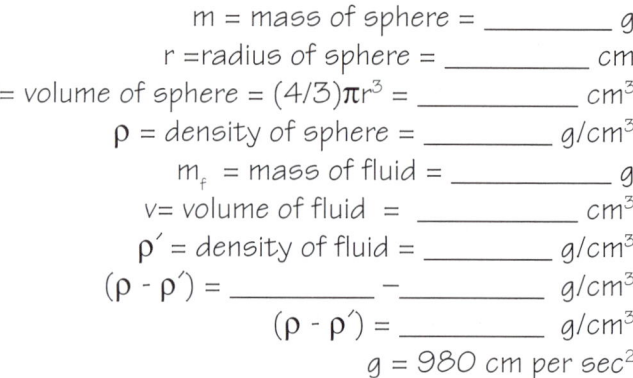

Observe and Measure

v_t = _____ cm/sec

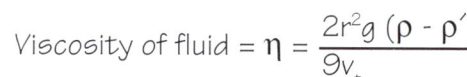

Viscosity of fluid = $\eta = \dfrac{2r^2 g\,(\rho - \rho')}{9 v_t}$

Viscosity has the centimeter-gram-second (cgs) units of $= \dfrac{\text{dyne} \cdot \text{s}}{\text{cm}^2}$

1 poise $= \dfrac{\text{dyne} \cdot \text{s}}{\text{cm}^2}$

A Parachuting Timeline

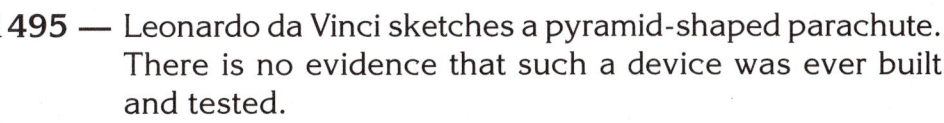

1495 — Leonardo da Vinci sketches a pyramid-shaped parachute. There is no evidence that such a device was ever built and tested.

1595 — Fausto Veranzio covered a square wooden frame with canvas and jumped from a tower in Venice, Italy.

1783 — In France, the Montgolfier brothers made the first balloon flight and later tested several parachute designs. They used a seven-foot canopy to safely lower a sheep.

1797 — On October 22, 1797, over a park located outside Paris, France, Andre Jaques Garnerin jumps from a balloon to become the first human to make a parachute jump.

1802 — Andre Jaques Garnerin jumps from a balloon 8000 feet over London, England. He used a silk parachute 23-feet in diameter.

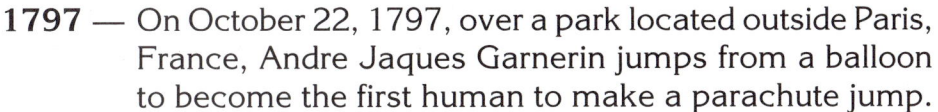

1808 — Warsaw, Poland. A Polish balloonist jumps from a burning balloon and successfully opens his parachute which saves his life.

1838 — The American John Wise twice let his balloon ascend to an altitude high enough to deflate the envelope. Each time, the deflated balloon assumed an inverted shape safely lowering him from heights of 13,000 feet.

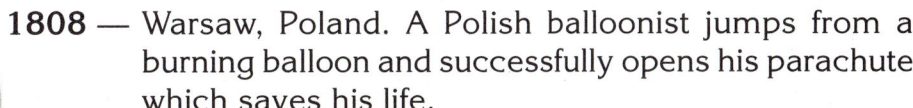

1865 — During the American Civil War, both sides used manned balloons to conduct reconnaissance flights. The observers did not have parachutes and many were lost to enemy fire and accident.

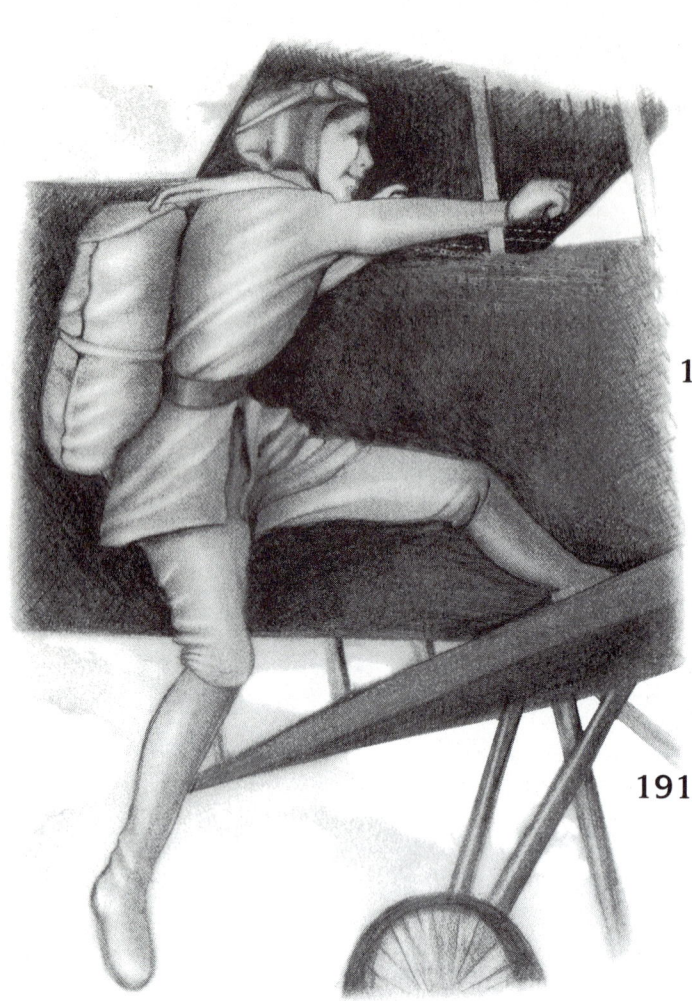

Tiny Broadwick

1908 — Georgia (Tiny) Broadwick, age 15, trained by her foster father, Charles Broadwick, makes her first jump from a balloon. This marks the beginning of Tiny's fourteen-year career as a parachutist in an aerial circus.

1911 — Grant Morton makes the first recorded parachute jump from an airplane flying over Venice, California.

1913 — Tiny Broadwick is the first woman to jump from an airplane. The jump was made over what is now the parking lot for the Los Angeles Zoo.

1914 — Tiny Broadwick demonstrates her father's Coatpack parachute for United States Government observers. The Coatpack is put on and worn like a coat. Impressed by her successful jumps, the U. S. Army ordered its first parachute.

1914-1918 — World War I. Balloon observers are issued parachutes.
Except for the Germans, near the end of the war, pilots did not use parachutes.

1918 — Leslie Irvin patents a manually-operated parachute. On April 28 of the following year he jumps from an airplane at 1500 feet over a field near Dayton, Ohio and pulls his own ripcord.

1922 — Tiny Broadwick retires from parachuting after more than 1100 jumps.

1923 — United States Army Air corps pilots are required to wear parachutes.

1925 — Steven Budreau, a United States Army flight instructor, jumps from an altitude of 7000 feet and freefalls to 3500 feet before opening his parachute. He demonstrates that a parachutist can remain conscious and fall without going out of control.

1926 — Charles Lindbergh makes his fourth emergency parachute jump. This was the year before he made his famous, solo transatlantic airplane flight. In the years before his famous flight, Lindbergh was a mail pilot, wing walker, and parachute jumper in flying circuses that toured the United States.

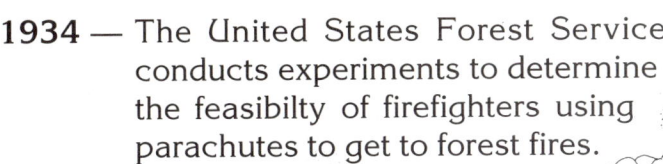

1934 — The United States Forest Service conducts experiments to determine the feasibilty of firefighters using parachutes to get to forest fires.

1938 — Du Pont invents nylon, a synthetic fiber that eventually replaces silk in parachute canopies.

1940 — German paratroopers drop *behind* the French Maginot Line. The Germans occupy Paris, France on June 14, 1940.

1940 — The United States Army begins training paratroopers at Fort Benning, Georgia. The jump school at Fort Benning is still in operation.

1944 — June 6th. Allied paratroopers lead the invasion by jumping at night into Nazi-occupied France.

1944 — Frank Derry modifies a surplus canopy by cutting six-foot-long vertical slits (*Derry Slots*) into the canopy to provide a measure of forward thrust and steerability to the canopy. Frank Derry was a civilian employee of the Eagle Parachute Company working with the *smoke jumpers* of the National Forest Service.

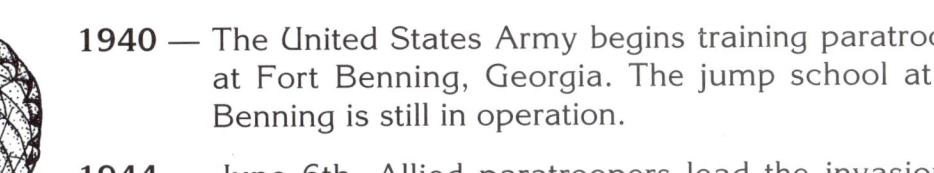

1958 — Charles Hilliard and Steve Snyder make the first freefall baton pass in the United States. The sport of two or more skydivers flying relative to each other is born.

1960 — On August 16th, United States Air Force Captain Joseph W. Kittinger, Jr. stepped out of a balloon at an altitude of 102,800 feet. A six-foot diameter drogue parachute was soon released to stabilize his fall. In the thin air, his freefall velocity reached 625 miles per hour by 90,000 feet. The gondola suspended beneath the balloon that carried Captain Kittinger to his launch point contained a placard that read, "This is the highest step in the world."

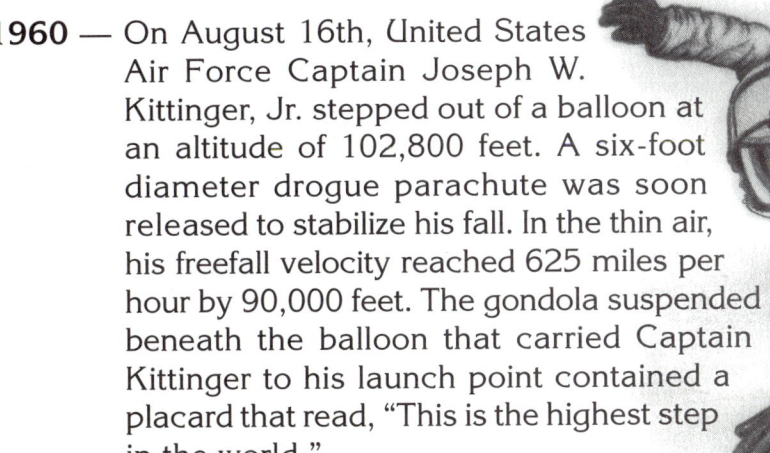

Domina Jalbert

1964 — Domina Jalbert invents the ram-air, fabric wing (called a *parafoil*) and flies it as kite.

1964 — The first 6-way formation is built over Arvin, California.

1966 — Jalbert receives patent number 3285546 for his multi-cell, wing type aerial device.

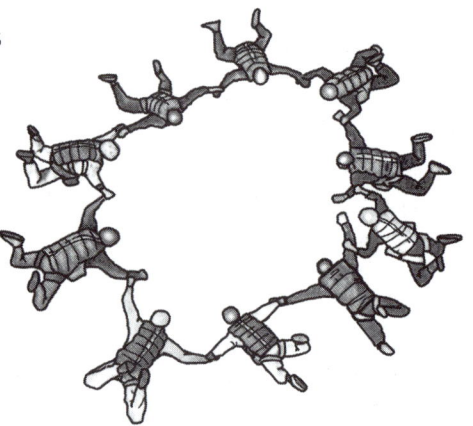

1965 — The first 8-way formation is built over Taft, California

1967 — The first 10-way star is built over Taft, California.

1968 — Steve Snyder, skydiver and aeronautical engineer, develops the Jalbert parafoil as a parachute.

1969 — Steve Snyder markets the Para-Plane ram-air canopy.

Steve Snyder

1972 — Tiny Broadwick is honored by the Adventurers Club of Los Angeles for her long and distinguished parachuting career. During the festive evening, Tiny is presented her Gold Wings, signifying 1000 jumps, by the United States Parachute Association (see *Tiny Broadwick and Bill Booth* at the end of the *Skydiver!* activity).

1976 — Bill Booth introduces the 3-ring release and hand-deployed pilot chute.

Bill Booth and Tiny Broadwick

1977 — The first tandem jump is made over DeLand, Florida by Mike Barber and Kirk Morrison.

1979 — Tiny Broadwick, "First Lady of Parachuting," dies at age 85.

1980 — Skydivers parachute into the Super Bowl football game as part of the opening ceremonies. The event is viewed on television by 125 million.

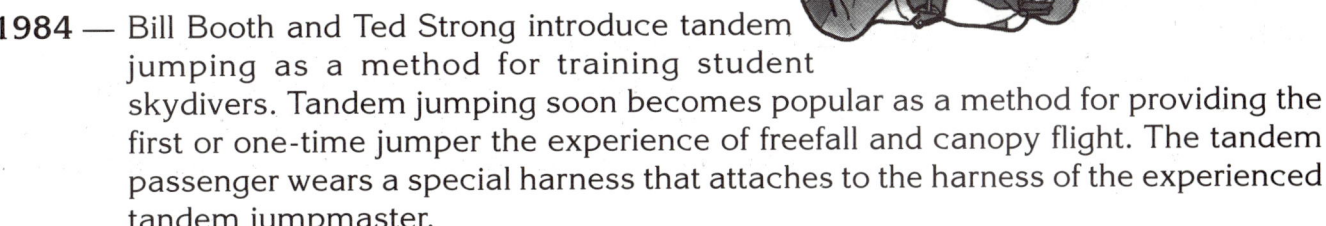

jumpmaster

passenger

1984 — Bill Booth and Ted Strong introduce tandem jumping as a method for training student skydivers. Tandem jumping soon becomes popular as a method for providing the first or one-time jumper the experience of freefall and canopy flight. The tandem passenger wears a special harness that attaches to the harness of the experienced tandem jumpmaster.

1986 — The world's first 100-way is built over Davis Field, Muskogee, Oklahoma.

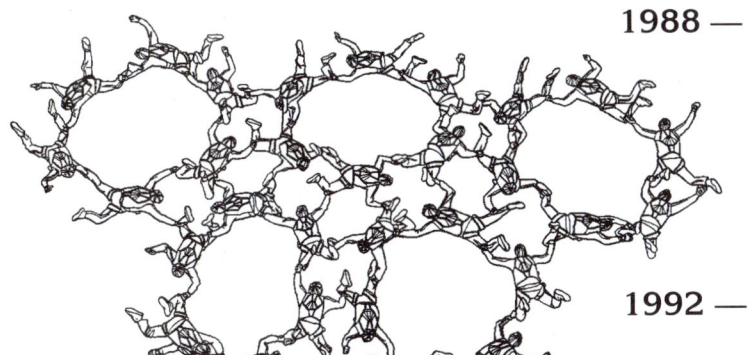

1988 — Thirty skydivers wearing color-coordinated jumpsuits and parachutes form the five Olympic Rings over the Olympic stadium in Seoul, Korea, to open the Olympic games. An estimated one billion view the ceremonies on television.

1992 — A 200-way is built over Myrtle Beach, South Carolina.

1995 — American Cheryl Stearns logs 352 jumps in 24 hours.

1996 — Three hundred male and female skydivers from 24 countries attempt a 300-way world record over Russia. They complete and fly a 297-way for over ten seconds. To be a record-breaking formation, the rules require that the planned 300-way formation be achieved.

1997 — A parachute safely delivers the *Pathfinder* to the surface of Mars.

1997 — March 25: George Bush, former President of the United States, completes accelerated freefall training and successfully does a Level I Accelerated Freefall skydive from an altitude 12,500 feet.

George Bush

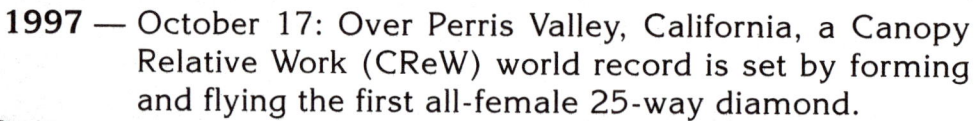

1997 — October 17: Over Perris Valley, California, a Canopy Relative Work (CReW) world record is set by forming and flying the first all-female 25-way diamond.

1997 — November 28: Yuma, Arizona. Jay Stokes makes 384 jumps in 24 hours.

1998 — Roger Nelson organizes a new world-record, 246-way, skydive. On July 26, 1998, 246 skydivers started building a formation 19,500 feet above Ottawa, Illinois. The formation held together and flew for 7.3 seconds.

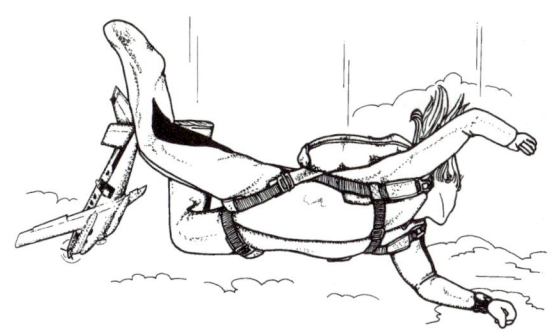

Note: Words or phases in italics are cross-referenced to other glossary entries. Only the first appearance of a word or phrase in an entry is italicized. Glossary entries that appear as video segments are cross-referenced by the video segment title — the Section (Roman numeral) — first subsection (numeral) — second subsection (letter) in which they appear in the *Video Companion* for the titled segment.

AAD — (*Automatic Activation Device*) An AAD is a small, computer controlled device that senses velocity (speed) and altitude. Preset by the skydiver, the AAD will activate and release the reserve canopy *if* the skydiver passes through a set altitude at a high rate of speed. An AAD is a life-saving device. By law, all student parachutes *must* be equipped with an AAD. (See *A Close Up Look at the Harness and Container* in the *Appendix*.)

AFF — (*Accelerated Freefall*) AFF is a seven-level sequence of skydives a student must complete before being allowed to jump alone. Two jumpmasters accompany the student on levels I, II, and III. Only one jumpmaster is in the air with the student on the remaining levels. (*Gravity Rules!*: I - 3)

AGL — (*Above Ground Level*) AGL is the vertical height above the ground as measured by an *altimeter*.

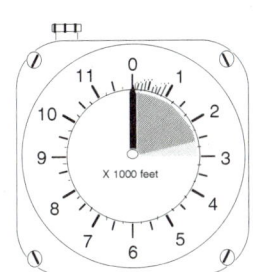

Altimeter — This is the instrument that indicates the skydiver's altitude above the level of the ground. Altimeters are typically worn on the wrist or attached to the chest strap. The single hand on the clock-like dial indicates the altitude in thousands of feet. Skydivers set their altimeters to 0 feet AGL before boarding the airplane. *Skydivers* usually open their parachutes at an altitude above 2000 feet. (*Gravity Rules!*: II - 7)

Arch — Arching his/her back lowers a skydiver's *center of gravity*. The lowered center of gravity puts the skydiver in a *face-to-Earth stable, body position*. Sometimes called a "hard arch." (*Gravity Rules!*: IV - 1 and VI - 2 - e)

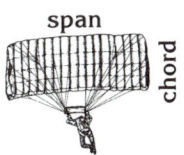

Aspect ratio — This is the ratio of the *span* of a ram-air canopy to its *chord*. Larger aspect ratios generate more *lift*.

BASE jumping — (**B**uilding, **A**ntenna, **S**pan, and **E**arth) A growing number of skydivers are jumping from tall buildings, TV antennas, bridges, and cliffs. (*BASE Jumping*: I - 1 - 10)

Beechcraft King Air — This is a popular airplane for carrying skydivers. Its two gas turbine engines help it quickly climb to altitude. (*Gravity Rules!*: VI - 1 - a and VI - 1 - e)

Break off — Skydivers performing a *relative work* (formation) skydive agree to the altitude at which they will stop their maneuvers. This is called the break off altitude. At break off, skydivers will *wave off* to signal no more maneuvers, turn 180 degrees, and *track* away from the center of the formation until they are clear to open their parachutes. (*Gravity Rules!*: III - 2 - b)

Bridle — This is an approximately three-foot long fabric band that connects the *pilot chute* to the *deployment bag*. The *main release pin* is attached to the bridle. The bridle pulls the main release pin, opening the *container*, and then pulls the deployment bag from the bottom of the container. (*Gravity Rules!*: II - 3)

Brown-blue — The term used to describe what it looks like to skydivers when they are tumbling through the air. The *brown* is the ground, the *blue* is the sky. (*Gravity Rules!*: I - 5 and III - 2)

Canopy — Synonymous with *parachute*, this is the fabric "umbrella" that lowers a skydiver safely to Earth. The first canopies were round (actually hemisphere-shaped) and are still the canopy of choice for paratroopers. For sport jumpers the "round" canopy has been replaced by the ram-air, airfoil-shaped canopy. (*Gravity Rules!*: II - 3)

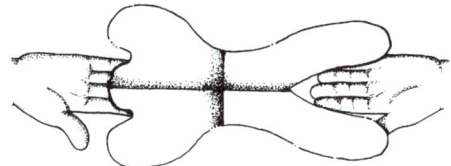

Cell — Two airfoil-shaped, fabric tubes sewn together (*Canopy Pilot*: II - 10)

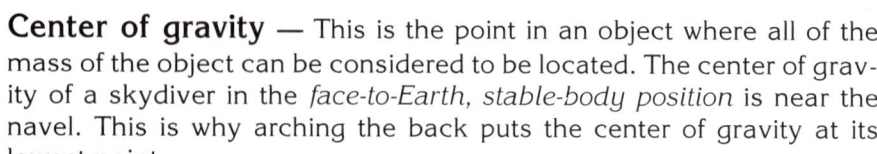

Center of gravity — This is the point in an object where all of the mass of the object can be considered to be located. The center of gravity of a skydiver in the *face-to-Earth, stable-body position* is near the navel. This is why arching the back puts the center of gravity at its lowest point.

Cessna 182, Cessna 206 — These single-engine airplanes are popular with drop zone owners and operators because they are cheap to fly. They carry the pilot and four skydivers.

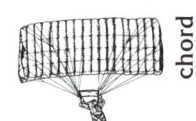

Chest strap — This is the part of the *harness* that, when buckled, keeps the *shoulders straps* on the shoulders of the skydiver. An *altimeter* is often attached to the chest strap. (*Gravity Rules!*: II - 1)

chord

Chord — The distance from the front, leading edge of an airfoil to its back, trailing edge

Container — This is the part of the parachute worn on the back of a skydiver that contains the packed *main* and *reserve* canopies. The container is basically a two-compartment bag, each with flaps held closed by a metal *main release pin* and *reserve release pin*. The container is attached to the harness. (*Gravity Rules!*: II - 2)

Creeper — The wheeled device that skydivers lay on and move and turn to practice a *relative work* (formation) skydive (*Gravity Rules!*: IV - 1)

CReW — An acronym for *Canopy Relative Work* which describes that class of skydivers that open their canopies as soon as they exit the airplane and then group themselves into formations

Cutaway handle — This is the pillow-shaped handle that, when pulled, activates the *three-ring release* located on each shoulder of the *harness*. When activated, each three-ring release separates the *main canopy* from the harness. (*Gravity Rules!* : II - 5)

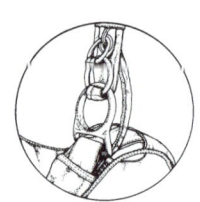

Deployment bag — This bag contains the packed *main* canopy. Rubber bands on the deployment bag grip the *suspension lines* to keep them from getting tangled. The *bridle* attaches to the bottom of the deployment bag. (*Gravity Rules!*: II - 3)

Dirt diving — When two or more skydivers plan a *relative work* skydive, they practice the exit from the airplane and the maneuvers they plan to do in *freefall*. They will often practice the freefall maneuvers by laying on wheeled platforms called *creepers*. (*Gravity Rules!*: IX - 7 - a, b)

Drop zone — This is the area, usually on or near an airport, designated for parachuting activity. Drop zone locations are indicated on the navigation maps used by pilots.

Drouge chute — This small parachute is used to slow down and stabilize a large suspended load. Tandem rigs have a drogue chute. [*Gravity Rules!*: 1-10)

Exit — This is the act of jumping out of an airplane. The exit is an important part of a skydive. A good exit puts a skydiver in a good body position or a good position relative to another skydiver. (*Gravity Rules!*: I -1, 2, VI - 2 - a, and IX - 7 - c)

Face-to-Earth, stable-body position — The safe body position taught to every first-jump student, the body position that is easily achieved and maintained by arching the back (*Gravity Rules!*: III - 1, 2)

Fall rate — This is the speed, usually expressed in feet per second, at which a skydiver is falling. Fall rate can be increased or decreased, within limits, by changing the body's frontal area. Fall rates between 140 feet per second (100 miles per hour) and 250 feet per second (170 miles per hour) are typical. (*Gravity Rules!*: V - 3)

Federal Aviation Administration (FAA) — The FFA is an agency of the federal government responsible for controlling and monitoring the nation's pilots, mechanics, airplanes, airports, and air space. The FAA recognizes the United States Parachute Association as the official representative of skydiving.

Flare — The action of pulling down on both steering lines is called a flare. This action creates a temporary reduction of vertical and forward speed. Skydivers flare when landing their canopies. (*Gravity Rules!*: VI - 2 -L)

Formation flying — This is the same as relative work. Formations are typically named for the number of jumpers in the formation; six jumpers make up a six-way formation. (*Gravity Rules!*: IX - 7)

Freefall — This is the portion of a skydive starting with the exit from the airplane and ending with the opening of the parachute. Freefall is the high-speed part of a skydive. A skydiver keeps a record in the log book of the amount of freefall time he/she accumulates. Awards are given for every 12-hours of freefall time accumulated.

Free flying — This is a high speed, heads-down form of skydiving. It is for experienced skydivers only. (*Gravity Rules!*: I - 6,7)

Funnel — A relative work skydive where the formation breaks up due to improper flying by one or more of the skydivers (*Gravity Rules!*: IX - 8)

g — The symbol g is used for acceleration due to gravity. Near the surface of the Earth g is approximately 32 feet per second per second.

Glide ratio — The ratio of the horizontal distance traveled to the altitude lost in traveling the distance (*Glide Ratio*: I)

Harness — This is the part of the parachute worn by a skydiver which attaches the parachute to the body. Each leg strap is adjustable and can be snugged down for a tight fit. The chest strap keeps the shoulder straps from slipping off the skydiver's shoulders. Many skydivers also attach their altimeters to their chest straps. (*Gravity Rules!*: II - 1)

Head-down flying — This is an extreme skydiving activity. Experienced and skilled skydivers will get into a head-down position and fly relative to one another. Extremely high terminal velocities can be reached in the head-down position since the area the skydiver presents to the relative wind is minimal. (*Gravity Rules!*: I - 6)

Jumpmaster — A jumpmaster is a skydiver certified by the United States Parachute Association to instruct student skydivers. Tandem jumpmasters are certified to carry a single passenger on a skydive. (*Gravity Rules!*: III - 1)

Jumpsuit — This is a special suit worn by skydivers. The suit is usually designed to fit the body tightly so the skydiver can fall fast. (*Gravity Rules!*: IX - 7 - a)

Jump run — This is when the airplane has reached the altitude at which the skydivers will jump, the pilot levels off and slows down the airplane. Based upon knowledge of the speed and direction of the winds on the ground and at altitude, the pilot or a qualified skydiver determines when to give the signal to jump. (*Gravity Rules!*: VI - 1 - h)

Lift — The force generated by air moving over and under an airfoil is called lift. Lift usually acts in a direction opposite to gravity.

Line stretch — This is the point in the opening sequence when the pilot chute, bridle, deployment bag, suspension lines, and risers are aligned. After line stretch is reached the main canopy is pulled from the deployment bag for inflation. (*Gravity Rules!*: X)

Load — The group of skydivers going in the airplane (*Gravity Rules!*: VI - 1 - d)

Log book — This is the book in which skydivers keep a record of their jumps. Besides the number of the jump, the date, location, airplane type, equipment, freefall time, and any special maneuvers are also described. If necessary, a licensed pilot or jumpmaster signs the log entry as a means of verifying the skydiver's performance. The log book is an important document. When a skydiver applies for a license or award, the signed entries in the logbook are accepted as proof of performance.

Main parachute (canopy) — This is the fabric, ram-air parachute packed in the deployment bag. The deployment bag is packed in the bottom of the container. Skydivers pack their own main parachutes after every jump. (*Gravity Rules!*: II - 2)

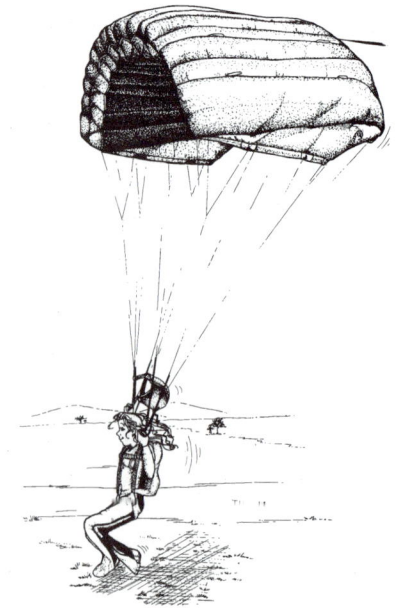

Main release pin — This is the curved metal pin sewn to the bridle that holds the container closed. The inflated pilot chute pulls the main release pin opening the container until it is pulled by the bridle. (*Gravity Rules!*: II - 3)

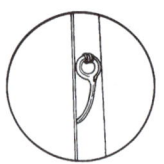

Malfunction — A malfunction occurs when something goes wrong with any part of the skydiver's equipment. If the main canopy malfunctions, the skydiver will generally pull the cutaway handle to release it from the harness. The skydiver will then pull the reserve handle to activate the reserve parachute.

Opening sequence — This is the sequence of events beginning with the throwing of the pilot chute into the air stream and ending with the successful opening of the main canopy. (*Gravity Rules!*: X)

Opening shock — The deceleration force felt by a skydiver during the opening of their parachute is called the opening shock. A typical skydiver will slow down from 180 feet per second to 15 feet per second as the parachute opens. The slider reduces opening shock. (*Gravity Rules!*: X)

Parachute — Synonymous with canopy, the fabric "umbrella" that lowers a skydiver safely to Earth

Pilot chute — This is the small (approximately 30 inches in diameter) parachute connected to one end of the bridle. The skydiver pulls the pilot chute from its pouch and throws it into the air stream. Its inflation starts the opening sequence. (*Gravity Rules!*: II - 3)

Pin check — This is a safety check that skydivers perform at least once before jumping from an airplane. The security of the main and reserve closing pins, the routing of the bridle, the three-ring release, and the leg and chest straps are checked. If the skydiver's rig has an automatic opener, it is checked to make sure it is switched on and properly set.

Potato chipping — The slightly unstable, side-to-side motion of a skydiver in the face-to-Earth position (*Gravity Rules!*: III - 2 - b)

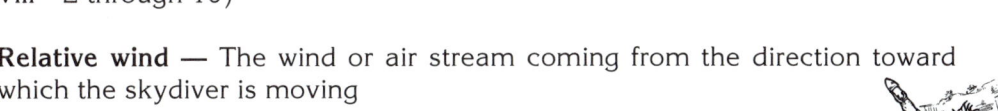

Ram-air parachute — A fabric, airfoil-shaped parachute invented by Domina C. Jalbert in 1964 (*Gravity Rules!*: I - 3, II - 3 through 4, and VIII - 2 through 10)

Relative wind — The wind or air stream coming from the direction toward which the skydiver is moving

Relative work — This is a freefall maneuver performed by two or more skydivers. Even though each skydiver is falling at a high rate of speed, one can still move relative to another. Relative work is a very competitive, team sport. (*Gravity Rules!*: IX - 8, 9)

Reserve parachute (canopy) — Only riggers certified by the Federal Aeronautics Administration (FAA) are allowed to pack the reserve parachute. The skydiver's reserve, whether or not it's been used, must be unpacked, inspected, and repacked by a rigger every four months. The rigger secures a small lead seal to the reserve release pin. As long as this seal is not broken, the skydiver knows the reserve was last inspected and packed by a certified rigger. (*Gravity Rules!*: II - 2 and II - 6)

Reserve handle — This is the metal, D-shaped handle stored in a pouch sewn on the left side of the harness. Pulling the reserve handle pulls the reserve release pin releasing the spring-loaded reserve pilot chute. (*Gravity Rules!*: II - 6)

Reserve release pin — This is the straight metal pin that holds the reserve section of the container closed. The reserve handle, when pulled, pulls the reserve release pin opening the reserve section of the container. (*Gravity Rules!*: II - 6)

Rig — The term skydivers use when referring to their harness, container, main, and reserve canopies (*Gravity Rules!*: II - 1, 2, 3)

Rigger — A person certified by the Federal Aviation Administration to pack reserve parachutes and repair parachute equipment

Risers — These are short, three-foot long fabric strips. A three-ring release system is attached to one end of the riser. This end of the riser is then attached to the harness at the shoulder. The other end of the riser has metal connecting links that attach to the suspension lines. Each harness has four risers, two front risers and two rear risers. (*Gravity Rules!*: X - 1,2)

Round — The name given to the traditional, umbrella-shaped parachute canopy still used by smoke jumpers and Army paratroopers (*Canopy Pilot*: II 14-19)

Sit flying — Instead of a face-to-Earth, stable position, the skydiver falls in a sitting position. This is done only by experienced skydivers.

Skydive — A parachutist exits an airplane, flies the body during freefall, opens the parachute to slow the descent rate, and then flies the wing-like canopy to a landing.

Skysurfer — A skydiver that attaches a surfboard to his or her feet and surfs the 100 plus miles per hour relative wind (*Gravity Rules!*: I - 3)

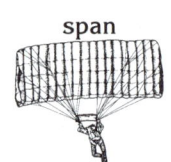

Slider — This is a rectangular piece of fabric that slides down the suspension lines to keep the suspension lines separated into four groups. It also slows the opening of a ram-air parachute to reduce opening shock. (*Gravity Rules!*: X -1,2)

Slot — The position assigned to each skydiver in a relative work formation (*Gravity Rules!*: IX - 9)

Span — The length of a wing or ram-air canopy from wing tip to wing tip

span

Spot — This is the positioning of the jump airplane over the drop zone. The spotter makes adjustments for any winds aloft and determines when skydivers can jump. Spotting is usually done by a qualified skydiver or the pilot.

Snivel — The slow opening of a parachute

Speed — Speed is the rate at which distance changes with time. For example, an automobile traveling on a highway at a speed of 65 miles per hour is changing distance at the rate of 65 miles every hour. Speed indicates the rate at which distance is changing with time but does not indicate the direction in which this change is occurring (see velocity).

Square — This is the name given to the ram-air canopy. It is not an accurate term since ram-air canopies are not square. The term is meant to describe the contrast between a round canopy and a square ram-air canopy.

Steering Lines — These are the lines attached to the rear of the main canopy that the skydiver pulls on to control the direction of flight. Pulling down on the right steering line causes the canopy to turn to the right. Pulling down on the left steering line causes the canopy to turn to the left. Pulling down on both steering lines causes the canopy to flare. The ends of the steering lines have loops, called toggles, that provide the skydiver good hand grips. (*Gravity Rules!*: II - 4)

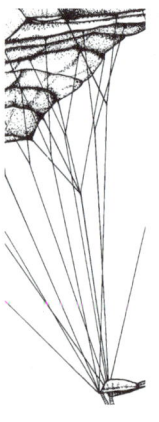

Step — A platform attached to the outside of the airplane on which skydivers stand (*Canopy Pilot*: II - 15)

Suspension lines — These are the thin but strong lines that connect the top of each riser to the bottom of the ram-air canopy. The suspension lines carry and distribute the weight of the skydiver over the bottom surface of the canopy without distorting the airfoil shape of the canopy. (*Gravity Rules!*: II - 3)

Taxi — An airplane in motion on the ground (*Gravity Rules!*: VI - 1 - a)

Tandem jump — This is a popular way to make the first skydive. The harness of a tandem jumpmaster connects to the harness of a passenger. The tandem jumpmaster carries the passenger during freefall and when the parachute opens. Ram-air canopies with large surface areas are used to carry the double weight of jumpmaster and passenger. (*Gravity Rules!*: VIII - 4)

Terminal velocity — This is the velocity attained in freefall at which the force due to air resistance balances the weight (the force due to gravitational attraction) of the falling object. A typical skydiver attains a terminal velocity of approximately 170 feet per second (120 miles per hour). Terminal velocity can be changed by changing the frontal area presented to the air stream thereby increasing or decreasing the force due to air resistance.

Three-ring release — There are three metal rings of decreasing diameters connected to the bottoms of the risers. The rings carry the suspended load of the skydiver. When the cutaway handle is pulled, the rings release the main canopy. (*Gravity Rules!*: II - 5)

Three-way — Relative work skydives are generally described by the number of skydivers in the formation. A three-way consists of three skydivers, a hundred-way consists of 100 skydivers. (*Gravity Rules!*: IX - 7, 8, 9)

Toggles — The loops at the lower end of the steering lines that the skydiver grips in order to steer the canopy (*Gravity Rules!*: II - 4)

Track — This is the body position in which skydivers sweep their arms backwards, close to their sides, and straighten their legs to achieve maximum horizontal movement. It is used to create separation between skydivers after break off from a relative work skydive. (*Gravity Rules!*: VI - b)

Turning points — Scores are attached to relative work skydives, one point is earned for every formation change. (*Gravity Rules!*: IX - 9)

United States Parachute Association (USPA) — The USPA is an organization officially recognized by the Federal Aviation Administration as the representation of the nation's skydivers. The USPA certifies jumpmasters and issues licenses. The organization is made up of over 30,000 skydivers, 15 per cent of which are women.

Velocity — Speed in a given direction is called velocity (see terminal velocity).

Wave off — The overhead crossing of the hands and arms used by a skydiver to signal that he/she is about to open the parachute (*Gravity Rules!*: III - 2 - b)

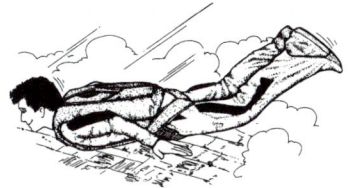

Wind sail — This is a wind sock (see next entry) which is shaped like a sail and is used to indicate wind direction.

Wind sock — This is a fabric tube, open at one end, mounted on a swivel attached to a vertical pole so that it can turn in any direction. If the wind is blowing, the sock fills with air and turns so that its open end faces into the wind. Skydivers — and pilots too — use the wind sock to determine which way the wind is blowing. Landings are made into the wind. (*Glide Ratio:* V)

The AIMS Program

AIMS is the acronym for "Activities Integrating Mathematics and Science." Such integration enriches learning and makes it meaningful and holistic. AIMS began as a project of Fresno Pacific University to integrate the study of mathematics and science in grades K-9, but has since expanded to include language arts, social studies, and other disciplines.

AIMS is a continuing program of the non-profit AIMS Education Foundation. It had its inception in a National Science Foundation funded program whose purpose was to explore the effectiveness of integrating mathematics and science. The project directors in cooperation with 80 elementary classroom teachers devoted two years to a thorough field-testing of the results and implications of integration.

The approach met with such positive results that the decision was made to launch a program to create instructional materials incorporating this concept. Despite the fact that thoughtful educators have long recommended an integrative approach, very little appropriate material was available in 1981 when the project began. A series of writing projects have ensued and today the AIMS Education Foundation is committed to continue the creation of new integrated activities on a permanent basis.

The AIMS program is funded through the sale of this developing series of books and proceeds from the Foundation's endowment. All net income from program and products flows into a trust fund administered by the AIMS Education Foundation. Use of these funds is restricted to support of research, development, and publication of new materials. Writers donate all their rights to the Foundation to support its on-going program. No royalties are paid to the writers.

The rationale for integration lies in the fact that science, mathematics, language arts, social studies, etc., are integrally interwoven in the real world from which it follows that they should be similarly treated in the classroom where we are preparing students to live in that world. Teachers who use the AIMS program give enthusiastic endorsement to the effectiveness of this approach.

Science encompasses the art of questioning, investigating, hypothesizing, discovering, and communicating. Mathematics is the language that provides clarity, objectivity, and understanding. The language arts provide us powerful tools of communication. Many of the major contemporary societal issues stem from advancements in science and must be studied in the context of the social sciences. Therefore, it is timely that all of us take seriously a more holistic mode of educating our students. This goal motivates all who are associated with the AIMS Program. We invite you to join us in this effort.

Meaningful integration of knowledge is a major recommendation coming from the nation's professional science and mathematics associations. The American Association for the Advancement of Science in *Science for All Americans* strongly recommends the integration of mathematics, science, and technology. The National Council of Teachers of Mathematics places strong emphasis on applications of mathematics such as are found in science investigations. AIMS is fully aligned with these recommendations.

Extensive field testing of AIMS investigations confirms these beneficial results.

1. Mathematics becomes more meaningful, hence more useful, when it is applied to situations that interest students.
2. The extent to which science is studied and understood is increased, with a significant economy of time, when mathematics and science are integrated.
3. There is improved quality of learning and retention, supporting the thesis that learning which is meaningful and relevant is more effective.
4. Motivation and involvement are increased dramatically as students investigate real-world situations and participate actively in the process.

We invite you to become part of this classroom teacher movement by using an integrated approach to learning and sharing any suggestions you may have. The AIMS Program welcomes you!

AIMS Education Foundation Programs

A Day with AIMS

Intensive one-day workshops are offered to introduce educators to the philosophy and rationale of AIMS. Participants will discuss the methodology of AIMS and the strategies by which AIMS principles may be incorporated into curriculum. Each participant will take part in a variety of hands-on AIMS investigations to gain an understanding of such aspects as the scientific/mathematical content, classroom management, and connections with other curricular areas. *A Day with AIMS* workshops may be offered anywhere in the United States. Necessary supplies and take-home materials are usually included in the enrollment fee.

A Week with AIMS

Throughout the nation, AIMS offers many one-week workshops each year, usually in the summer. Each workshop lasts five days and includes at least 30 hours of AIMS hands-on instruction. Participants are grouped according to the grade level(s) in which they are interested. Instructors are members of the AIMS Instructional Leadership Network. Supplies for the activities and a generous supply of take-home materials are included in the enrollment fee. Sites are selected on the basis of applications submitted by educational organizations. If chosen to host a workshop, the host agency agrees to provide specified facilities and cooperate in the promotion of the workshop. The AIMS Education Foundation supplies workshop materials as well as the travel, housing, and meals for instructors.

AIMS One-Week Perspectives Workshops

Each summer, Fresno Pacific University offers AIMS one-week workshops on its campus in Fresno, California. AIMS Program Directors and highly qualified members of the AIMS National Leadership Network serve as instructors.

The Science Festival and the Festival of Mathematics

Each summer, Fresno Pacific University offers a Science Festival and a Festival of Mathematics. These festivals have gained national recognition as inspiring and challenging experiences, giving unique opportunities to experience hands-on mathematics and science in topical and grade-level groups. Guest faculty includes some of the nation's most highly regarded mathematics and science educators. Supplies and take-home materials are included in the enrollment fee.

The AIMS Instructional Leadership Program

This is an AIMS staff-development program seeking to prepare facilitators for leadership roles in science/math education in their home districts or regions. Upon successful completion of the program, trained facilitators may become members of the AIMS Instructional Leadership Network, qualified to conduct AIMS workshops, teach AIMS in-service courses for college credit, and serve as AIMS consultants. Intensive training is provided in mathematics, science, process and thinking skills, workshop management, and other relevant topics.

College Credit and Grants

Those who participate in workshops may often qualify for college credit. If the workshop takes place on the campus of Fresno Pacific University, that institution may grant appropriate credit. If the workshop takes place off-campus, arrangements can sometimes be made for credit to be granted by another college or university. In addition, the applicant's home school district is often willing to grant in-service or professional development credit. Many educators who participate in AIMS workshops are recipients of various types of educational grants, either local or national. Nationally known foundations and funding agencies have long recognized the value of AIMS mathematics and science workshops to educators. The AIMS Education Foundation encourages educators interested in attending or hosting workshops to explore the possibilities suggested above. Although the Foundation strongly supports such interest, it reminds applicants that they have the primary responsibility for fulfilling *current* requirements.

For current information regarding the programs described above, please complete the following:

Information Request

Please send current information on the items checked:

___ *Basic Information Packet* on AIMS materials
___ *Festival of Mathematics*
___ *Science Festival*
___ *AIMS Instructional Leadership Program*

___ *AIMS One-Week Perspectives* workshops
___ *A Week with AIMS* workshops
___ Hosting information for *A Day with AIMS* workshops
___ Hosting information for *A Week with AIMS* workshops

Name _____   Phone _____

Address _____
        Street   City   State   Zip

We invite you to subscribe to *AIMS* !

Each issue of *AIMS* contains a variety of material useful to educators at all grade levels. Feature articles of lasting value deal with topics such as mathematical or science concepts, curriculum, assessment, the teaching of process skills, and historical background. Several of the latest AIMS math/science investigations are always included, along with their reproducible activity sheets. As needs direct and space allows, various issues contain news of current developments, such as workshop schedules, activities of the AIMS Instructional Leadership Network, and announcements of upcoming publications.

AIMS is published monthly, August through May. Subscriptions are on an annual basis only. A subscription entered at any time will begin with the next issue, but will also include the previous issues of that volume. Readers have preferred this arrangement because articles and activities within an annual volume are often interrelated.

Please note that an *AIMS* subscription automatically includes duplication rights for one school site for all issues included in the subscription. Many schools build cost-effective library resources with their subscriptions.

YES! I am interested in subscribing to *AIMS*.

Name _____   Home Phone _____

Address _____   City, State, Zip _____

Please send the following volumes (subject to availability):

_____ Volume V	(1990-91)	$30.00	_____ Volume X	(1995-96)	$30.00
_____ Volume VI	(1991-92)	$30.00	_____ Volume XI	(1996-97)	$30.00
_____ Volume VII	(1992-93)	$30.00	_____ Volume XII	(1997-98)	$30.00
_____ Volume IX	(1994-95)	$30.00	_____ Volume XIII	(1998-99)	$30.00

_____ **Limited offer: Volumes XIII & XIV (1998-2000) $55.00**
(Note: Prices may change without notice)

Check your method of payment:

❏ Check enclosed in the amount of $ _____

❏ Purchase order attached (Please include the P.O.#, the authorizing signature, and position of the authorizing person.)

❏ Credit Card   ❏ Visa   ❏ MasterCard   Amount $ _____

Card # _____   Expiration Date _____

Signature _____   Today's Date _____

Make checks payable to **AIMS Education Foundation.**
Mail to *AIMS* magazine, P.O. Box 8120, Fresno, CA 93747-8120.
Phone (209) 255-4094 or (888) 733-2467   FAX (209) 255-6396
AIMS Homepage: http://www.AIMSedu.org/

AIMS Program Publications

GRADES K-4 SERIES

Bats Incredible

Brinca de Alegria Hacia la Primavera con las Matemáticas y Ciencias

Cáete de Gusto Hacia el Otoño con la Matemáticas y Ciencias

Cycles of Knowing and Growing

Fall Into Math and Science

Field Detectives

Glide Into Winter With Math and Science

Hardhatting in a Geo-World (Revised Edition, 1996)

Jaw Breakers and Heart Thumpers (Revised Edition, 1995)

Los Cincos Sentidos

Overhead and Underfoot (Revised Edition, 1994)

Patine al Invierno con Matemáticas y Ciencias

Popping With Power (Revised Edition, 1996)

Primariamente Física (Revised Edition, 1994)

Primarily Earth

Primariamente Plantas

Primarily Physics (Revised Edition, 1994)

Primarily Plants

Sense-able Science

Spring Into Math and Science

Under Construction

GRADES K-6 SERIES

Budding Botanist

Critters

El Botanista Principiante

Mostly Magnets

Ositos Nada Más

Primarily Bears

Principalmente Imanes

Water Precious Water

GRADES 5-9 SERIES

Actions with Fractions

Brick Layers

Conexiones Eléctricas

Down to Earth

Electrical Connections

Finding Your Bearings (Revised Edition, 1996)

Floaters and Sinkers (Revised Edition, 1995)

From Head to Toe

Fun With Foods

Gravity Rules!

Historical Connections in Mathematics, Volume I

Historical Connections in Mathematics, Volume II

Historical Connections in Mathematics, Volume III

Machine Shop

Magnificent Microworld Adventures

Math + Science, A Solution

Off the Wall Science: A Poster Series Revisited

Our Wonderful World

Out of This World (Revised Edition, 1994)

Pieces and Patterns, A Patchwork in Math and Science

Piezas y Diseños, un Mosaic de Matemáticas y Ciencias

Soap Films and Bubbles

Spatial Visualization

The Sky's the Limit (Revised Edition, 1994)

The Amazing Circle, Volume 1

Through the Eyes of the Explorers:
    Minds-on Math & Mapping

What's Next, Volume 1

What's Next, Volume 2

What's Next, Volume 3

For further information write to:

AIMS Education Foundation • P.O. Box 8120 • Fresno, California 93747-8120

AIMS Duplication Rights Program

AIMS has received many requests from school districts for the purchase of unlimited duplication rights to AIMS materials. In response, the AIMS Education Foundation has formulated the program outlined below. There is a built-in flexibility which, we trust, will provide for those who use AIMS materials extensively to purchase such rights for either individual activities or entire books.

It is the goal of the AIMS Education Foundation to make its materials and programs available at reasonable cost. All income from the sale of publications and duplication rights is used to support AIMS programs; hence, strict adherence to regulations governing duplication is essential. Duplication of AIMS materials beyond limits set by copyright laws and those specified below is strictly forbidden.

Limited Duplication Rights

Any purchaser of an AIMS book may make up to *200 copies* of any activity in that book for use at *one school site*. Beyond that, rights must be purchased according to the appropriate category.

Unlimited Duplication Rights for Single Activities

An individual or school may purchase the right to make an unlimited number of copies of a single activity. The royalty is $5.00 per activity per school site.

Examples: 3 activities x 1 site x $5.00 = $15.00
                   9 activities x 3 sites x $5.00 = $135.00

Unlimited Duplication Rights for Entire Books

A school or district may purchase the right to make an unlimited number of copies of a single, *specified* book. The royalty is $20.00 per book per school site. This is in addition to the cost of the book.

Examples: 5 books x 1 site   x $20.00 = $100.00
                  12 books x 10 sites x $20.00 = $2400.00

Magazine/Newsletter Duplication Rights

Those who purchase *AIMS* (magazine)/*Newsletter* are hereby granted permission to make up to 200 copies of any portion of it, provided these copies will be used for educational purposes.

Workshop Instructors' Duplication Rights

Workshop instructors may distribute to registered workshop participants a maximum of 100 copies of any article and/or 100 copies of no more than eight activities, provided these six conditions are met:

1. Since all AIMS activities are based upon the *AIMS Model of Mathematics* and the *AIMS Model of Learning,* leaders must include in their presentations an explanation of these two models.
2. Workshop instructors must relate the AIMS activities presented to these basic explanations of the AIMS philosophy of education.
3. The copyright notice must appear on all materials distributed.
4. Instructors must provide information enabling participants to order books and magazines from the Foundation.
5. Instructors must inform participants of their limited duplication rights as outlined below.
6. Only student pages may be duplicated.

Written permission must be obtained for duplication beyond the limits listed above. Additional royalty payments may be required.

Workshop Participants' Rights

Those enrolled in workshops in which AIMS student activity sheets are distributed may duplicate a maximum of 35 copies or enough to use the lessons one time with one class, whichever is less. Beyond that, rights must be purchased according to the appropriate category.

Application for Duplication Rights

The purchasing agency or individual must clearly specify the following:
1. Name, address, and telephone number
2. Titles of the books for Unlimited Duplication Rights contracts
3. Titles of activities for Unlimited Duplication Rights contracts
4. Names and addresses of school sites for which duplication rights are being purchased.

NOTE: Books to be duplicated must be purchased separately and are not included in the contract for Unlimited Duplication Rights.

The requested duplication rights are automatically authorized when proper payment is received, although a *Certificate of Duplication Rights* will be issued when the application is processed.

Address all correspondence to: **Contract Division**
AIMS Education Foundation
P.O. Box 8120
Fresno, CA 93747-8120